"This lovely book transforms a rigorous psychometr[...] mindfulness into a compassionate and user-friendly guide for teaching clients to live in the present moment, in ways that will change how they see the world and live their lives."

—**Ruth Baer, PhD**, professor of psychology at the University of Kentucky and author of *The Practicing Happiness Workbook*

"In this well-written and thoughtful book, Kirk Strosahl, Patricia Robinson, and Thomas Gustavsson have paved a path to my personal clinical heart. They have tapped into and conveyed, with a clear and engaging voice, my favorite 'quality' of psychotherapy—the present moment. In *Inside This Moment*, the authors provide a truly useful guide for clinicians, assisting them to understand and build life-changing moments in the therapeutic process and relationship. The five essential tasks involved in creating these powerful moments—noticing, naming, detaching, holding, and expanding—are explored with clinical acuity and neuroscience backing. This book will help you to help your clients transform their lives. It is my belief that working to develop present-moment awareness is the soul of acceptance and commitment therapy, and Strosahl, Robinson, and Gustavsson have beautifully and knowledgably put this process into words."

—**Robyn D. Walser, PhD**, past president of the Association for Contextual Behavioral Science, associate director for dissemination and training at the National Center for PTSD, assistant clinical professor at the University of California, Berkeley, and coauthor of *The Mindful Couple* and *Learning ACT*

"They've done it again. The cocreators of FACT (focused acceptance and commitment therapy) have written another innovative, creative, and incredibly practical guide to brief therapy with ACT, this time expertly explaining their interventions in terms of the underlying neuroscience. It's novel, powerful, and cutting-edge; a breath of fresh air in the ever-growing pantheon of ACT literature. Highly recommended!"

—**Russ Harris**, author of The Happiness Trap and ACT Made Simple

"This is a beautifully written book that masterfully combines science, theory, and practice. An invaluable tool for clinicians who want to engender more mindfulness and self-compassion in their clients, it maximizes the power of acceptance and commitment therapy to change lives."

—**Kristin Neff, PhD**, associate professor in human development and culture at the University of Texas at Austin, and author of *Self-Compassion*

"There are several reasons why I feel this book is a significant contribution to our field. First, as a longtime practitioner who uses the notion of 'present moment' in my work with clients, the authors have cleared up a sticky concept that I have struggled with—that is, what is actually meant by the 'present moment.' They do so in a way that covers its function, rather than a topographical description. For example, they clearly indicate that mindfulness practice is not the only way to contact the present moment. Second, there's a constant theme throughout the book in which either theory, research findings, and methods are described and then related to clinical practice. In particular they emphasize what happens during the therapy session—a topic of particular interest and importance from my perspective. Third, they cover a topic close to my heart in which they ask the clinician to use the same methods applied to clients to heal themselves. Fourth, their approach is coherence with contextual behavioral science. Finally, the authors keep their eye on the ball of providing an approach that clinicians can use by detailing how-to application to common clinical problems. I highly recommend this book."

—**Robert J. Kohlenberg, PhD, ABPP**, professor of psychology at the University of Washington, cofounder of functional analytic psychotherapy (FAP)

inside this moment.

A CLINICIAN'S GUIDE *to* PROMOTING RADICAL CHANGE USING ACCEPTANCE *and* COMMITMENT THERAPY

KIRK D. STROSAHL, PhD
PATRICIA J. ROBINSON, PhD
THOMAS GUSTAVSSON, MSc

CONTEXT PRESS
An Imprint of New Harbinger Publications, Inc.

Publisher's Note

This publication is designed to provide accurate and authoritative information in regard to the subject matter covered. It is sold with the understanding that the publisher is not engaged in rendering psychological, financial, legal, or other professional services. If expert assistance or counseling is needed, the services of a competent professional should be sought.

Distributed in Canada by Raincoast Books

Elements of the section "Self-Assessment: Taking Inventory of Your Present-Moment Processing Skills" have been adapted from the Five-Facet Mindfulness Questionnaire (FFMQ) in R. Baer, G. Smith, E. Lykins, D. Button, J. Kreitemeyer, S. Sauer, et al. 2008. "Construct Validity of the Five Facet Mindfulness Questionnaire in Meditating and Non-Meditating Samples." *Assessment*, 15:329–342. Used by permission of the authors.

Context Press
An Imprint of New Harbinger Publications, Inc.
5674 Shattuck Avenue
Oakland, CA 94609
www.newharbinger.com

Cover design by Amy Shoup
Acquired by Catharine Meyers
Edited by Jasmine Star
Indexed by James Minkin

Library of Congress Cataloging-in-Publication Data

Strosahl, Kirk, 1950- author.
  Inside this moment : a clinician's guide to promoting radical change using acceptance and commitment therapy / Kirk D. Strosahl, Patricia J. Robinson, Thomas Gustavsson.
    pages cm
  Includes bibliographical references and index.
  ISBN 978-1-62625-324-7 (paperback) -- ISBN 978-1-62625-325-4 (pdf e-book) -- ISBN 978-1-62625-326-1 (epub) 1. Acceptance and commitment therapy. 2. Awareness. I. Robinson, Patricia J., author. II. Gustavsson, Thomas, author. III. Title.
  RC489.A32S773 2015
  616.89'1425--dc23
                                2015018132

Printed in the United States of America

17   16   15

10   9   8   7   6   5   4   3   2   1   First printing

To Patti: How lucky am I? I get to write about things that inspire me with a coauthor and life partner who inspires me even more. To my brother, Mark Strosahl: I'll never forget you, pal. This one's for you. And to Jasmine Star, our insanely talented copy editor, thought generator, and cheerleader. You are awesome.

—KS

To Kirk, a masterful mindful therapist and a master writer. I am honored to write another book with you.

—PR

I would like to thank everyone who has taught me the value and practice of being present, especially my dog, Ella, who demands me to do so; my lovely daughters, Edith and Alice, who are natural teachers in present-moment activities; and the sunshine of my life, my wife, Ika, who I'm looking forward to being present with during the rest of my days. Thanks also to all of my inspiring colleagues at Segesholms. And Mom, without you none of this would have been, and that's a FACT!

—TG

Contents

Dear reader,

Welcome to New Harbinger Publications. New Harbinger is dedicated to publishing books based on acceptance and commitment therapy (ACT) and its application to specific areas. New Harbinger has a long-standing reputation as a publisher of quality, well-researched books for general and professional audiences.

As part of New Harbinger's commitment to publishing books based on sound, scientific, clinical research, we oversee all prospective books for the Acceptance and Commitment Therapy Series. Serving as series editors, we comment on proposals and offer guidance as needed, and use a gentle hand in making suggestions regarding the content, depth, and scope of each book.

Books in the Acceptance and Commitment Therapy Series:

- Have an adequate database, appropriate to the strength of the claims being made.

- Are theoretically coherent. They will fit with the ACT model and underlying behavioral principles as they have evolved at the time of writing.

- Orient the reader toward unresolved empirical issues.

- Do not overlap needlessly with existing volumes.

- Avoid jargon and unnecessary entanglement with proprietary methods, leaving ACT work open and available.

- Keep the focus always on what is good for the reader.

- Support the further development of the field.

- Provide information in a way that is of practical use to readers.

These guidelines reflect the values of the broader ACT community. You'll see all of them packed into this book. This series is meant to offer professionals information that can truly be helpful, and to further our ability to alleviate human suffering by inviting creative practitioners into the process of developing, applying, and refining a better approach. This book provides another such invitation.

Sincerely,

Steven C. Hayes, Ph.D.
Georg H. Eifert, Ph.D.
John Forsyth, Ph.D.
Robyn Walser, Ph.D.

Introduction

The present moment is filled with joy and happiness.
If you are attentive, you will see it.

—Thich Nhat Hanh

This book is intended to help you, the clinician, learn to organize and deliver powerful present-moment-awareness interventions in therapy. This involves helping clients who habitually escape from the present moment learn to stay in the here and now and integrate their immediate affective and cognitive experience in a way that promotes long-lasting benefits. Our many years of clinical experience suggest that anchoring clients in present-moment awareness can have a transformative effect on their view of themselves and the world. This transformational moment, which we call *radical change*, can happen at any time or at any point in therapy. Radical change allows clients to walk through a door, figuratively speaking, and begin to relate to the past, present, and future in a whole new way. In most cases, this doesn't happen serendipitously; it happens because you take advantage of an opportunity to use clients' present-moment awareness to change how they relate to what's going on inside. You use the present moment to open that door so clients can walk through it. In this book, we'll help you learn how to open these transformational doors, often within minutes of seizing an opportunity to do so.

Psychological Flexibility

The principles and practices described in this book are based upon a treatment approach called acceptance and commitment therapy, or ACT (Hayes, Strosahl, & Wilson, 1999, 2012), and a brief intervention model called focused acceptance and commitment therapy, or FACT (Strosahl, Robinson, & Gustavsson, 2012). A guiding premise is that human suffering and human resiliency are two sides of the same coin. They are both determined by three underlying psychological processes, which produce either psychological rigidity or psychological flexibility. We call these important psychological processes the "pillars of flexibility":

- Being open

- Being aware

- Being engaged

Psychological flexibility involves the ability to be open and nonjudgmental toward private experiences like negative thoughts, unpleasant feelings, painful memories, or distressing physical sensations. It requires being able to contact present-moment awareness in order to integrate these experiences into a coherent sense of self. And it entails living a life that's guided by personal values rather than social conventions.

There are two major barriers to being psychologically flexible. One is *experiential avoidance*. This involves being unwilling to accept the presence of distressing, unwanted thoughts, feelings, memories, or physical sensations. Clients who are struggling with this problem avoid their distressing internal experiences by trying to push them out of awareness or by staying out of real-life situations that might trigger them. The second barrier is *rule following*. Clients who are struggling with this problem live life on autopilot; they're just going through the motions of daily existence and following socially transmitted rules about how to live life. Thus, within the ACT/FACT framework, the goal is to strengthen the underlying core processes of flexibility to make clients less susceptible to the pernicious effects of emotional avoidance and rule following.

Present-Moment Awareness and Psychological Flexibility

We believe that being aware and present is the single most important determinant of psychological flexibility. This ability allows us to make contact with distressing private experiences without being dominated by them. Simply put, if you can't stay in contact with what's in your awareness, you can't learn from those experiences, and you won't be able to change your behavior to better fit the demands of whatever life situation is provoking the experiences. Clients with deficits in present-moment awareness tend to repeatedly engage in the same unworkable behaviors (most of which are avoidance based) even while the emotional costs of doing so escalate.

From a clinical perspective, one nice thing about experiential avoidance and rule following is that clients can't help but engage in these practices during therapy sessions. In fact, you, the clinician, *want* clients to engage in their habitual avoidance strategies so that you can teach them how to do something different: contact and accept the presence of distressing experiences within the frame of present-moment awareness. This is when the healing can begin, and it requires the clinician to be highly observant and also to be guided by a mental model of what needs to happen, when, and in what order. Clinicians often report that this is the most difficult aspect of dealing with present-moment-awareness interventions. Therapy is necessarily a verbal enterprise, and words always lag behind the present moment. A common result is that the clinician and client talk about present-moment experience instead of immersing themselves in the present moment. We liken working in the present moment to dancing; you, the clinician, must pay close attention to the dance steps that occur in the therapeutic conversation while keeping from stepping on the client's toes or from getting so far out of sync that present-moment awareness disappears from the conversation altogether.

While being able to pay attention to the client's every dance step is a huge plus, there are many other things that need to be accomplished within a present-moment-awareness intervention. You must be able to effectively probe for and recognize failures of present-moment awareness when they occur. Then you must figure out how to help the client learn to relate to whatever shows up in present-moment awareness in a flexible, clinically productive way. Our goal in writing this book is to give you a solid theoretical and practical framework that will provide guidance as you do this dance with your clients.

Five Phases of Present-Moment Awareness

We maintain that present-moment awareness involves both the dynamic allocation of the finite, higher-order attention resources of the brain, and five distinct, dynamic psychological tasks (we call them phases) to perform while sustaining focus. These five essential processing tasks are as follows:

- Noticing what's there

- Naming what's there

- Detaching from what's there (which we refer to in this book as letting go)

- Holding what's there softly (in short, practicing self-compassion)

- Reframing the personal meaning of what's there (which we refer to as expanding)

To some extent, these tasks are progressive; completion of one makes it possible for clients to move to the next. This is one of the fun challenges of using present-moment awareness as an intervention tool. Every client is different in terms of strengths or weaknesses in performing each task. Thus, you must learn to assess each client's present-moment processing strengths and weaknesses—often while a present-moment-awareness intervention is underway—and then make rather instantaneous decisions about where to go next in terms of the intervention.

Present-moment-awareness interventions need to happen quickly, because most people have a limited ability to remain in the present moment. The human mind doesn't do the present moment very well, so before too long, the mind's chatter begins to interfere with the client's present-moment awareness. The five tasks might unfold over a period of minutes in a single therapeutic intervention, and there might be abrupt shifts backward such that a phase that seemed to be completed resurfaces. Like the captain of a ship sailing in stormy waters, the therapist must use probes, higher-order clinical formulations, and interventions to steer the client through each of these phases. Don't worry! We'll go into each phase of present-moment awareness in exquisite detail, teaching you how to probe for strengths and weaknesses, how to interpret the results of probes, and then how to implement real-time clinical interventions.

Present-Moment Awareness and Mindfulness Traditions

Readers familiar with meditation and mindfulness practices will notice a distinct parallel between the five-phase approach and many mindfulness traditions. We often joke that the correct term for how to stay in present-moment awareness is to be *mindless*, because one major task is to let go of attachment to the busy, problem-solving mind and instead enter into a state of simple awareness. Mindfulness skills are a key ally in the client's progression through the five phases of present-moment awareness:

- The ability to adopt an observer perspective

- The ability to apply descriptive, nonevaluative verbal labels to experience

- The ability to detach oneself from the provocative and evocative aspects of private experience

- The ability to practice self-compassion for one's flaws and past mistakes

- The ability to convert distressing, unwanted life experiences into motivation to live a principled life

This aspect of our present-moment-awareness intervention approach is influenced by the pioneering work of Ruth Baer and her colleagues examining the core features of mindfulness (Baer et al., 2008).

Contributions from Cognitive and Affective Neuroscience

Our approach to present-moment-awareness interventions also has been heavily influenced by neuroscience studies of mindfulness, emotion processing, and attention, most notably the work of Richard Davidson (Davidson & Begley, 2012). The two most important principles we've integrated are the concepts of neurospecificity and neuroplasticity. *Neurospecificity* means that specific neuroanatomical structures and neural pathways, alone or in synchronous interaction with other pathways, support such basic present-moment processing skills as paying attention, simple awareness, verbal labeling, and practicing detachment. The concept of *neuroplasticity* means that practicing present-moment-awareness skills strengthens the neural circuitry in areas of the brain responsible for each specific skill. In other words, using mindfulness interventions in therapy is really a form of brain training. Neuroplasticity challenges the traditional belief that the brain is a fixed entity that changes only in a limited way and very slowly over time. It now appears that fairly remarkable changes in the brain's neural circuitry can happen in weeks or months, rather than years or decades. For example, research has shown that a relatively brief experimental regime of mindfulness training increased gray matter density in an area of the brain associated with meditative states of awareness (Lutz, Greischar, Rawlings, & Davidson, 2004).

Organization of This Book

We've organized this book so that part 1 is more theoretical, giving those who are interested in broader theoretical issues something to chew on. Parts 2 and 3 are successively more pragmatic and clinically focused to meet the needs of clinicians who are interested in learning specific techniques and seeing how they're applied in practice.

In part 1, we explore foundational concepts related to both understanding and intervening with present-moment-awareness processes and give you, the clinician, a chance to assess your own present-moment-awareness skills. Chapter 1 examines the composition of present-moment awareness from a number of different perspectives: neuroscience, mindfulness, and psychology. We explain a neuroscience-based approach to attention and how different types of attention color the inner world of present-moment awareness. Chapter 2 first explores barriers to present-moment awareness, including experiential avoidance and rule following. These barriers typically originate in the problem-solving mind, where distressing private experiences may be perceived as a threat to well-being. We then introduce the five-phase present-moment clinical approach in some detail. In chapter 3, we give you, the reader, a chance to assess your strengths and weaknesses in regard to present-moment-awareness skills, both in your clinical work and in your personal life.

In part 2 (chapters 4 through 8), we examine each of the five phases of present-moment-awareness interventions in great detail. Each chapter includes a case example, with sequential therapeutic dialogues demonstrating how to probe the client's skills, how to interpret the results of probes (termed "reads"), and how to implement interventions designed to address skills deficits. In each chapter, we provide practical clinical tips on how to be even more effective with the clients you serve.

In part 3 (chapters 9 through 14), we examine how to apply present-moment-awareness interventions to a wide range of clinical problems: depression, anxiety and panic, post-traumatic stress, addictive behaviors, self-harming behaviors, and making difficult lifestyle changes. In each of these chapters, we analyze the target problem from a present-moment-awareness perspective. This will help you better understand how different weaknesses in present-moment-awareness skills are linked to different types of clinical presentations. For example, the problems in present-moment awareness that produce depression are cut from a different cloth than those that produce anxiety. Each chapter includes a case example with extensive clinical dialogues to illustrate how to help clients with each type of difficulty move through all the phases of present-moment awareness.

An Invitation

Present-moment-awareness work doesn't just empower clients; it stimulates spiritual growth for clinicians too. The look of positive recognition on the face of a client who has been transformed by a powerful present-moment-awareness intervention is something you will never forget. It dignifies and makes purposeful all of the work you've put in to be in a position to help those who suffer. We found the process of writing this book to be a powerful spiritual experience for each of us. We hope the process of reading it will be a powerful spiritual experience for you.

PART 1

The Present Moment Inside Out

CHAPTER 1

In Search of Present-Moment Awareness

> The present moment, if you think about it, is the only time there is.
> No matter what time it is, it is always now.
>
> —Marianne Williamson

We all have the capacity to create present-moment awareness. However, on a moment-to-moment basis in daily living, we don't usually step back and try to deconstruct what present-moment awareness consists of in the first place. And there's no real cost to taking this position; we can be as sloppy as we want moving from moment to moment in life. However, you, the clinician, cannot afford to adopt a sloppy approach to present-moment-awareness interventions in the therapy room. You need to have a firm grasp of the core processes that collectively create the experience of present-moment awareness, because you need to directly or indirectly manipulate these processes to help clients. To get you started on your journey toward excellence in this area, we're going to address some foundational concepts that will help you better understand the core features of present-moment awareness.

First, we'll review growing and compelling evidence that present-moment awareness and related experiences of self are firmly rooted in the anatomy and neural circuitry of the brain and experientially processed via the verbal and symbolic operating system of the mind. This means that when you elicit present-moment awareness in therapy in the appropriate way, you are not just training the client to use symbolic processing skills but also strengthening the brain circuitry responsible for producing them.

Second, we'll describe a neuroclinical approach to attention. Being able to allocate attention in a flexible way is a prerequisite condition for therapeutic contact with present-moment awareness. Our approach emphasizes that attention is a dynamic and finite brain resource, supported by specific neural pathways in the brain. In addition, there are different forms of attention that are closely tied to structurally distinct neural pathways within the brain; these different forms of attention have distinctive, evolutionarily significant functions that determine what's screened into present-moment awareness. In turn, what's screened into present-moment awareness influences motivation and behavior. We'll show how this approach can be used not only to predict specific types of clinical problems, but also to determine what types of present-moment-awareness interventions are likely to be effective.

Finally, we'll take on the challenge of defining what we mean by present-moment awareness, particularly with reference to contemporary concepts of mindfulness and acceptance. We will argue that simply equating mindfulness or meditation practice with present-moment awareness is both theoretically and clinically limiting. This is an important set of concepts to understand, particularly in light of the growing popularity of acceptance, perspective taking, and mindfulness-based interventions in psychotherapy.

Neuroscience Considerations

Without being pedantic about it, it is worth saying that *all* forms of self-aware human experience ultimately originate in the neurobiology of the brain. So any attempt to understand something as basic as present-moment awareness must ultimately be linked to basic brain science as the primary reference point. This doesn't mean clinical interventions are going to involve brain surgery, but rather that we can structure present-moment-awareness interventions to take advantage of the neurospecificity and neuroplasticity of the brain.

It is an appropriate analogy to think of the brain as the computer that's responsible for the operating system of mind, anchored as it is in such core processes as language and nonverbal functions, including consciousness, attention, and self-awareness. The field of cognitive and affective neuroscience is rich with clinical studies showing how mindfulness and present-moment awareness are produced within the brain's anatomical structures and associated functional neural networks (see Braboszcz, Hahusseau, & Delorme, 2010, for a well-written, clinically relevant synopsis). This information is directly pertinent to how clinical interventions designed to strengthen present-moment-awareness interventions should be organized and delivered.

Psychological Distress and Fight-or-Flight Circuitry

The brain consists of an elaborate system of neural circuitry designed to help us maintain a continuous dynamic balance between the activating and regulatory portions of the autonomic nervous system. This balancing act is achieved through an ongoing interaction between two different regions of the brain. One is the reticular activating system; it consists of the primitive part of the brain that produces emotional arousal and the well-known fight-or-flight response. This is the part of the brain that first evolved to protect us from all kinds of natural threats to survival. Thus, it is exquisitely sensitive to and triggered by the presence of any kind of threat—real or imagined. The branch of the nervous system that supports all of these stress-related changes is the *sympathetic nervous system* (SNS).

Activation of the SNS initiates a cascade of changes in the body. The hypothalamic-pituitary-adrenal axis of the hormone system works closely with the SNS and releases stress hormones, such as epinephrine and cortisol, into the bloodstream. These neurochemicals have an immediate impact on blood pressure, heart rate, skin temperature, and blood flow. The release of stress hormones is why clients with high levels of emotional distress complain about feeling confused, being unable to concentrate, and having trouble making decisions.

The Result: Busy Mind

A particularly germane consideration is that the mind's definition of what constitutes a threat or danger has expanded so indiscriminately that even normal human experiences can trigger high levels of SNS arousal. This is why a rejection letter or a bad interaction with a coworker or classmate can have the same physiological impact as seeing an eighteen-wheeler careening toward you. More importantly, even mild levels of chronic SNS arousal are associated with mental states involving low-grade anxiety, restlessness, and narrowly focused, easily distracted attention. Readers with any meditation experience will instantly recognize this state of mind; it's the busy, "fix-it," problem-solving state of mind you may notice when you start to meditate. We call this state of awareness *busy mind*. As the name suggests, it doesn't do the present moment very well.

Countering the SNS: The Portal to Present-Moment Awareness

Responsibility for counterbalancing the pernicious effects of chronic SNS arousal lies in the left dorsolateral and left ventrolateral prefrontal cortex. This region of the "new brain" is involved in producing most of the higher-order functions typically associated with being human: attention, emotion regulation, planning, abstract reasoning, and so on. Some of these important human abilities are actually the result of synchronous interactions among different functional structures spread throughout the brain, including the primitive brain. In other words, an activity like paying attention is partly generated by primitive brain functions, which are then regulated and controlled by functions in the "new brain." These functional brain structures exert their regulatory influence on the SNS through activation of the parasympathetic nervous system (PNS). The PNS is responsible for regulating the level of SNS activation through what amounts to a physiological dampening process. Thus, the physical and mental signs of PNS activation are the exact opposite of those noted in SNS activation: blood pressure decreases, as does blood pulse volume, skin temperature, heart rate, and respiration rate.

The Result: Quiet Mind

Prolonged PNS activation is associated with experiences of calmness, tranquility, transcendent awareness, self-compassion, empathy, and connectedness. We call this state of awareness *quiet mind*. In this mode of mind, the normal mental clutter of busy mind gives way to clarity of thought and purpose. If busy mind is responsible for creating clouds that obscure the sky, quiet mind is the wind that gently moves the clouds away to reveal the clear blue sky beyond. It is from this perspective—one of clarity of thought and purpose—that we can benefit directly from the self-knowledge available in present-moment awareness. Not surprisingly, activation of the PNS is achieved through psychological techniques that many would associate with mindfulness and meditative traditions: sustained deep breathing, mental focusing, prayer, and compassion meditations, to name but a few.

Present-Moment-Awareness Interventions as Brain Training

Although there are still skeptics out there, in our view the findings of brain training studies clearly indicate that repeated practice with present-moment-awareness skills results in perceptible changes in the areas of the brain responsible for those skills. And it isn't necessary to practice mindfulness or meditation strategies for years to reap these benefits; rather, they appear to accrue quite quickly (Hölzel et al., 2011; Lutz et al., 2004). However, the differences disappear over a relatively short period of time when attention training is discontinued. The take-home message is that having clients practice various aspects of present-moment awareness in and out of session is likely to strengthen their present-moment awareness at the brain circuitry level.

A Neuroclinical Approach to Attention

Clinical experience suggests that the ability to flexibly allocate and maintain attention is a prerequisite condition for developing and sustaining present-moment awareness. The ability to pay attention to what is in present-moment awareness doesn't guarantee radical change, but it's nearly impossible to succeed if clients can't sustain attention as you move through the phases of an intervention. We often hear clinicians talk about attention as if it were a static entity—for example, the client is or is not paying attention to what the clinician is saying. Our approach to attention is a bit different. We maintain that attention is a finite brain resource that's often being requested by competing neural networks. These networks are activated or downregulated based upon specific internal or external inputs. In this section, we'll address the two core determinants of the experience of present-moment awareness as it unfolds in the moment. One is the type of attention that's being applied within awareness itself. The second is the underlying neural network that's supporting the phenomenological experience of what's present in awareness.

The Problem of Paying Attention

The commonly used phrase "pay attention" is quite apt. Because there's only so much attention available, attending to one thing results in that much less attention being available for other things. It's useful to think of attention as a finite, functional resource. There is no attention gland in the brain. Instead, attention is a composite result of complex interactions involving multiple structures in the brain. Thus, it isn't surprising that the functions of attention span the full range of human experiences, from detecting basic threats to survival to supporting transcendent forms of present-moment awareness. Being such a complex human ability, attention is intricately interwoven throughout the entire brain, from the primitive reptilian brain to the complicated networks of the "new brain."

Bottom-Up Attention

Bottom-up attention is a primitive type of attention that originates in the older regions of the human brain. The fundamental purpose of this system is to detect real or imagined threats to survival; therefore, it is heavily biased toward selecting and weighting negative cues. It was undoubtedly the first form of attention available to the progenitors of the human race and was highly adaptive as a survival protection system. Notably, bottom-up attention is very unstable, shifting from one potential threat to the next. The presence of bottom-up attention is associated with distortions in cognitive processing, particularly with complex, multistage tasks. Because of its negative information bias, bottom-up attention is also associated with (and likely produces) primitive affective states such as anxiety, fearfulness, and abject depression.

Top-Down Attention

Top-down attention is more cognitively complex than bottom-up attention. It is flexible yet focused and provides the foundation for complex problem solving and emotional processing. Top-down attention is thought to originate in synchronous activity between the thalamus and the right frontal and right parietal cortical structures, also known as the thalamo-cortical loop (Posner & Rothbart, 2007). Executive control, sometimes referred to as working memory capacity, allows us to both manage and shift attention when conflicts between emotions, thoughts, and intentions arise. This complex cognitive ability is associated with increased activation of the dorsal anterior cingulate nucleus and the dorsolateral prefrontal cortex. These specific neural networks are also activated during periods of self-awareness, suggesting that they have a superordinate role to play in the overall experience of consciousness and self-focused attention (Braboszcz et al., 2010).

Clinical Implications

If the pathway to suffering is being dominated by bottom-up attention, then the ability to apply top-down attention is the doorway to present-moment awareness and radical change. It may seem obvious, but it is worth saying that what the client pays attention to is what the client will respond to overtly (behaviorally) and covertly (mentally). Your goal is to get clients to apply top-down attention to experiences they have been unwilling or unable to attend to in the past.

Often, clients have previously attended to and made contact with distressing and unwanted private experiences and then made a conscious choice to turn their attention elsewhere. The saying "Out of sight, out of mind" applies quite well here. If you suppress or redirect awareness away from distressing or painful experiences, they will exert less regulatory influence on your immediate reactions and behaviors.

The problem here is busy mind, which is capable of turning even normal human emotional experiences into threats to self-survival. The imperative, once an experience is evaluated as a threat, is to either attack it (suppress it) or run away from it (distract attention). This means clients are processing the distressing experience from the perspective of bottom-up attention. Clients bring these threats into the therapy room all the time (traumatic memories, sadness, guilt, anger, self-destructive thoughts, and so on).

Ultimately, substantial attention resources are required to ensure that avoided experiences don't enter into awareness. If attention resources are depleted beyond a certain point due to other competing demands on the brain (such as having to perform a very complex and stressful task), there will be inadequate attention resources to keep the suppressed experience at bay and it will rebound into awareness. Further, when such experiences show up in present-moment awareness, applying bottom-up attention results in numerous distortions in how such experiences are mentally processed.

Conversely, there are situations in which clients are simply unable to pay attention to whatever is in their present-moment awareness in a productive way. This can be seen with clients who suffer from attention deficit disorder, developmental delays, organic brain damage, psychosis, or acute drug or alcohol intoxication. For one reason or another, these clients are unable to organize and deploy their attention resources in an effective way.

A more clinically interesting example of being unable to pay attention is clients who haven't made the mental connection between a particular life problem and a corresponding set of private reactions. There are actually a fair number of clients like this, and clinicians often view them as lacking insight into their current situation. For example, such clients might not see a fairly obvious link between earlier painful life events and how they're reacting to a current life event that's somehow similar. These clients aren't struggling with willingness to make contact with distressing private experiences; they just haven't made the mental connection that will generate the experience. Fortunately, present-moment-awareness interventions can have a very profound effect on these clients.

The Funnel of Attention

Psychologist and colleague Steve Humm has developed a very elegant and clinically useful approach that involves using a funnel as a visual metaphor for attention (personal communication, September 14, 2014). The figure below offers annotations for clinicians. In session, this intervention usually starts with just a picture of a funnel. The clinician customizes what's written on the sheet based upon a given client's presenting complaints. This exercise allows clinicians to help clients better understand how different kinds of attention control what's allowed into their awareness.

Attention, like a funnel, has one very narrow end and one very broad end. At the narrow end of the funnel, awareness is quite constricted in scope, so a lot of details that lie outside this limited field of perception are missed. This is what bottom-up attention feels like: it produces a narrow perspective on whatever situation is being looked at. Conversely, at the other end of the funnel, the field of attention is very broad, and consequently, a lot more information is available. This is what top-down attention looks like. It inherently produces a broader perspective because it includes much more information.

When using this metaphor with clients, to cement their understanding you can have them curl the fingers of one hand to create a very small opening to look through. Have them look at you through this small opening, then ask what's missing from the picture. Next, have them open their hand so that their fingers touch their thumb, creating a much bigger opening to look through. Have them look at you through this much bigger opening, and ask them to comment on what new information comes into view. You can then ask them to identify which end of the funnel is likely to be the most workable, given the personal issue they're dealing with.

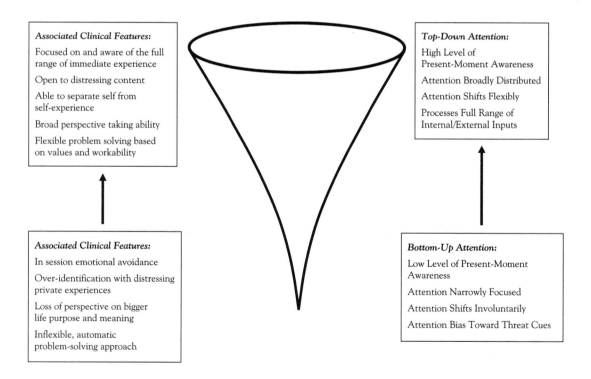

Figure 1.1 The Continuum of Attention and Associated Clinical Features

The Neuroscience of Present-Moment Awareness

To create a better understanding of how attention and present-moment awareness are linked requires a discussion of how the brain's neural networks are organized to perform the incredibly broad range of functions the brain is charged with. There are three widely discussed neural networks that interact in complex ways to produce complex human behavior: the default mode network, the task-positive network, and the executive control network. In this section, we'll briefly discuss each of these networks in relation to both attention and the experiences that populate present-moment awareness.

The Default Mode Network

You're probably familiar with the old adage "An idle mind is the devil's playground." This saying turns out to be quite prophetic when it comes to understanding the neural basis of attention. Over the last decade, neuroscientists have become increasingly interested in what the brain does when it isn't doing anything. They have discovered what's called the *default mode network*, a broadly distributed network of synchronous neural activity that we liken to the screen saver function of a computer. When you aren't using the computer, the screen saver randomly produces images that require engaging the functions of the monitor. Interestingly, the default network appears to lack significant connectivity to somatosensory areas of the brain and is strongly supported by brain structures responsible for memory retrieval and mental rehearsal and representation. It appears that not being engaged in any particular task at the neural level results in an ongoing self-focused mental narrative that's "self-stoking" and more or less cut off from the sensory world.

The brain's default network is so dominant in our daily life that it has been termed the "dark energy" of the mind (Raichle, 2010). Overactivation of the default network likely results in becoming overidentified with and lost in mental content such that external inputs are ignored and the individual suddenly loses contact with present-moment awareness. A term used in the neuroscience literature to describe this loss of present-moment awareness is "mind wandering" (Smallwood, Beach, Schooler, & Handy, 2008). Mind wandering involves daydreaming, worrying, ruminating, mentally representing the perspectives of others, or creating mental representations and rehearsals of events yet to come (Buckner, Andrews-Hanna, & Schacter, 2008; Spreng, Sepulcre, Turner, Stevens, & Schacter, 2013). Most of us can identify many examples of mind wandering in daily life. For example, you might be reading a magazine and suddenly realize that you aren't reading anymore—your mind has wandered off and is doing something else.

Default mode network activation isn't intrinsically a bad thing; not all daydreams are just empty pipe dreams. For example, imagining the perspective of others leads to empathy, and creating mental representations of the future leads to inspiration, vision, and imagining new valued life directions. It's also likely that outward-focused meditation practices, such as compassion meditation, are supported by activation of the default mode network. However, excess activation of the default mode network has been associated with negative psychological outcomes. For example, mind wandering correlates with reduced capacity for processing externally relevant stimuli, and individuals who exhibit high levels of mind wandering during cognitive processing tasks tend to report higher levels of dysphoria and depression (Carriere, Cheyne, & Smilek, 2008). Similarly, negative affective states themselves tend to be correlated with increased frequency of mind wandering (Smallwood, Fitzgerald, Miles, & Phillips, 2009). It doesn't take much of a theoretical leap to arrive at the idea that negative mental processes such as depression, daydreaming, and rumination and behaviors that produce emotional numbing, such as addictive behaviors or overeating, are linked to excessive activation of the default mode network.

The Task-Positive Network

A second major neural network that competes for the brain's attention resources is the *task-positive network*, also called the dorsal attention network (Spreng et al., 2013). The task-positive network is activated whenever there's a specific task for the brain to perform, regardless of whether the task is internally or externally focused and whether it has a positive or negative valence. Neuroscience studies show that the default mode network and task-positive network share few positive synchronicities. Indeed, the task-positive network actively competes with the default mode network for finite resources and is associated with deactivation of the default network.

The task-positive network recruits the perceptual and somatosensory resources of the brain and also increases activity in areas of the brain responsible for abstract reasoning and mental representation—two core attributes of complex problem solving. Not surprisingly, task-positive network activation is associated with marked changes in how the brain's attention resources are used. Whereas attention resources are widely dispersed in the default mode, they are much more tightly organized in the task-positive mode.

In our view, the name "task-positive" is somewhat misleading because task-positive network activation can have a dark side when put to tasks involving self-protection or survival. When this happens, task-positive activation recruits bottom-up attention resources, often leading to a host of negative cognitive outcomes, such as worry, obsession, catastrophic thinking, analysis paralysis, and hypervigilance, and also painful emotional outcomes, such as anxiety, fearfulness, and paranoia.

The Executive Control Network

The third and, from a clinical perspective, most salient neural network is called the *executive control network*, also referred to as the fronto-parietal control network (Spreng et al., 2013). This network performs a gatekeeper role in the ongoing competition between the task-positive and default networks for finite brain resources. The executive control network has strong neural connections with both the task-positive and default mode networks, suggesting that it can exert regulatory influence over either, depending upon its higher-order situation assessment. One major function of this network is to utilize top-down attention resources to regulate the degree and type of network dominance. When the executive control network interacts with the default mode network, rumination about previous life failures (associated with bottom-up attention) might be transformed into contact with core values and a sense of life purpose (associated with top-down attention). When the executive control network interacts with the task-positive network, self-focused anxiety (associated with bottom-up attention) might be transformed into highly focused and motivated personal problem solving (associated with top-down attention).

Clinical Implications

As shown in the following figure, common clinical problems can be characterized in terms of the relative dominance of the brain's three attention networks. One axis is whether the task-positive or default network is the dominant mode. A second axis is the degree of involvement of the executive control network, with its associated influence on the ratio of top-down to bottom-up attention. The figure below suggests that low executive control network activation is highly problematic, regardless of which of the other two neural networks is dominant. This is because bottom-up attention will predominate, leading to a host of information biases and cognitive processing errors. The distress generated by skewed processing of unwanted private experiences is generally what brings clients to therapy.

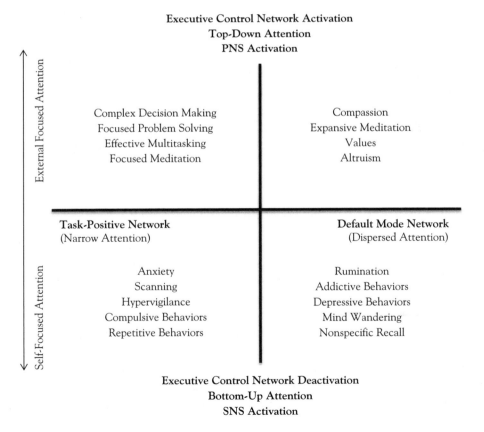

Figure 2.1   A Neuroclinical Model of Attention

The form of the client's suffering is directly linked to which neural network is overly dominant. Task-positive dominance generally results in anxious, fearful, agitated, overly ideational, and escape-oriented clinical presentations. Default mode dominance generally produces apathetic, withdrawn, ruminative, self-absorbed, or numbed-out presentations in which escape is achieved through collapsing into the self. In general, the goal of present-moment-awareness interventions is to increase activation of the executive control network so that clients can process emotionally salient material using top-down attention. The type of present-moment-awareness strategy to use depends on which of the two networks (default mode or task-positive) is dominant. With clinical problems driven by the default mode, it's generally best to use present-moment-awareness interventions that require the client to engage with somatosensory and perceptual information (for example, body scans, focused meditation, speeding up the rate of interaction, or physical exercises and metaphors) while disengaging memory retrieval and passive activities like daydreaming and mind wandering. Clinical problems driven by the task-positive network respond better to interventions that deactivate the client's task focus (such as deep breathing, focusing on just one issue, slowing the rate of interaction, or detachment metaphors and exercises).

Present-Moment Awareness and Mindfulness

In this section, we want to take on the challenge of defining what the term "present-moment awareness" means in our clinical approach. We also want to offer a new perspective on the role mindfulness and meditation practices might play in promoting present-moment-awareness interventions.

Present-Moment Awareness: A Timeless Perspective

The first question that naturally arises is "What is present-moment awareness?" This isn't a rhetorical question! It's actually a pivotal question, because how you think about the composition of present-moment awareness influences what you look for and respond to in session. The term "present moment" is heavily imbued with temporal connotations, and these are fundamentally misleading. In actuality, present-moment awareness is a timeless perspective in which we are simply aware of being here, now, on a moment-to-moment basis. Whatever we are aware of, whether an emotion, memory, thought, or sensation, is what we're aware of—nothing more, nothing less. Contrast this perspective on self-experience to some other perspectives that are commonplace. For example, when we look from the present at the past, it changes our self-experience; we're relating to ourselves based on what we did or what we used to be like. Similarly, looking from the present at the future involves anticipating what we might be like or how we might respond if a specific event happens. So a very simple yet powerful definition of present-moment awareness is that it's the immediate experience of being oneself (what's going on in the body, what emotions and memories are present, and so on) without interference from competing perspectives. In a simple sense, the goal of clinical work is to recognize when these interfering perspectives show up, and then neutralize their impact while strengthening the client's core skills for adopting the present-moment perspective.

A New Perspective on Mindfulness

The tenets of the neuroclinical approach can help us make better sense of the sometimes vague and confusing discourse about what mindfulness is, and how it applies to present-moment-awareness interventions. We agree with Kabat-Zinn (1994) that mindfulness involves learning to pay attention—on purpose and in a particular way. Basically, mindfulness practice teaches us how to use top-down attention. Thus, almost anything can be a vehicle for a mindfulness intervention, and indeed, almost anything you can imagine has been used that way: walking, breathing, gardening, eating, praying, music, art, literature, and the list goes on. As diverse as these practices might seem in form, they all share a common underlying feature: they recruit top-down attention. So in the process of practicing them, the underlying neural pathways that promote top-down attention skills are strengthened. This is undoubtedly why mindfulness is such a versatile clinical intervention. The reality is that most clients initially lack the ability to limit the pernicious effects of bottom-up attention, which increases the likelihood that the self-relevant meaning of distressing, unwanted private experiences will be skewed in a negative direction. Mindfulness practices supply clients with an antidote that stops this destructive spiral.

An Important Distinction

Mindfulness techniques are often thought of as being synonymous with present-moment-awareness interventions; however, while the two are clearly related, they are not one and the same. Mindfulness interventions are basically a form of attention control training, and, yes, clients have to be able to control their attention to make much headway in a present-moment-awareness intervention. As far as present-moment-awareness interventions are concerned, we regard the ability to focus and sustain attention on what has shown up in the present as a means to an end, which leads us to the bigger question: What is that end?

When clients enter into present-moment awareness and possess the attention control resources needed to stay present, they aren't suddenly, automatically healed from whatever ails them. Once the problem of attention control is solved, the real fun begins! What clients will immediately make contact with is the full gambit of private experiences that were previously inaccessible or systematically avoided. This is what everyone who has ever meditated knows all too well. You can get as quiet and focused as you can possibly imagine, but that doesn't mean your mind will shut up. While for many of us the typical problem is having a very busy mind that won't shut up, for clients it is having a very busy mind that won't shut up, combined with major, emotionally salient life experiences that haven't been integrated in a cohesive, healthy way. Once the client can control attention, the problem becomes what to do with the material that's showing up in the field of present-moment awareness.

The Clinical Benefits of Present-Moment Awareness

We should emphasize that our approach to utilizing present-moment-awareness interventions in therapy doesn't require clients to meditate, as is a common practice in some therapeutic approaches. We also don't assume that radical change is dependent upon how long clients are in therapy. Our goal is to help clients enter into the space of present-moment awareness, make sustained contact with feared content, and use top-down attention resources to reframe and expand the psychological meaning of the present-moment experience. In this sense, change triggered by present-moment-awareness interventions is a qualitative rather than a quantitative event. Not surprisingly, we see some clear and obvious clinical benefits associated with focusing on and utilizing present-moment-awareness interventions in therapy.

First, as we've pointed out, there really isn't a role for busy mind in the space of present-moment awareness. Busy mind is only capable of representing the past and future perspectives, whereas present-moment awareness involves being present, here and now, without interference from competing symbolic perspectives. Typically, when we have clients enter into the space of present-moment awareness, busy mind immediately attempts to pull them into a symbolically derived perspective of the past or future. Assuming clients learn how to tame this beast, they can create an accessible space where busy mind's activities are largely irrelevant. We like to call this "the sanctuary." When people are in the sanctuary, they are able to simply be aware of what they're aware of—nothing more, nothing less. When clients are stressed-out, the sanctuary offers respite from the endless negative chatter of busy mind.

Second, present-moment awareness is the only place where people can experience the immediate products of the interface between their inner and outer worlds without interference from the symbolic activities of busy mind. We like to remind clients that emotions are never wrong, and they are never accidental. They are the result of thousands of years of evolution, and it makes no evolutionary sense whatsoever to argue that they're bad for a person. Emotions are good for people; they're a powerful form of feedback about what's working in life and what isn't. Practicing present-moment awareness allows clients to absorb the information in their emotions, rather than getting lost in the mind's evaluations of emotions and directives about what should be done about them. In reality, nothing should be done about the way you feel except to feel the way you feel. Contact with this form of nonverbal intelligence often allows clients to override the directives of mind and behave in new, flexible, and effective ways.

Summary

In this chapter, we've explored the core features of present-moment awareness from the perspectives of neuroscience, evolution science, and contextual as well as clinical psychology. The picture that results tells us much about the probable clinical benefits of present-moment-awareness interventions. Clients who engage in these interventions are likely to experience improved health and well-being as a result of enhanced attention control skills and the resulting opportunity to reprocess distressing, avoided private experiences. This powerful clinical impact shouldn't be surprising, since most of the world's religious traditions implicitly or explicitly assume that sustained present-moment awareness functions as a portal to more transcendent forms of self-understanding. There is something extraordinarily powerful residing within the timeless perspective of being inside the moment, as anyone with a long-standing mindfulness practice will certainly attest to. On a more practical level, developing present-moment awareness creates the opportunity to learn new and more effective ways to live a vital, purposeful life.

For clinicians, the main barrier to optimizing the impact of present-moment-awareness interventions is the lack of a clinically useful framework for assessing specific present-moment-awareness skills, profiling the client's strengths and weaknesses in each skill area, and then designing interventions to improve skills as needed. For clients, the main barrier is having a mind that doesn't necessarily want to cooperate with interventions designed to improve present-moment awareness. In the next chapter, we'll address each of these topics in detail.

CHAPTER 2

Therapeutic Uses of Present-Moment Awareness

Mind is blocking the fountain of intelligence like a rock.

—Bhagwan Shree Rajneesh

When asked directly, most clients readily admit that being in the present moment is often associated with a positive sense of being alive. They seem to vaguely recognize that being here, now, is a good thing for their mental health. Unfortunately, it's difficult for clients (and all the rest of us) to create and sustain contact with present-moment awareness. Most clients come to therapy seeking help for their psychological pain, not realizing that this pain originates in how they process their ongoing present-moment experience. They want to talk about their problems endlessly and are loath to stop attaching to the endless evaluative activities of busy mind so that they can refocus their attention on the natural flow of emotions, thoughts, memories, and physical sensations that make up raw human experience.

Fundamentally, it is only in the present moment that the battle between experiential avoidance and acceptance can be won. Immersing oneself in busy mind's narratives about the past or future is, for most clients, the highway to hell. Our clinical experience is that helping clients stay in the present moment allows them to reconnect with personal motives that have been obscured by the mental clutter of the conceptual mind. The therapeutic conversation often turns to the client's life and what values or principles of living will guide the client's journey. Sometimes the clarity of the present moment brings into focus the need for game-changing moves in life, like quitting a job, leaving a dysfunctional relationship, or fundamentally reorganizing big-picture priorities. It is exactly this transformative power that strikes fear in clients and causes them to avoid the present moment like the plague.

In this chapter, we'll delve more deeply into the everyday barriers to developing sustained contact with present-moment awareness and how to use present-moment-awareness interventions to help clients confront and overcome these barriers. First, we'll examine the core features of busy mind that tend to set it at odds with present-moment awareness, leaving people bombarded with messages that the private experiences that lie in the present moment are toxic and must be avoided at all costs. Next, we'll examine how experiential avoidance fosters lifestyles and daily habits that essentially rob people of the opportunity to practice present-moment awareness. In contemporary life, we are socially conditioned to live an avoidance-based lifestyle. This is so widespread in our culture that we're facing an epidemic of mental disorders, addictions, and unhealthy lifestyles that kill people long before their time. Not surprisingly, clients bring their avoidance behaviors with them into therapy. Some of them are verbal (such as refusing to talk about something painful or changing the topic in session), and some are nonverbal (such as breaking eye contact, fidgeting in the chair, or pulling at a lip).

If you, the clinician, have an ace in the hole, it's that clients can't help but engage in their avoidance behaviors right in front of you. This puts you in perfect position to block experiential avoidance behaviors through the therapeutic use of present-moment-awareness interventions. To help guide you in this important endeavor, we'll introduce and describe a process model of present-moment-awareness interventions. This model holds that there are distinctly different phases within a present-moment-awareness intervention as it unfolds in session. Further, each phase places qualitatively different demands on the client's attention control and mindfulness skills. If you learn this model, you'll be able to pinpoint client weaknesses within each phase of present-moment awareness and build interventions to address those weaknesses. Bear in mind that the ultimate goal of therapeutic present-moment-awareness interventions is not only to undo the toxic impact of experiential avoidance, but also to give clients the skills they need to capitalize on the wisdom contained in present-moment experiences. It's one thing to learn to allow feared and avoided experiences to show up; it's a different matter entirely to convert emotional pain into a new frame of reference that makes it personally useful.

Busy Mind and Loss of Present-Moment Awareness

Earlier, we defined present-moment awareness as a timeless perspective on direct experience that's free from the competing perspectives of past or future. One might wonder what makes it so difficult for us to make contact with and stay in a state of present-moment awareness. The short answer is because we have a mind that doesn't like us to go there! Busy mind is ill equipped to participate in present-moment awareness because the symbolic activities of mind are always located, temporally, in the past or future. The mind will take any present-moment experience and render it in a past- or future-oriented form. At that exact moment, the human is given the choice of whether to simply be here, now, or to participate in the mind's version of here and now, which involves categorizing, predicting, comparing, and evaluating the here and now, not participating in it. Since the present moment is always unfolding in the here and now, the experience of being human is to choose one of the two alternatives just described on a moment-by-moment basis. We believe that the ever-present evaluative chatter of busy mind is what's most responsible for the common problem of not being here, now. Clients literally get lost in their mind and cannot shed its interfering perspective.

The fact that busy mind seems to win this competition over and over again, even though the result is suffering, is probably due to a negative interaction between the protect-and-survive imperative of busy mind and the intrinsic qualities of present-moment experience. Busy mind is an incredible tool. It helps us use the past to foresee and be prepared for the future. This seminal feature of busy mind is the reason we're at the top of the food chain, rather than being another animal's lunch. Think of how our chances of survival would drop if we couldn't learn from past experiences, predict future hazards, or find solutions to potential dangers before they arise. Thus, in addition to the evaluative and predictive activities of the mind being essentially hardwired, we are also evolutionarily predisposed to act based upon input from busy mind. We tend to take its products as facts and rarely challenge them. This lack of skepticism is where problems with busy mind start.

As discussed earlier, busy mind's definition of what constitutes a danger or threat is socially conditioned to include private experiences such as negative emotions, painful memories, intrusive thoughts, and unpleasant physical states. Busy mind tends to treat every possible threat as cut from the same cloth. It can become as reactive to a perceived slight as it is in the face of an actual threat to physical well-being. As a result, feelings related to either type of situation are distressing and painful and therefore are seen as bad for health and well-being.

It goes without saying that at least some of the private experiences that await us within the space of present-moment awareness are going to be painful. In therapy, distressing and unwanted thoughts, emotions, and memories that have been systematically avoided lie in wait for clients. The practical impact is that, because of the continuous proximity to the present moment, we are all bombarded with warning messages from the mind on a nearly continuous basis. And if emotional pain were, in fact, a threat to personal health, busy mind would be a godsend. The problem is, making sustained contact with distressing and unwanted private experiences is actually good for you. These experiences are part and parcel of the process of psychological integration and personal healing. In this scenario, the protection and survival activities of busy mind are the single biggest threat to the health and well-being of the human race.

A related issue is that busy mind isn't just equipped with a noisy warning system; it's equipped with a specific problem-solving model that's applied across the board when threats to survival are encountered. Threats are converted into problems to be solved. So if sadness is a problem to be solved, how would you know the problem has been solved? Answer: You wouldn't be sad; you'd be happy. And how do you solve the problem of being sad? Answer: Figure out what's causing you to be sad and then control or eliminate the cause. Then the sadness will go away.

While this approach works fantastically in the external world, it's a total flop in the world of emotions, thoughts, memories, and sensations. These private experiences are the natural by-products of human existence. Their causes cannot be controlled or eliminated without eliminating the human being. Further, attempts to control or eliminate the threats contained in private experience divert attention resources away from making healthy, sustained contact with private experience. The resulting blockage in the natural integration process amplifies the experience of distress and personal pain. But busy mind is like a one-trick pony. This is the only problem-solving rule it has to offer, and it will keep offering it come hell or high water. The result is that contact with distressing, unwanted private experiences actually *is* aversive—not because the experiences themselves are unhealthy, but because what we try to do with them is unworkable and actually ratchets up emotional pain.

In the darkest depths of this process, someone has to take the blame for the fact that nothing is working. Is busy mind going to confess to its inadequacies? Or is busy mind going to point the finger at the human being for not following the problem-solving rule well enough? For a clue, think about clients who ruminate incessantly about what's wrong with them, why they can't control their depression, or why they can't be happy like everyone else, and then conclude that they must have a major defect of character. Their rumination itself is a source of great suffering, but getting them to stop ruminating (following the problem-solving rule to control the distress they feel over the fact that the problem solving doesn't work) is an even greater source of anxiety.

Experiential Avoidance: The Ostrich Approach

If for whatever reason contact with distressing unwanted experiences contained in present-moment awareness becomes aversive and can't be directly controlled or eliminated, people often feel the next best thing to do is run from the threat. Experiential avoidance is, in effect, running from the threat posed by distressing private experiences. There are two problems that experiential avoidance attempts to address. One is the ubiquitous nature of the threat itself. We are always just a stone's throw away from contact with present-moment awareness. The other is that we've already learned from direct training that if we do busy mind's version of present-moment awareness, it's going to be very unpleasant. So the "problem" of negative private experience not only continues unabated; it actually seems to get worse. This creates anticipatory anxiety and fear at the mere prospect of contacting present-moment awareness. This shows up in therapy when clients start to exhibit anxiety and experiential avoidance behaviors in response to nothing more than the conversation turning to the topic of practicing present-moment awareness.

A threat this aversive and ubiquitous can only be dealt with by developing a continuous stream of experiential avoidance behaviors that constitute an avoidance-based lifestyle. This problem isn't restricted to clients in therapy; nearly everyone practices experiential avoidance in their daily routines. Some of these routines are so automatic that we aren't even aware that we do them. A formidable array of avoidance behaviors can be seamlessly integrated into daily living. Here's a somewhat small sampling:

- Driven household activities like cleaning, mopping, or doing laundry

- Daydreaming

- Getting overinvolved in other people's problems

- Ruminating about the past

- Worrying about the future

- Fidgeting, foot tapping, or restless movements

- Using drugs or alcohol

- Overeating

- Suppressing awareness

- Pretending to be okay when asked

- Not talking about emotions or personal issues

- Nonstop talking

- Distracting activities like TV, video games, or surfing the web

- Mindless self-preening behaviors (hair pulling, skin picking)

- Organizing and reorganizing things

Clearly, people use a wide variety of strategies to deal with the unpleasant reality that not only is busy mind's version of present-moment awareness quite unpleasant, but with it, things just seem to get worse. So why go there? We maintain that the main reason clients present for help is that experiential avoidance strategies aren't working. They can't help but make contact with distressing, unwanted experiences, but they aren't doing so in the healing environment that present-moment awareness provides. Instead, they are contacting the harsh, self-critical version of present-moment awareness that's constructed by busy mind. Instead of strengthening their top-down neural circuitry, clients are trapped in a cycle of practicing behaviors that strengthen the neural networks that produce SNS activation, bottom-up attention, and avoidance and escape behaviors.

The reason experiential avoidance leads people into therapy is because it gets converted into behavioral avoidance. As the list of activities above demonstrates, we can adopt a set of behaviors that effectively minimize contact with the present moment. A key feature of behavioral avoidance is that it functions like a preemptive strike on experiences that could potentially induce painful, present-moment awareness. For example, if participating in a social gathering is going to trigger social anxiety, the best way to deal with that preemptively is to avoid going to the gathering in the first place. Likewise, if sitting still in a recliner brings a person into contact with traumatic childhood memories, that person may very well get up and start cleaning as a distraction. When this simple, universal principle is applied to life overall, it creates a sense of aimlessness that contributes to a high level of symptoms and distress.

The Tipping Point

Our perspective is that no single act of experiential avoidance determines a person's fate; in fact, most of us practice avoidance on a regular basis and still do quite well in life. The tipping point is when checking out of present-moment awareness becomes the habitual response to highly salient forms of private experience. For example, if a person consistently avoids experience of negative emotions and thoughts about an intimate partner, he's likely headed for trouble in his relationship if the couple hits difficult times that strain intimacy. Or if someone tries to integrate sexual trauma she experienced as a child by suppressing all private responses related to it, she's going to struggle with rebounds of thoughts and emotions. And ultimately, if she simply refuses to enter into the social world of friendships and dating, she can't learn how to be anxious while at the same time being vulnerable.

The goal of present-moment-awareness interventions isn't to turn clients into little Buddhas, but rather to equip them with the knowledge and skills they need to check in when it's in their best interests to do so. Fortunately, when clients present for therapy, they have usually stumbled into a highly salient life area where checking out is exacting a terrible emotional toll on them. You, the clinician, don't have to cull through hundreds of potentially significant life situations to find the problem; the problem will be sitting right in front of you. When you simply observe the client's behaviors in response to the appearance of distressing content, you'll see the lapses in present-moment awareness that the client is using to cope with emotionally charged life challenges. You'll also have the distinct opportunity to help the client learn how to do the present moment a little differently.

The Functions of Present-Moment-Awareness Interventions

In chapter 1, we described present-moment awareness not as a temporally anchored event, but as a dynamic process of flexibly deploying top-down attention to foster ongoing psychological wholeness. This means present-moment awareness exists inside of time, because time itself is a symbolically derived perspective of busy mind. When we cease to be concerned about busy mind's time perspectives, what's left is just the direct, unhindered experience of contact with the contents of self. We call this "the zone." When you're in the zone, time seems to stand still. Present-moment-awareness interventions often have this feel; it can be hard to gauge how long the intervention lasted. Sometimes it seems like forever, even though it might be only two or three minutes by the clock. There's a lot happening inside of this short time frame, because the client's learning curve is exponential, not linear.

This being said, the reality is that each present-moment experience gives way to the next one over this two- to three-minute period of time. Our clinical experience suggests that present-moment-awareness interventions unfold in a predictable way over even very short periods of time. For lack of a better word, we'll call these quali-tatively distinct processes phases. The transition between one phase and another is time dependent because emotional processing involves a series of progressive actions taken over time. However, what happens *inside* any particular phase isn't time depen-dent. So the overall experience you, the clinician, will have is that of a warped time perspective. For the amount of time you've actually spent, the amount of change will be disproportionately large. Inside the moment itself, you will have the distinct feeling that everything is slowing down and coming into clarity. This is what it feels like to be in the zone.

Five Phases of Present-Moment Awareness

The approach we follow involves teaching clients how to handle the experiences they contact within present-moment awareness in a more effective way. This will allow them to experience present-moment awareness not from the self-evaluative perspec-tive of busy mind, but from the perspective of self-reflective awareness. Doing so requires clients to move through five qualitatively distinct phases, each of which makes different demands on their attention and mindfulness skills. We like to dis-criminate between these phases in terms of whether they have an orienting, counter-inhibitory, or generative function. *Orienting functions* involve bringing clients' attention resources to bear in a productive way. *Counter-inhibitory functions* involve actions that remove barriers produced by busy mind while in the midst of present-moment-awareness interventions. *Generative functions* involve transforming toxic or counterproductive meanings associated with previously avoided experiences into self-affirming, values-consistent meanings. Typically, traditional mindfulness skills are more appropriate when the function is to orient the client to what's present or to address inhibitory processes such as cognitive fusion. Generative functions tend to occur in the later phases of present-moment-awareness interventions and involve transformative events such as reframing toxic self-narratives, linking personal pain to values, or forming commitments to pursue activities that produce present-moment awareness in daily life.

Because our clinical approach involves teaching a blend of attention control, self-compassion, and mindfulness skills, we often administer self-report measures of mind-fulness, such as the Five Facet Mindfulness Questionnaire (Baer et al., 2008) or the Self-Compassion Scale (Neff, 2003), to clients at the outset of treatment to help us zero in on particular areas they perceive as weak spots in present-moment processing. Here's a summary of the overall clinical process model.

Phase: Noticing

Description: The ability to simply observe what's present in the moment and maintain an observer perspective

Function: Orienting function

Underlying process: Recruiting top-down attention resources, activating the executive control network, and organizing attention, focus, and the ability to shift between salient external and internal cues

Phase: Naming

[handwritten: thought / feeling / memory / sensation]

Description: The ability to name and describe private experiences contacted in present-moment awareness objectively and nonjudgmentally

Functions: Orienting and counter-inhibitory functions

Underlying process: Allowing for verbal mediation of private experiences at the self-reflective level, and enabling semantic processing and cognitively mediated emotion regulation networks

Phase: Letting go

Description: The ability to both recognize and detach from provocative evaluations or competing time perspectives injected by busy mind, and the ability to separate self from mental activities of mind

Function: Counter-inhibitory function

Underlying process: Using top-down attention and self-reflective awareness to override the negative information bias of bottom-up attention, as well as being a powerful emotion regulation strategy

Phase: Softening

Description: The ability to release oneself from imperfections and attachment to negative self-narratives, and the ability to connect with the universal nature of self-inflicted suffering

Functions: Counter-inhibitory and generative functions

Underlying process: PNS activation *[handwritten: breath]* increases perspective taking on self-defeating personal rules and self-stories, allowing for the existence of personal flaws or failures and the experience of self as part of humanity

Phase: Expanding

Description: The ability to find new purpose and life meaning that allows for making voluntary contact with previously avoided painful private experience

Function: Generative function

Underlying process: Using top-down attention and semantic processing networks to reprocess previously avoided experience, and activating the task-positive neural network and higher-order value-based problem-solving operations

In the sections that follow, we'll briefly introduce each phase and describe its relevance to healthy present-moment experience. In part 2 of the book, we'll delve into each component in much more detail to show how to assess it and how to develop interventions to improve clients' skill level in each.

Notice

The doorway into the present moment is to first elicit painful content in the therapeutic interaction and then help clients show up and make contact with it. Often, the signal that painful content has been triggered within clients is some type of verbal or nonverbal emotional behavior; clients might cover their mouth, put their head in their hands, or start to cry. Alternatively, you might observe verbal or nonverbal behaviors that indicate clients are trying to suppress or avoid whatever is present. They may change the topic, look away, sigh repeatedly, or engage in nervous movements like lip biting or playing with part of their clothing. Some clients may even directly communicate their desire to avoid making contact with the painful material, saying things like "I don't want to talk about this right now" or "I just want this to go away and to not think about it."

The act of noticing basically involves having clients remain motionless, figuratively speaking—just being aware of whatever has shown up. This means they have to round up their scattered attention resources (orienting response) and then direct those resources toward whatever is in their awareness in a sustained way (focusing response). When the content is painful, bottom-up attention is the dominant mode, and if this is left unchecked, it will result in clients' attention being scattered and unstable. Thus, the goal of noticing interventions is to help clients transition from bottom-up to top-down forms of attention so they can orient toward the pain, rather than avoid or deflect it. The next goal is to help them sustain attention on the pain to allow for subsequent emotional processing. All of this typically happens within a matter of seconds to just a few minutes.

Name

When all is said and done, humans are intensely verbal creatures. Relational frame theory, a post-Skinnerian account of human language, holds that the very experience of self is a symbolic activity that is created by and evolves in parallel with the acquisition of increasingly complex uses of language (Hayes, Barnes-Holmes, & Roche, 2001; McHugh & Stewart, 2012). We use verbal behavior not only to relate to the external world, but also to relate to whatever is inside our experiential world. An observation like "I'm feeling sad right now," even if it remains unspoken, is an example of how verbal behavior interacts with and organizes immediate experience. Indeed, we regard the ability to attach verbal labels to discriminate between and among private experiences as a core skill of emotional processing. You won't get very far in present-moment-awareness interventions if clients can't supply verbal labels that accurately correspond with core features of their present-moment experience.

The practice of applying verbal labels to distressing private experiences activates areas of the frontal cortex responsible for downregulating the amygdala and the bottom-up attention it recruits. The first step in emotion processing is to be able to put a name to each experience showing up in awareness, whether it be a thought, feeling, memory, or physical sensation. One significant barrier to being present is the inability to discriminate between various experiences that are occurring in the present moment. Clients may complain that the emotions they're experiencing are overwhelming and scary. Yet when asked to name the emotions they're aware of, they draw a total blank. Thus, a goal of this phase is to help clients begin to attach verbal labels to discrete elements of their self-experience.

The second goal of this phase is to help clients avoid using a type of verbal behavior that we don't want to see: implicitly or explicitly inserted evaluations, comparisons, or categorizations of private experience. As described earlier, busy mind will quickly impose its evaluative processes on any painful private experience. This is one of the main reasons clients avoid these experiences in the first place. They're under the sway of messages that these experiences are unhealthy and need to be controlled, eliminated, or avoided. Thus, the goal is to help clients develop the lexicon needed to simply describe the discrete components of their painful private events without injecting toxic evaluations or narratives that will distort the wisdom of the moment.

Let Go

No matter how good a client is at detecting and neutralizing busy mind's evaluations, comparisons, categorizations, and predictions, some of these mental activities are going to slip through the first level of defense (naming without evaluating). When this happens, the continuity of the moment will suddenly be disrupted as the client attaches to a provocative message from busy mind. The ACT term for this event is *fusion*, meaning the client and the mental activity meld together. The client's behavior will instantly be governed by implicit messages from the mind such as "I deserve to suffer because of my flaws" or "This sadness is going to kill me." The risk in the moment is that the client's attention will be diverted from simply noticing and naming experiences as they show up and instead turn to the task of following busy mind's problem-solving rule. The signs of this discontinuity are typically pretty obvious. Clients start talking about a present-moment experience rather than just having the experience. They may show nonverbal signs of divided attention, such as shifting around in their chair, nervously moving their hands, or breathing irregularly.

The antidote for fusion is to let go of any attachment to the literal meaning of what has shown up. If fusion is overidentifying with the literal meaning of a private experience, then letting go is disidentifying with it. In effect, letting go is the act of acknowledging what is in awareness (a thought, feeling, memory, or sensation) without attaching any significance to it. There are lots of different terms for this process: detachment, defusion, and stepping back, to name a few. In the moment, letting go is really a move to recapture and reorganize attention resources so the focus can remain on simply being aware of and naming whatever is showing up. Letting go is distinctly different from cognitive reappraisal in that the clinician isn't asking the client to substitute one meaning for another; the clinician is instructing the client to not believe anything at all. Belief or disbelief is irrelevant in the present moment. In fact, the minute belief or disbelief enters into the conversation, we are, by definition, no longer located in the present moment; instead, we're playing the mind's game of evaluating, rather than just having direct experience.

Soften

Similar to the permeable line of defense between naming and letting go, no amount of detachment is going to neutralize every closely held self-evaluation. The ones that slip through the filters of detachment are usually the real-life killers. They stick to clients like Velcro and color their view of how the world works, often functioning like a sort of self-fulfilling prophecy. We all carry narratives like this and deal with them primarily through experiential and behavioral avoidance strategies. People try to steer clear of situations that directly provoke this dark material, and when it is stimulated, they typically try to put the lid on it as soon as possible. This is, of course, exactly what clients have been doing, often exchanging any sense of vitality in life for escape from the harsh glare of the self-narrative. The pain that clients are experiencing is often decades old and based in terrible life experiences such as abuse, neglect, addiction, sexual violence, or the capricious giving or denial of parental affection and attachment. Alternatively, the client may have been hiding out with a carefully guarded narrative full of self-criticism that was acquired in the most innocent of ways.

Softening is a sublime form of acceptance designed to deal with the harsh self-narratives that can surface in the midst of the intense personal pain that often arises in present-moment-awareness interventions. It involves the ability to take a deep, relaxed, cleansing breath and lean into the pain that's present. This pain usually originates in the evaluative and storytelling functions of busy mind. The goal is for clients to accept themselves, flaws and all, recognizing that they are not alone in having flaws and imperfections. The life-altering question that's on the table at this moment is "Even if it were true that you have this flaw, could you accept that you still deserve your own kindness and love?" The act of embracing one's flaws like this is sometimes referred to as *self-compassion*.

Softening also requires clients to let go of their self-narrative and instead view it as a feature of busy mind. They can then develop a transcendent new perspective built on the realization that they are not bound to their stories. The storytelling functions of busy mind are basically useless when it comes to the life imperatives that really matter:

belonging, compassion, universal understanding, spiritual awakening, and a sense of meaning and vitality in life. Only in a state of quiet mind can we pursue these things.

Expand
- sealing the deal

As clinicians, we don't elicit painful present-moment experience and help clients integrate it because we believe in contemplating one's navel. Stewing in pain for the sake of stewing in pain is just therapeutic sadism. Bringing clients into contact with previously avoided private experiences needs to lead to something wonderful and eye-opening; otherwise present-moment-awareness interventions are a waste of time. The temptation after an emotionally powerful and draining experience with the present moment is to fall back into talking about it. Left to its devious ways, busy mind will quietly slip into the process and co-opt what has just happened, reframing it as some type of intellectual concept: "Oh, I see it now! If I just let my thoughts or emotions go, I won't have to experience the pain that goes with them."

Therapists often fail to see the risk of this type of regression during the most generative phase of present-moment-awareness interventions. They incorrectly assume that simply contacting the present moment in itself breeds powerful change, so no further therapeutic guidance is required. Nothing could be further from the truth; indeed, this phase requires the highest level of therapist activity. We sometimes refer to this phase as "sealing the deal," because the client and therapist have to jointly construct a new frame of reference for the painful experiences that have been the focus of the present-moment-awareness intervention.

So the last phase of the present-moment experience is to help clients develop a more expansive meaning for what happened during the intervention. This might involve leaving the room with a more compassionate, accepting, and transcendent form of self-awareness and sense of life purpose. The best analogy for this process within the client is two large soap bubbles floating into contact with one another. As they quiver and shake, their respective membranes meld to form one big bubble. One of these bubbles is the client's busy mind; the other is the client's quiet mind. The air inside the new, larger bubble is the client's ongoing moment-to-moment experience of both minds.

As clinicians, we aren't interested in preserving the sovereignty of busy mind. Rather, we're focused on joining it with quiet mind to create a more elegant form of ongoing contact with the here and now. Unshackled from the life-constricting, self-defeating impact of busy mind, clients are running in an open field, figuratively speaking. The question is what they wish to do with this newly discovered freedom. The conversation should naturally evolve to focus on how this new relationship with the self will influence their daily activities and priorities. How will clients change the ways they do business in all of the areas of life that matter? Ultimately, radical change means walking through a door into a new way of dealing with life on life's terms.

Summary

In this chapter, we've explored the barriers that clients experience as they try to deal with distressing, unwanted private experiences that tend to show up in present-moment awareness. The main culprits are the evaluative and problem-solving functions of busy mind, which make contact with painful private experiences terribly aversive. The main clinical implication is that clients won't be able to arrive at the restorative, transcendent aspects of present-moment-awareness interventions without first working through the barriers that busy mind puts in their way. This is where you, the clinician, get paid the big bucks to help out!

To help guide your clinical interventions, in this chapter we introduced a process model of present-moment-awareness interventions consisting of five distinct phases: notice, name, let go, soften, and expand. As one of two people trying to promote radical change, you, the clinician, are a core active ingredient in the process. Thus, it is imperative that you be able to model the same present-moment processing skills you're attempting to teach the client. In the next chapter, we invite you to take a closer look at your own strengths and weaknesses with respect to present-moment awareness skills.

CHAPTER 3

Clinician, Heal Thyself

Healing yourself is connected with healing others.

—Yoko Ono

In clinical practice, promoting radical change requires that you, the clinician, have the ability to be here, now, so that you can function as a role model and also observe and react to both verbal and nonverbal aspects of clients' present-moment experience. We've found that many clinicians have as much trouble being in the present moment as their clients. This may sound like an unwarranted generalization, but it actually isn't all that surprising that clinicians struggle with present-moment experience as it unfolds in session. Indeed, a core ACT philosophy is that clinicians are really no different or better than the clients they're working with. Both of you have your issues, and recognizing that is an important, humanizing way of forging the intense, horizontal therapeutic relationship that characterizes good ACT.

What clinicians can improve upon is deliberately structuring therapeutic interactions such that they increase the likelihood that clients will show up and contact the present moment in a productive way. To achieve this goal requires developing and utilizing insight into how we move inside our own present moment. Consider which issues or themes in therapy cause you emotional discomfort and possibly trigger your own experiential avoidance behaviors. How does your in-session behavior change when your buttons are pushed? What are the behaviors you use to avoid the moment on a more consistent basis in your daily life? Are there certain phases of present-moment processing that you struggle with or have especially strong skills in?

Without this kind of self-awareness, clinicians can only hope that the present moment spontaneously erupts on its own or occurs as an accidental by-product of some other intervention. In the end, the move into the present moment is a two-way street: both you and the client have complete control over the appearance or disappearance of the present moment in your interaction. You can cultivate present-moment experience, or you can discourage it. As the old saying goes, "It takes two to tango."

In this chapter, we'll help you build a better sense of your present-moment processing strengths and weaknesses. We'll start by having you look at your own out-of-session lifestyle behaviors to help you identify your higher-level escape and avoidance routines—those you manifest as behavior in day-to-day life. We call these *escape routines*. Then we'll examine some fairly typical in-session avoidance behaviors that clinicians can fall prey to so you can consider whether any of them apply to you. Finally, we'll have you complete a self-assessment of your present-moment processing skills using the phase model we described in chapter 2. We encourage you to take a good-faith approach to the self-exploration exercises in this chapter. There's nothing toxic about acknowledging that you have weaknesses and hot-button situations that trigger them. In fact, if you're unwilling to admit that you even have weaknesses, it's going to be very hard for you to correct them. So try to take an objective view of both your strengths and your weaknesses. If you have weaknesses that show up in this process, we welcome you to the human race!

General Escape Routines

To tell the truth, we are all escape artists, some of us just more so than others. The human nervous system is hardwired to trigger escape or avoidance behaviors at the drop of a hat. As discussed in chapter 2, the initial emotional tone of contact with the present moment is often negative and painful. Thus, it's fairly routine for people to just opt out of staying present. There are lots of things to do in daily life that require little or no contact with the present moment. We would argue that most people, including most clinicians, are checked out and living on autopilot for a good portion of each day. If you don't believe this, try to go through an entire day consciously choosing each action you engage in. We guarantee that it will drive you crazy to do so! The fact is, in many respects it's actually very convenient to just turn on the autopilot switch and let the mind do its thing. The tipping point occurs when escape routines become so pervasive that we no longer know how to make contact with the present moment when it's vital to our emotional welfare to do so.

Self-Assessment: What Are Your Escape Routines?

While the number of ways to escape is seemingly unlimited, our clinical experience suggests that most people use a smaller number of preferred escape tactics over and over again in daily life. As mentioned, we call these programmed responses escape routines. They are well-practiced, automatic behaviors you might use to avoid making contact with painful stress reactions. As you read through each of the short descriptions that follow, try to determine whether that escape routine is something you do frequently in your daily life. One important note: We think it's far more useful to treat escape routines in a lighthearted, humorous way, rather than taking a heavy-handed, judgmental approach. If you can, just notice which, if any, of these escape routines applies to you and let it go at that.

The busy bee escapes the present moment by staying busy all the time. If this is your main mode, most of the activities you engage in will be rather simple and can be done somewhat mindlessly. The busy bee moves quickly from one completed task to another and may sometimes repeat an activity, like cleaning the countertops in the kitchen, mopping floors, or waxing the car, several times. The busy bee may also go overboard by making tasks larger than they need to be—for example, washing all of the towels in the entire house, even those that have barely been used. A more technical term for this escape routine is "activity defense," with excess activity functioning to keep unpleasant and stressful internal experiences from seeping into awareness.

The butterfly escapes the present moment by shifting attention and focus constantly, like a butterfly flitting from bloom to bloom in a flower garden. This may occur with activities at work or at home. The butterfly starts activities, then quickly moves on to other activities, and then others. When sitting still, the butterfly often finds it difficult to focus on any one thing, making it difficult to complete simple activities such as reading a brief newspaper article or watching a TV program from beginning to end.

The ostrich escapes the present moment by ignoring distressing, unwanted private experiences by not allowing any thoughts about them to creep into awareness. When others ask questions like "How are you doing?" the ostrich typically says, "Fine." Around others, the ostrich avoids participating in conversations that might trigger contact with unpleasant internal experiences that have been carefully buried. The ostrich often changes the subject if a partner or family member starts talking about topics that might bring up this material. The goal of the ostrich is to remain unaware of and out of contact with distressing private content.

The twiddler is a bundle of nervous energy, escaping the present moment by zoning out in a rather limited space at home or at work. Whether seated, standing, or lying down, the twiddler's hands, arms, legs, or feet are usually in continuous motion. Anxious movements might include tapping a foot, twiddling fingers, mindlessly handling an object, hair twirling or pulling, or other small, repetitive behaviors. The twiddler has a hard time staying in one position for very long and often alternates between sitting and standing. The twiddler uses these minor, repetitive behaviors to bleed off energy due to unpleasant internal experiences and keep related emotions at bay.

The rationalizer is aware of distressing, unwanted private content, but escapes by explaining it away. The goal is to effectively disavow the existence of this content by insisting that it's something else—something much less serious. This is sometimes called denial, and it's a powerful defense against coming to grips with the reality that a problem is serious. The rationalizer may attempt to normalize stressful situations (for example, thinking, *Anyone who's expected to work that many hours is bound to be pretty tired*), minimize the impact of the problem (*I can make it even if I'm only sleeping four hours a night; I just can double up on my energy drinks*), or compare the current level of difficulty to that of others who "have it much worse." Usually, the rationalizer falls back on these strategies as a way to deflect the concern of others, such as a partner, friend, or coworker.

The busybody escapes the present moment by overfocusing on someone else, creating a lot of drama and emotional arousal around the other person's problems. Often this attention is directed at a family member with some type of substance abuse or behavioral problem. The busybody is often fixated on controlling the other person's behavior. This consumes most of the busybody's free time and mental energy, limiting opportunities for the busybody to directly experience distressing private content.

The worrier escapes the present moment by worrying about anything and everything *other* than present-moment experiences. Worrying all the time draws attention away from painful emotions related to unwanted private content. The worrier may not sleep well due to thinking about one worrisome topic after another into the wee hours of the night. Like the butterfly, the worrier tends to flit about, shifting from one worry to another when discussing concerns with a partner, friend, or coworker. Often, a difficulty that's glaringly apparent to others is conspicuously absent in these conversations.

The stoic escapes the present moment by bottling distressing private content up inside and often takes the stance that strong people don't show their emotions. The stoic may even deny that unpleasant private experiences are present. In fact, the stoic often denies having *any* emotional reactions and therefore may seem emotionally flat and numb. Topics that would typically give rise to emotions seem to have no impact on the stoic. Allowing even a trace of emotion to show up endangers the stoic's strategy of complete emotional shutdown.

The numbster escapes the present moment by using any means necessary to numb out the effects of unpleasant internal experiences, from drinking excessively, using drugs, or overeating to gambling, cutting, or sleeping the day away. The guiding philosophy of the numbster's approach is that you can't feel something if you aren't there to feel it. This pattern of behavior often is accompanied by a pattern of self-isolating behavior.

Again, when considering these escape routines and which might apply to you, try to take a lighthearted approach. You aren't the only one out there who's practicing avoidance strategies, and of course the point isn't to compare yourself to others. We instead urge you to remember the particular escape routine you tend to use most frequently in your daily life. In-session versions of those same routines are likely to appear when your buttons have been pushed during therapeutic interactions.

In-Session Escape Routines

Clinically speaking, the present moment is the space in which you and the client can simply make contact with what shows up in awareness, based upon the immediate context of the interaction. Cognitions, emotions, memories, and sensations are incredibly state dependent. When an interaction triggers a particular thought, feeling, or memory in you, your entire learning history with that private experience can wash over you. You might drift off into your own personal stories, recall similar painful events in your life, or get hooked by dire predictions about your own life fortunes. Faced with this onslaught of personally relevant and painful material, most clinicians are tempted to do the same thing their clients are tempted to do: escape from or avoid whatever is there.

An example might help make this more personally relevant. Imagine feeling totally lost with a client. The client has just disclosed an extremely painful story, and you feel stuck about how to respond. Then you get defensive because you don't know what to do next. What would be your strategy here? Would you break eye contact and instead look at your clipboard and pretend to be making some notes? Would you paraphrase what the client told you just to buy time? Would you get up, walk to your whiteboard, and draw an ABC diagram to avoid having to acknowledge the client's emotional distress? Would you start talking about what the research says about the client's particular issue in an effort to get the client to feel better? We confess that we've tried each of these strategies on more than one occasion.

It is, in fact, all too easy to be as experientially avoidant as clients, because that's how we create a sense of safety around unpleasant private reactions. If this supposedly works for clients, why shouldn't it work for us? Unfortunately, the end result is that it can be very easy for both clinician and client to end up in a dance of experiential avoidance, rather than a dance of present-moment-awareness processing.

Self-Assessment: What Are Your In-Session Hot Buttons?

In this section, we'll give you the opportunity to examine some of the in-session escape techniques you might use on more than an occasional basis. Again, remember the tipping point concept, first discussed in chapter 2. Using an in-session escape behavior isn't necessarily toxic by itself; what will severely compromise your effectiveness is if you, the clinician, persistently engage in escape behaviors across clients and across opportunities to cultivate present-moment awareness.

Each of the authors has been involved in the training and supervision of ACT therapists for many years. While many different hot-button situations arise in therapy that tempt clinicians to check out of the moment, certain clinical themes seem to consistently be high-risk situations. We've described these situations briefly below. As you read through the descriptions, consider whether any of them frequently elicit escape behavior on your part. For any issues that are hot buttons for you, you might want to write a few sentences about the escape behavior you typically engage in when confronted with that situation.

Failing

Many clinicians, if not most, choose their profession due to a genuine interest in helping other people. It would be fair to say that most of us believe deep inside that not being able to help a client is a personal failure, even though we know intellectually that we won't succeed with every single client. The moment when it becomes clear to you and the client that you haven't been able to help the client and won't be able to is a very intense present-moment experience. Knowing that someone is disappointed with you, or perhaps thinking that you may not be a very good therapist or that you've let someone down, can lead you to engage in escape behaviors. One of the main escape behaviors in this situation is to avoid thoughts of not being good enough by getting offended and blaming the client: "She wasn't motivated and didn't really want to change." "He wasn't ready to expose himself to a social situation." "I followed a treatment approach that's worked for everyone else, but she just didn't get it." We, the authors, are quite sure that you've heard things like this from colleagues, but never in a thousand years would you say something like this yourself!

Flaws

Kirk was once "fired" by a client, who said in a very polite and respectful manner, "You know, you're a really nice man, and I'm sure you really are trying to help people as best you can. But I just don't think you know what you're doing with people like me. I'm sorry to tell you this, but you should probably just refer me to another therapist who knows more about my type of problem. And maybe you should work with people with different kinds of problems than mine." Ouch!

This type of feedback might even come from colleagues, a boss, or a clinical supervisor. As difficult as it might be to field this kind of client feedback, there is always the possibility that the client might have something useful to share with you. Consider the example of professional baseball. An offensive superstar in baseball fails to get on base 66 percent of the time and gets to *that* level of failure because of an unrelenting work ethic and physical training that often spans decades. The reality that you will make mistakes or not be particularly effective in some clinical situations is both obvious at some level and emotionally threatening at another. How you deal with this obvious fact and the emotional threat associated with it is what matters. Some typical escape behaviors in this situation are to rationalize why it's impossible for you to be good at everything or to disqualify the source with thoughts like *She's probably a chronic malcontent. I'm probably one in a long line of therapists who haven't been good enough for her.*

Countertransference

Most of us are familiar with the concept of countertransference, or overidentifying with a client due to our own unresolved issues with the same situation the client is facing. It's useful to think of countertransference not as a thing, but as an ongoing escape behavior in which the clinician is using the client to vicariously process present-moment experience that the clinician is unwilling to face directly. The take-home message here is that countertransference happens all the time in therapy—not necessarily in the ways specified by psychodynamic theories, but in the broad sense that every therapist is prone to identifying with clients who are struggling with the same things the therapist has struggled with. In fact, ACT encourages a kind of voluntary countertransference reaction on the part of the therapist—with certain strings attached. The main string is that countertransference must be used to validate the client, not the therapist. When therapists fall into this escape routine, it is often hard to figure out who is actually receiving treatment. The therapist consistently overuses self-disclosure to bring the discussion back to how the therapist has dealt with that particular issue. The therapist may actually look to the client for validation, instead of vice versa. This version of countertransference radically compromises the integrity of any present-moment-awareness intervention because it isn't really designed to address the clinical needs of the client.

Codependency

Here, we define "codependency" as the act of knowingly or unknowingly conspiring with clients to help them avoid making contact with painful present-moment experience. This is usually done to please clients, to get their approval, and to help therapists avoid the same issues clients are avoiding. Codependency is sometimes revealed by client comments such as "I always feel so good when I'm finished talking with you. You make me feel good for at least a day or two." The real question is what the client is doing with painful private experience after two days, and whether it's working to promote the client's sense of vitality and purpose. The codependency pact is generally fatal to the goal of developing a healing therapeutic relationship. If the therapist is supposed to act like a role model, avoiding discussions of painful experiences is a bad idea. Still, sometimes when potentially painful issues arise, at the critical moment the therapist retreats from immersing the client in the painful material. In such cases, the therapist is hindering the client from directly learning that exposure to distressing emotions, thoughts, associations, memories, and physical sensations isn't toxic, but rather can lead to healthy life outcomes.

Self-Assessment: Taking Inventory of Your Present-Moment Processing Skills

Assuming that you, the clinician, are able to resist the temptation to engage in escape behaviors during therapy, you're still left with an important question to answer: "If I don't shoot myself in the foot by using escape behaviors, will I be able to make it through the various phases of present-moment processing as they unfold in front of me and my client?" We'll help you answer this question with the following self-assessments. Just as some clients are stronger than others at one present-moment processing skill, clinicians also potentially have an uneven skill profile. The bare-bones reality is that you can't fake doing the present moment. Your present-moment processing skills in each phase of the unfolding process need to be reasonably strong.

In this section, we'll ask you to complete a self-assessment of your present-moment processing skills using a subset of items from two self-report inventories: the Five Facet Mindfulness Questionnaire (FFMQ; Baer et al., 2008) and the Self-Compassion Scale – Short Form (SCS-SF; Raes, Pommier, Neff, & Van Gucht, 2011). Several FFMQ subscales map nicely onto the phases of present-moment processing we described in chapter 2. The Self-Compassion Scale is particularly relevant to the phases of softening and expanding. We often have clients complete these inventories as part of their initial assessment; this helps correlate our direct observations of their present-moment processing skills with their self-perceptions.

In the sections that follow, we will once again provide you with a brief description of each phase of present-moment processing and then have you complete a set of self-assessment items. Review the items and then rate your own personal experience during the past month in regard to frequency of experience, using the following scale of 1 to 5:

1 = never or very rarely true

2 = not often true

3 = sometimes true, sometimes not true

4 = often true

5 = very often or always true

Answer according to what really reflects your experience rather than what you think your experience should be. Also try to think about how you might experience the quality described in each item in the context of trying to help a client. We'll offer some suggestions about how to translate items in each of the processes to the clinical environment.

Notice

As mentioned in chapter 2, noticing requires top-down attention directed toward both internal experience (physical sensations, thoughts, feelings, and memories) and external events (sounds, sights, colors, faces, the activities of others, and so on). This observer mode of awareness involves development of a singular focus, and clinicians often vary in their abilities in this area, with some being more able to tune in to experiences within their own skin and others being more skillful in noticing even minute changes in client behavior. Skills in noticing are fundamental to powerful clinical interventions, so you may need to strengthen your abilities in order to be skillful in a variety of ways and with a wide range of clients.

Remember to translate the items below to reflect how they might show up in your experience as a clinician. For example, you might translate item 1, "When I'm walking, I deliberately notice the sensation of my body moving," to "When I walk with a client to my office, I'm aware of the sensations in my feet as they touch the floor." For item 4, you might translate it to "I pay attention to sensations in my hands, such as their connection with my keyboard or pen, when I'm working with a client."

Now, using the scale of 1 to 5 previously shown, indicate on the line to the left of each statement how frequently or infrequently you've had each experience in the last month.

____ 1. When I'm walking, I deliberately notice the sensations of my body moving.

____ 2. When I take a shower or a bath, I stay alert to the sensations of water on my body.

____ 3. I notice how foods and drinks affect my thoughts, bodily sensations, and emotions.

____ 4. I pay attention to sensations, such as the wind in my hair or sun on my face.

____ 5. I pay attention to sounds, such as clocks ticking, birds chirping, or cars passing.

____ 6. I notice the smells and aromas of things.

_3_ 7. I notice visual elements in art or nature, such as colors, shapes, textures, or patterns of light and shadow.

_3_ 8. I pay attention to how my emotions affect my thoughts and behaviors.

_26_ Notice score (the sum of your answers)

Take a moment to think about your strengths and weaknesses in this area. If you're aware of certain clinical situations in which it's easier or harder for you to practice and model noticing skills, take a few minutes to write about your impressions.

Name

Naming is the ability to use words to organize and convey what you're aware of either inside or outside you at any moment in time. Some people use the term "witnessing" to describe this process. A witness tells the truth and remains anchored in the present moment as an experience unfolds. Take, for example, the experience of a client beginning to cry in a therapy session and your almost immediate emotional response. Strong naming abilities involve being able to label a strong emotion the moment you make contact with it and using labels that are descriptive rather than evaluative. Strong naming skills also involve noticing possible urges to interpret and explain your experience rather than just naming it.

Using the same scale of 1 to 5 previously described, indicate on the line to the left of each statement how frequently or infrequently you've had each experience in the last month. Note that for items 3, 4, and 5, you need to subtract the number associated with your answer from 6 to obtain the score for the item. For example, if your answer to statement 3 is 4 (often true), you'll subtract 4 from 6, resulting in a score of 2.

_3_ 1. I'm good at finding words to describe my feelings.

_4_ 2. I can easily put my beliefs, opinions, and expectations into words.

6 − _2_ _4_ 3. It's hard for me to find the words to describe what I'm thinking.

6 − _2_ _4_ 4. I have trouble thinking of the right words to express how I feel about things.

6 − _3_ _3_ 5. When I have a sensation in my body, it's hard for me to describe it because I can't find the right words.

_3_ 6. Even when I'm feeling terribly upset, I can find a way to put it into words.

_3_ 7. My natural tendency is to put my experiences into words.

_2_ 8. I can usually describe how I feel at the moment in considerable detail.

_26_ Name score

Take a moment to think about your strengths and weaknesses in this area. Do you find it easier to label your experiences in some contexts than in others? If you're aware of any particular clinical situations in which it's easier or harder for you to name what you're aware of in the present moment, take a few minutes to write about your impressions.

Let Go

For clinicians in the therapy room, letting go involves the ability to allow any thoughts, feelings, memories, and sensations that arise in clinical work—to simply be present and allow them to come and go. Letting go is an ongoing process, given the tendency to become absorbed in mental evaluations of our experience (for example, _I'm not really helping this person. This isn't good. I have to do something effective now!_). Letting go is sometimes referred to as practicing detachment. If you have strong skills in this area, you're almost always able to make contact with difficult thoughts and feelings without becoming absorbed in them, even in very challenging therapeutic moments.

Now, using that same scale of 1 to 5, indicate, on the line to the left of each statement, how frequently or infrequently you've had each experience in the last month.

_2_ 1. I perceive my feelings and emotions without having to react to them.

_2_ 2. I watch my feelings without getting lost in them.

_3_ 3. In difficult situations, I can pause without immediately reacting.

_2_ 4. When I have distressing thoughts or images, I am able to just notice them without reacting.

_1_ 5. When I have distressing thoughts or images, I feel calm soon after.

_1_ 6. When I have a distressing thought or image, I sit back and am aware of the thought or image without getting taken over by it.

_2_ 7. When I have distressing thoughts or images, I just notice them and let them go.

_13_ Let go score (the sum of your answers)

Take a moment to think about your strengths and weaknesses in this area. Do you find it easier to detach in some contexts than in others? If you're aware of any clinical situations in which it's easier or harder for you to practice letting go, take a few minutes to write about your impressions.

Soften

Softening involves the ability to step away from harsh and critical narratives about yourself or your client and instead practice compassion—for the client and yourself. Most clinicians find it easier to practice compassion for their clients than to practice self-compassion. Self-compassion is an act of love and kindness that doesn't depend on your performance or accomplishments or the approval of others—a good thing, as we often need to be self-compassionate at precisely those times when we've made a mistake or disappointed someone. Clinicians with strong self-compassion skills tend to show concern for their own well-being, are able to tolerate their own distress without excessive self-criticism, and seek to understand what triggers any distress they feel— and they do all of this with a sense of warmth, gentleness, and curiosity.

The items below are taken from the Self-Compassion Scale – Short Form (Raes et al., 2011) and are reproduced with the permission of the authors. Using the same scale of 1 to 5, indicate, on the line to the left of each statement, how frequently or infrequently you've had each experience in the last month. Note that for items 1, 4, and 8, you need to subtract the number associated with your answer from 6 to obtain the score. For example, if your answer to statement 8 is 2 (not often true), you'll subtract 2 from 6, resulting in a score of 4.

6 – _3_ _3_ 1. When I fail at something important to me, I become consumed by feelings of inadequacy.

_2_ 2. When something painful happens, I try to take a balanced view of the situation.

_2_ 3. When I feel inadequate in some way, I try to remind myself that feelings of inadequacy are shared by most people.

6 – _3_ _3_ 4. When I'm feeling down, I tend to feel like most other people are probably happier than I am.

_2_ 5. I try to be understanding and patient toward those aspects of my personality that I don't like.

_25_ 6. When I'm going through a very hard time, I give myself the care and tenderness I need.

_2_ 7. I try to see my failings as part of the human condition.

6 – _4_ _2_ 8. I'm disapproving and judgmental about my own flaws and inadequacies.

_18·5_ Soften score

Take a moment to think about your strengths and weaknesses in this area. Do you find it easier to show kindness to yourself in some situations and more difficult in others? If you're aware of specific clinical situations in which it's easier or harder for you to practice softening or self-compassion, take a few minutes to write about your impressions.

Expand

Expand refers to a group of skills that support your ability to both reframe and transform the meaning of distressing private experiences so they don't function as barriers in your life journey. Reframing entails redefining a negatively charged situation in a way that allows for personal growth. In a clinical context, an example might involve being fired by a client and experiencing anxiety related to the thought that you're somehow inadequate. Strong reframing skills would promote acceptance of the situation and help you redefine the situation in a way that promotes growth, such as thinking, *This is a very courageous move for this client. My job is to create a positive ending to our relationship.*

Using the same scale of 1 to 5, indicate, on the line to the left of each statement, how frequently or infrequently you've had each experience in the last month. Note that for items 2 and 5, you need to subtract the number associated with your answer from 6 to obtain the score. For example, if your answer to statement 5 is 2 (not often true), you'll subtract 2 from 6, resulting in a score of 4.

    _3_ 1. When something upsets me, I try to keep my emotions in balance and focus on what they mean for my life direction.

6 – _3_ _3_ 2. During and after a difficult emotional time, I often end up "running on automatic" without much awareness of what I'm doing.

    _2_ 3. I use difficult emotional times as an opportunity to grow inside and learn more about myself.

    _2_ 4. Even when I'm very upset, I can still see the big picture of my life and what is important to me.

6 – _4_ _2_ 5. When I'm upset emotionally, I find it difficult to try new ways of reacting to how I'm feeling.

    _3_ 6. I think painful emotional experiences are as important to my growth and well-being as my positive emotional experiences.

    _3_ 7. I'm able to use difficult emotional moments to help motivate me to be a better person.

 8. When I'm feeling upset, I am able to adjust my actions in response to what my emotions are telling me.

___ Expand score

Take a moment to think about your strengths and weaknesses in this area. Do you find it easier to transform difficult present-moment experiences in some situations and more difficult in others? If you're aware of any clinical situations in which it's easier or harder for you to reframe present-moment experience, take a few minutes to write about your impressions.

Summary

You've arrived at the end of part 1 of this book. You've learned a set of concepts that will help you implement powerful present-moment-awareness interventions in your clinical practice. And because cultivating present-moment awareness promotes personal vitality, this will be as beneficial for you as for the clients you serve. This is why we encourage you to develop your own present-moment-awareness skills by adopting some type of regular mindfulness-based brain training practice in your daily life. This doesn't mean you have to start sitting in meditation or go on a retreat or to a monastery. It just means carving out some time in your daily routine to practice showing up and just noticing whatever exists in the present moment for you.

As we've noted already, it appears that a little bit of mindfulness can go a long way, especially if you can integrate mindfulness moments into your lifestyle. To demonstrate the benefits to yourself, after you've identified a small mindfulness routine that you can integrate into your life, practice it for three months, then take the preceding assessments once again. We think you'll be pleasantly surprised by the results!

PART 2

The Five Processes of
Present-Moment-Awareness Interventions

CHAPTER 4

Notice

The faculty of voluntarily bringing back a wandering attention, over
and over again, is the very root of judgment, character, and will.

—William James

In this chapter, we will thoroughly explore the first phase of present-moment-awareness interventions: noticing. This is the act of showing up and becoming aware of what's transpiring on both the inside and the outside. In ACT, we speak of the *observing self*, and it is the observing self that notices. Clinical experience suggests that the most destructive impact of experiential avoidance and fusion with mental rules that drive avoidance is that clients live their lives out of touch with important private experiences that are, in fact, a source of guidance. The problem is that these experiences are often painful in their own right and, evolutionarily speaking, they are neurologically designed to be that way. After all, the Latin root of the word "emotion" literally means movement. Private experiences move us to behave in different and more adaptive ways. If people are checked out and ignoring these important signals, their behavior becomes fixed, rigid, and largely controlled by socially-instilled rules, rather than being flexible and responsive to immediate contingencies. For example, if you refuse to make contact with a gut-level feeling that you're in a dead-end relationship, you will probably stay in that relationship—in large part to avoid making contact with that gut-level feeling and the fear of loss that it provokes. The result might be staying with a person you don't really love, with avoidance of the pain related to losing an attachment being the overriding factor in deciding not to leave.

Clinical Relevance

We propose that the first and most important skill clients need to learn is to just notice whatever is there in awareness. It isn't an overstatement to say that the main job of the therapist is to get clients to make immediate contact with feared or avoided private experiences in session so that higher-order processing of those experiences can unfold in the therapeutic moment. As simple as this sounds, it can be terribly difficult to implement in clinical practice. Most clients arrive in therapy armed with various well-practiced present-moment escape routines similar to those we described in chapter 3. They disappear from the interaction in any number of ways when the heat of the emotional moment reaches a critical level. You, the clinician, need to both recognize these maneuvers and gently and compassionately channel the client back toward the feared or avoided experience. In practice, this often feels a bit like a chess match, with the client matching your moves with new moves you haven't seen before.

In this chapter, we'll introduce a number of important clinical principles and associated practices that can guide you as you try to identify, assess, and intervene with this critical phase of a present-moment-awareness intervention. First, we'll examine three levels of observing, which you can describe to clients to help them understand how attention and awareness can be aimed at an experience. These three levels are being a participant, being a participant-observer, and being an observer. Second, we'll examine three core attention allocation skills to develop in session: orienting, focusing, and shifting. We will also briefly describe evidence from cognitive neuroscience indicating that noticing skills are supported by specific neural pathways. These pathways can be strengthened with practice, both in session and between sessions. We will then present a case example, which we'll refer to in the remainder of the chapter as we examine various ways to probe for deficits in noticing, how to read or assess the results, and finally how to intervene appropriately to target noticing skills that need to be strengthened.

Different Modes of Noticing

A good way to think about the act of noticing is to draw a direct parallel with the observation methods used in cultural anthropology. For the sake of simplicity, let's imagine that the task at hand is to understand what the experience of riding a roller coaster is like, from the inside out. The first level of observation is that of a *participant*. At this level of observation, you climb into the front car of the roller coaster and take the ride as if you were just another thrill seeker. You directly experience the excitement and terror of the ride in order to gain firsthand appreciation of what a roller-coaster ride feels like. When you take this approach, you aren't interested in anyone else who's riding with you or any other aspects outside of your immediate experience. Clients entering therapy are generally on this type of roller coaster ride with their private experiences.

A second way you could approach this task is to become a *participant-observer*. In this approach, you once again hop on the roller coaster, but this time you're both experiencing the thrills and studying the reactions of your fellow riders. Your attention is divided between your direct experience of being on the roller coaster and noticing all of the different verbal and nonverbal reactions of your fellow riders. You might even notice your own reactions and compare them with what you observe in others. When we train therapists, we encourage them to adopt this level of observational awareness in session—to be tuned in to both what they're experiencing inside and what the client is experiencing.

A final way you can approach this task is to study the roller-coaster experience from an *observer perspective*. As an observer, you don't even board the roller coaster; rather, you position yourself so you can see all aspects of the roller coaster in a larger context, such as how the platform and rails are designed, how the ride is powered, how people arrange themselves in the cars, and the various emotional reactions riders display. Your focus is on what you observe, detached from the ups and downs of the roller coaster itself. An important feature of this level of noticing is that it's nonjudgmental. There's an age-old saying in certain meditative traditions that describes this stance of simple awareness: "Don't say no and don't say yes to what is there." You don't react in any way that would cause you to push the experience away or bring it into yourself. Helping clients adopt this level of self-observation is often the conduit to immediate and powerful present-moment experience.

As should be obvious, the level of noticing chosen in response to a private or public experience directly affects which information will be screened in as relevant to the individual. In a participant state, clients' behavior will likely be governed by the immediacy of present-moment forces, and they may lose all perspective on the experience. Readers familiar with ACT concepts will probably see this as an example of fusion—the state of being melded with an immediate experience. This lies at the extreme end of participant-level experience, with clients forgetting that the experience is being "studied" at all. But it is also possible to be in a participant mode within an experience without necessarily being fused with it. In fact, we believe it is highly adaptive for clients to be able to shift between modes of noticing depending on the context. For example, the participant-observer mode might be useful in enhancing empathy and understanding of the emotional reactions of others. The ability to simultaneously observe—and understand—both your own reactions and those of someone else is a key attribute of empathic responding. Indeed, one client we worked with described this ability to shift between modes of noticing as a critical coping skill: "When my anxiety level is going up, I just need to change my level of participation!"

Basic Noticing Skills

As is true of most higher-order cognitive skills, noticing requires contributions from a number of component skills. In this section, we'll briefly discuss three attributes of noticing that collectively, or individually, can be strengthened by therapeutic intervention.

Orienting

We regard orienting as a basic attention skill that's internally triggered in clients in response to entering into the social context of therapy. From a social-evolutionary perspective, orienting taps into our initial response to the social command "Be prepared to see something!" The therapist is asking the client to get attention resources ready to be deployed in the immediate future. Does the client look in the direction you're pointing toward, metaphorically speaking?

The act of greeting a client for the first time is really an inquiry of sorts, asking the client to get ready to pay attention. There's a social purpose to getting a client and a therapist together in the same room. The question is whether, over and above the need for informed consent, the client can organize attention such that his or her behavior is properly in alignment with the original purposes of the meeting. The orienting response includes the ability to recognize the social-communicative nature of this purpose. For example, it's understood that the time allowed for the interaction is limited, that the relationship is different from other relationships, that the purpose is to talk about personal problems and solutions, and that there's a level of social etiquette involved that includes being cooperative and responsive to the therapist's lead, sitting a safe social distance apart from one another, avoiding asking the therapist inappropriately personal questions that exceed the level of the relationship, and so on.

Now consider clients who might be struggling to orient themselves in this rather basic way. For example, this might be a client who's already talking about intensely personal problems as you walk down a public hallway to the therapy room—even though you might be walking in front of or behind the client. Effectively, the client is either talking to the back of your head or to a wall ahead. Or it may be a client who sits in a chair in the therapy room taking a position perpendicular to you and staring out a window or at a picture while talking to you. Or perhaps it's a client who immediately begins asking probing, intensely personal questions about you, or seems to be interrogating you about your skills and qualifications as a therapist before you've even started your informed consent speech. Or maybe it's a client who immediately launches into a long story of personal woe before you've even introduced yourself or described the purposes of therapy. While it's certainly possible that some of these behaviors are due to lack of knowledge about the purposes or methods of therapy, far more often these behaviors are harbingers of deficits in attention.

Focusing

Focusing is the ability to bring attention to bear upon a particular target—in this case, a distressing private experience that might have occurred in response to a therapeutic probe. From a social-evolutionary perspective, focusing taps into the social command "Look at that, there!" The therapist is essentially telling the client to deploy attention resources in a specific direction, a step above just being ready to pay attention to something yet unseen. When clients can focus, they demonstrate the ability to hold still and show up for their present-moment experience. They exhibit awareness of not only private experiences like emotions, memories, and thoughts, but also internal physical sensations such as breathing rate or symptoms like muscle tightness, pain, or sweating. In almost every meditative tradition, focusing is regarded as the portal to transcendent awareness. If you can't focus attention on something, be it one particular experience (targeted meditative training) or the experience of "everythingness" (expansive meditation practice), then it's very hard to move toward deeper states of internal awareness and experiential processing.

Now consider clients who might be struggling with focusing skills in therapy. There are a multitude of verbal and nonverbal indicators of such difficulties. Clients may repeatedly change the subject, ask you to repeat questions over and over again, give vague or even completely nonresponsive answers to even simple probes, and so forth. Nonverbal behaviors—for example, breaking eye contact, engaging in repetitive nervous movements with hands or feet, suddenly changing body position, or sighing repeatedly— are also important indicators. These are signs of ongoing struggles the client might be having with focusing attention on something unpleasant. This is particularly likely to happen when the client is emotionally aroused, with bottom-up attention and the threat-scanning programs it commands vying for the client's limited attention resources.

Shifting

Clients' attention must be flexibly applied within a present-moment experience, because the clinically useful targets of attention might shift from moment to moment. From a social-evolutionary perspective, shifting taps into the ability to obey the social command "Stop looking there; look over here!" The therapist is instructing the client to move attention from one target to another. For example, a client might first experience an emotion, followed by an intense physical sensation, followed by a social interaction with the therapist—all within a matter of a few seconds. The client's attention has to follow along with these important contextual shifts. Noticing one experience and then shifting to another experience unfolding in time is a higher-order use of noticing skills and promotes the linking of seemingly unrelated experiences into coherent stream-of-consciousness processing. There are few emotionally meaningful moments in life that are comprised of one experience only; they're much more likely to be lodged in a network of associated experiences encompassing past and present-moment experiences.

Now consider clients who might be struggling with the skill of shifting in therapy. Signs of difficulty with shifting focus frequently involve lapses in verbal processing— perhaps due to persistent rumination, worry, or perseverating—or even comments from clients indicating that they feel lost and don't know what to do next. Nonverbal indicators might involve sitting motionless with no perceptible change in facial expression for an unusually long time after being encouraged to make a shift from one private experience to another. Another important indicator of trouble is when clients can't seem to shift from internally to externally focused attention; rather, they seem to be lost in what's happening inside and, despite verbal prompts, can't reorient toward the therapist or reenter the therapeutic conversation.

Neuroscience Considerations

Much of what we've learned about the neuroscience of attention comes from research on the impacts of meditation on brain structures. This field of neuroscience has grown exponentially over the last decade. Indeed, meditation can be thought of as an ornate form of attention control training. This probably explains the profoundly positive effects that treatments incorporating meditation have upon conditions like depression, as these conditions are theorized to originate in problems with attention bias and failures of attention control (Rawal, Park, & Williams, 2010). There appear to be neural pathways that support each of the three forms of noticing we've already described (Lutz, Brefczynski-Lewis, Johnstone, & Davidson, 2008). First, orienting, which involves selecting specific information targets from the ongoing flow of sensory input available to the brain, seems to recruit cortical structures known to serve as gatekeepers for information, such as the temporoparietal junction, the ventrolateral prefrontal cortex, the frontal eye field, and the intraparietal sulcus. Second, focused attention involves the ability to maintain a state of high sensitivity to an internal or external stimulus over time and most likely involves sustained synchronous activity between the thalamus and the right frontal and right parietal cortical structures. (As mentioned, this neural pathway is also known as the thalamo-cortical loop.) Finally, shifting attention, such as when disengaging from one stimulus and redirecting to another equally salient but competing stimulus, recruits cortical structures responsible for executive control. As explained in chapter 1, executive control is the ability to both monitor and resolve conflicting demands for attention in the presence of emotionally salient cues—in this case, staying present with whatever is held in awareness, even while emotionally aroused. This function is managed by the dorsal anterior cingulate cortex and the dorsolateral prefrontal cortex, brain structures that have also been shown to be activated during tasks that require high levels of self-awareness.

• Case Example: Rafael

Rafael is a thirty-four-year-old married Latino with three sons. He's worked at the same job for fifteen years and describes it as very stressful but positive. He presented for help because of increasing problems with depressive experiences and anger outbursts at his oldest son. Although Rafael was a reasonably good student in high school, he was never part of the in crowd. He was self-conscious about his physical appearance and social skills and often felt like he was on the outside looking in during classes or social occasions. Despite this, he had a few very close friends. He married his one and only girlfriend, and their fifteen-year marriage has been solid. He describes his wife as his best friend. In fact, it was she who urged him to come in for help because of his increased self-isolating, brooding behavior at home and his frequent outbursts of anger toward his oldest son, Jesus.

Rafael is also highly concerned about his growing irritability and how it's so easily triggered by Jesus's mocking behaviors. These behaviors include refusing direct instructions to do his chores, mimicking Rafael's voice and emotion tone, and coaching his father in how to pronounce certain words correctly. Rafael says he's starting to go ballistic when his son engages in these provocative behaviors.

When first greeted in the waiting area, Rafael looked down and made only partial eye contact. His handshake was very passive, with a weak grip, and he hesitated and seemed uncertain about leading the way to the therapy room even though its location had been pointed out to him beforehand. During the initial interview, he tended to look down and away when talking about his boyhood experiences and his frustration at being unable to control his temper. Initially, his answers to questions were somewhat vague and incomplete, and at times he abruptly changed the conversation by asking a question that was superficially relevant but really out of the flow of the conversation. In addition, he sometimes paused for an unusually long amount of time before responding to comments or questions. It appeared that he was distracted by his reactions to questions.

Probe, Read, and Intervene

In this section, we'll describe clinical methods and strategies designed to help you both recognize and assess clients' noticing skills as a session unfolds. Once you've made your on-the-fly assessment, you'll need to intervene. To give the processes of recognition, assessment, and intervention a more practical basis, we'll illustrate these methods using Rafael's case each step of the way.

Probe: Noticing Initial Impressions

You, the clinician, are entering into the therapeutic conversation with the explicit goal of promoting a powerful and life-changing present-moment experience for the client. This is a real possibility for any client with any type of problem, regardless of the length of the client's struggles with mental health problems or substance abuse issues. Because this is your goal, think of every communication from you as a probe. Like a dentist, you're poking and testing each experience the client brings to the table. The purpose is not to be sadistic, but rather to uncover sources of unprocessed pain that could lead the client to powerful present-moment realizations. Notice, for example, that the clinician is already probing Rafael while shaking his hand and seeing if he'll make eye contact. Even at this early juncture, the therapist is already beginning to size Rafael up. How firm is his handshake? How does he handle eye contact in the waiting room? How does he handle the uncertainty of who's going to walk in the lead position down the hall to the therapy room? While exchanging pleasantries with him before heading off to the therapy room, does he appear to be in sync with the social purpose of pleasantries? Indeed, there is much to be learned in the first one to two minutes you spend with a client, before the mission of therapy is even started.

Probe: Mouse Perspective Interviewing

We view the presenting problem a little differently than many clinicians might. We aren't trying to eliminate the presenting problem; we're trying to make it happen in the therapy session. To really see how clients handle present-moment experiences, you have to elicit whatever is painful and then see what they do when the pain shows up. One good way to do this is to develop the "mouse perspective" of the problem. This means breaking down situations in which the presenting problem occurs into very small pieces and beginning to tug at each one to see if it's connected to the client's pain. The following dialogue demonstrates how the therapist took the mouse perspective approach with Rafael.

Clinician: Rafael, help me understand how this goes down with you and your son, Jesus. Just take me through it step-by-step—maybe the last time you went ballistic with him.

Rafael: Oh, that was yesterday. I was so angry that my wife basically told me to leave the house and cool off. [Read: This is a good, clean, responsive answer, indicating that Rafael is oriented.]

Clinician: Okay, cool. Can you give me a blow-by-blow description of who said what? Try to stay focused on just this one incident.

Rafael: Well, I had just gotten home from work, and I was tired and stressed-out. I think I told you that I'm the only machine operator, and I keep getting more and more work because I'm the only one there. Well, it just stresses me out because I really like my boss and I know he's trying to find another operator. [Read: Rafael starts out focused and then starts to get distracted by his other problem. The clinician will intervene to bring him back on track.]

Clinician: Okay, so tell me what happened with you and Jesus when you got home and were stressed and tired.

Rafael: Okay, sorry. I got a little off track. [Read: This is a good response, indicating that Rafael has the ability to notice that he was getting off track.] So, as usual, he hasn't done the dishes from breakfast and lunch, and that's his chore. I basically said, "The dishes aren't done. Go in and get them done before dinner." Then he said, "You said 'deeshes.' Dad, it's pronounced 'dishes,'" in this smart-ass tone of voice.

Clinician: So, what showed up right away was this thought that he was being a smart-ass.

Rafael: (*Drops his head and looks down.*) Yeah, and he's acting like I'm some kind of retard that can't speak English right. [Read: The fact that Rafael dropped his head slightly suggests there might be something emotionally painful that just showed up. The clinician will follow up on this.]

Clinician: Okay. I noticed you just looked down a little bit, like something showed up that caught you by surprise. Can you tell me what just showed up?

Rafael: I don't like being made fun of—never did and never will. [Read: He's bouncing off the pain by giving the clinician a semiresponsive answer, but he isn't really touching whatever is there. The clinician is going to try to get Rafael to contact the painful experience again to see if he'll engage with it.]

Clinician: Yeah, I don't know many people who enjoy being mocked or made fun of. So, did anything else come along with the part about being made fun of?

Rafael: Well, I told him that he isn't going to talk to me that way and he can get the fuck out if he isn't going to do his chores. Then he rolled his eyeballs in that special way he does to say, "Fuck you!" [Read: Rafael bounced off the second probe by shifting the topic back to the fight with his son. He has created more distance between himself and the painful experience by doing so. His body posture has also changed to being upright and tense looking, with his fists clenched and arms crossed.]

Clinician: So, you went ballistic?

Rafael: Yep.

The beauty of getting inside any problematic experience is that it offers a gold mine of direct observational data about how the client handles that experience. Because most clients aren't used to talking about something like anger in such exquisite detail, they can be surprisingly candid in walking clinicians through their experience. There's a lot that's loaded in that experience: not just particular aspects that clients want to avoid ("I don't like being made fun of"), but also other aspects of the experience that clients may be completely out of contact with. These are often the most painful aspects. We often liken the mouse perspective interview to pulling on a ball of string. We just keep pulling and pulling until no string remains.

Read: Formulating a Clinical Impression

It's crucial to take on-the-fly assessment data and quickly formulate an impression of the client's strengths and weaknesses. In the previous interaction, the clinician is testing Rafael, and taking a humane and compassionate approach to doing so. The clinician is methodically bringing up painful content for Rafael to interact with. The initial goal is to see how Rafael reacts when painful experience shows up. Does he seem willing to engage with the pain? Does he lose his focus and get distracted easily? Does he change the subject? Does he explicitly ask to talk about something else? Does he hunker down in his chair and begin to restrict his range of movement or facial expressions or flatten his tone of voice? These are all fairly typical signs of failures in noticing skills.

One of the best ways to elicit noticing skills is to ask questions that encourage clients to deploy these skills. Here are a few examples:

- "I'm curious—what just showed up for you as we were talking about this?"

- "Can you just sit with what's here without saying yes or no to it?"

- "Can you just let this stuff be here without doing anything but noticing that it's here?"

- "Can you point to the area of your body where you feel whatever is showing up?"

A variation on that approach is to make gentle suggestions about what you've just observed in the client's verbal or nonverbal behavior—suggestions that indicate a meaningful experience may be there to be noticed. For example, you might use the following questions:

- "I noticed that you slumped over a little bit and dropped your eyes just now [or a minute ago]. Did you notice that you did that? What was going on at that exact moment?"

- "I noticed that your eyes looked sad just now. Did something just happen for you while we were talking about this?"

- "You look more restless—almost like you're uncomfortable in your chair. What's going on for you right now?"

Based upon the brief exchange above, the clinician concludes that Rafael is sitting on some painful private experience that he's been avoiding. When confronted directly by this experience, his noticing skills get fragmented. He can catch a glimpse of what's painful, but then his ability to sustain his attention breaks down. He bounces off his experience by changing the subject or processing the experience in an oblique way—for example, stating that he doesn't like to be made fun of rather than talking directly about his emotional reactions to the experience of being mocked. The fact that he refused to make contact with that experience even after being redirected suggests that his focusing skills need to be strengthened.

Intervene: What's the First Emotion?

Based upon this brief but highly revealing test of Rafael's noticing skills, the clinician decided to bring him back to the reactions he was having when his son was mocking him by posing an interesting idea: "What if anger is always the second emotion you have? What if your problem isn't anger management, but that you use anger as a means of deflecting contact with whatever your first emotion is?" Here's how the clinician presented this to Rafael.

Clinician: I noticed when you were talking about how much you dislike being made fun of that you kind of slumped a bit and looked down at your hands. Did you notice yourself doing that?

Rafael: Yeah, I was remembering being back in high school. I wasn't very athletic and I had really bad acne. I always felt like everyone was looking at my face, maybe thinking I was ugly or feeling sorry for me. [Read: This is a very self-revealing present-moment type of response both in content and in terms of Rafael's nonverbal demeanor, which is quite sad. The clinician will try to amplify this moment of just noticing what's there.]

Clinician: Wow! That must have been really painful. (Pauses.) Sounds like it went on for a long time. That must have made you feel like you were on the outside looking in. (Pauses.)

Rafael: (Looks down again and is silent for ten seconds.) I don't like to think about it. It's in the past and I've moved on—no point in going over it again. I've told my wife that I had a painful teenage life, but there's nothing she or I or anybody can do about it. [Read: Rafael is starting to pull away from his painful memories and feelings by rationalizing his experience, rather than simply contacting it. The clinician is going to block his escape route.]

Clinician: Sounds like the past is still here to me. Maybe it isn't done. Maybe the past is what shows up when your son mocks you?

Rafael: What do you mean? [Read: This is a good reorienting response. Rafael isn't getting lost in his rationalizing escape route. He seems to be curious and is looking for additional information.]

Clinician: Well, can you tell me what you're feeling right here, right now, as we talk about you having acne, being kind of a nerd and not in the in crowd, and being teased about your appearance? (Pauses.)

Rafael: Well, geez, it's sad, you know? I haven't thought about it in a long time. I'm kind of surprised that it's come up in just a little while like this. [Read: This is a positive sign of an orienting and focusing response. The clinician wants to see if Rafael can keep a sustained focus on his sadness without saying yes or no to sadness.]

Clinician: Okay. So can we just sit here with sadness for a few minutes? You don't have to do anything about the sadness. Don't try to push it away or swallow it; just quietly stand your ground and notice it.

Rafael: It's hard. I don't like feeling this way. [Read: Rafael looks up and away with a strained look on his face, and his body language is starting to look more restless. This indicates that he's struggling to maintain focus as he shifts attention from one element of his emotional experience to another. The clinician will try to have Rafael practice shifting his attention while maintaining focus on the overall experience.]

Clinician: I know it doesn't feel good to be sad... Can you just let yourself breathe in this sadness? You don't have to do anything with it. Just breathe and stay here. Are you aware of anything else that's showing up inside right now?

Rafael: Well, I have a specific memory of being called "pit bull face" by a girl who was trying to show off for a bunch of guys. I remember getting really angry and yelling at her that I was going to kick her face in if she didn't shut up. I ended up getting a referral to the principal for threatening her. [Read: This is a very positive, multielement disclosure, and Rafael is staying focused as he shifts from element to element. The clinician is going to expand his flexibility by introducing emotionally salient content while helping him stay present.]

Clinician: So, she really hurt you and then you got really angry, right?

Rafael: Yeah, I pushed back after she jerked me around.

Clinician: And as you have this memory—and remember, we're still sitting here with sadness too—what do you sense was the very first feeling that showed up right at the exact moment she called you "pit bull face"?

Rafael: Well, it was sadness about being rejected and being different in a bad way. [Read: This is a very strong noticing response, combining different feelings in a highly congruent way. The clinician is going to push on!]

Clinician: So, it seems like what you're making contact with is that first you get sad, and then, to cover it up, you get mad. Is that what you're telling me?

Rafael: Well, I'd say you're right. I didn't realize those two things came together, but I think they do. And I've done this at other times with people when I think they're judging me or laughing at me. I have a hard time putting up with teasing, even from my wife. [Read: Rafael hasn't been thrown off track by the appearance of historical material and now is making contact with other, more generalized emotionally salient memories. The clinician is now ready to help Rafael connect the dots.]

Clinician: Would I be out-of-bounds to suggest that maybe this is what's going on when you and your son butt heads? He does something that makes you sad, then you cover up your sadness by being mad?

Rafael: That's exactly what I do, now that you talk about it this way.

Clinician: What if every time your son pushed your buttons like this, you first looked for sadness and just sat with it for a few seconds? Then, when anger shows up, if it does, don't say yes or no to it. Just let anger be there without doing anything about it. Inside your heart, you know what the anger is all about. It's inviting you to not let your sadness into the room. And you want to feel sadness as sadness, not as something else. That doesn't mean you like feeling sad. I know I don't like to feel sad. You could almost be grateful to your smart-ass son for giving you the opportunity to learn to feel sad. How cool would that be?

Rafael: *(Smiles.)* I would just walk away, because there's nothing to fight over.

In this dialogue, the clinician is gently directing and redirecting Rafael to practice noticing his emotions, memories, and thoughts as they appear inside the moment within the conversation. Even though this entire interaction took just five to seven minutes, the clinician exercised extreme patience throughout. Every step was guided by a question or a gentle proposal that was left at the client's feet, figuratively speaking. In the next section, we'll examine some of the technical errors that therapists often make when the conversation is about noticing experience.

Practical Clinical Tips

Therapists often struggle with the mechanics of maintaining an appropriate conversational flow when working to elicit noticing skills. This is primarily due to the fact that we're transitioning from the verbal enterprise of therapy into the far less verbal world of immediate experience. Although words are a necessary feature of the present-moment experience, it's essential to use them in ways that maximize their impact.

Slow the Pace

The natural tendency of therapists is to keep plowing ahead even though the content involved is emotionally and cognitively complicated. It's important to build a solid step-by-step noticing experience. This requires the therapist to slow down the pace, not speed it up. Your voice should typically be softer than usual, your sentences shorter, and your rate of speech slower. It's okay to let clients linger inside the moment with fresh experiences. Again, inside the moment there is often the mental illusion that the intervention is taking a long time. You might start looking at your watch and worrying about running late. Stay located in the present moment with the client and remind yourself that your normal sense of time doesn't work in the zone. If you appear to be relaxed and not in any particular hurry, the client will pick up the idea that noticing really requires being able to relax, slow down, and control attention.

Don't Talk, Do!

Noticing is facilitated by silent observation and the sparse use of words. So choose your words carefully. They should be designed to help focus the client's attention on something or help the client shift attention in an effective, flexible way. The aim is not to talk about experiences, but to get the client to directly experience whatever is there. You can almost think of yourself as a coach who's teaching a player to hit a baseball. You let the player take several swings at pitches, then you might make a limited comment or two about the mechanics of the swing. When you see clients drifting away from the noticing stance, you might make a comment to that effect and encourage them to try something a little different.

Gentle Reminders

In this chapter, we introduced noticing, the first phase of present-moment processing, a touchstone without which all hope is lost. Clients must be able to get present and make contact with whatever is going on inside. This requires that they be able to first orient toward a private experience, then focus on it without having all of their attention resources absorbed in the process. They must be able to flexibly shift attention between and among relevant targets as present-moment processing begins to unfold. Asking clients to show up in this way requires the clinician to be acutely observant of what clients are (and are not) doing in the interaction. There are usually numerous, subtle cues that signal whether the client is checked out or tuned in.

When you learn to reliably lead clients into the stance of noticing whatever is there, you've helped them develop the attention control skills needed to begin making sense of what's going on in the present moment. The first of these important processing skills is learning how to use verbal labels to describe various private, nonverbal experiences such as emotions, memories, and sensations. This is the skill we'll address in the next chapter.

CHAPTER 5

Name

Just because you didn't put a name to
something did not mean it wasn't there.

—Jodi Picoult

It's somewhat paradoxical that, in ACT, words are both the medium for processing and integrating experience and, at the same time, treated as the "enemy within." The reality is that present-moment experiences cannot be processed and integrated in any meaningful way without engaging the client's cognitive abilities. Three of the four major components of present-moment architecture (sensations, memories, and emotions) are best thought of as perceptual and somatosensory experiences. Thus, they aren't located in a client's verbal world. They are often bundled (along with associated cognitive appraisals) and experienced as being overwhelming in intensity or complexity. Other than difficulties with paying attention in the first place, this is the major reason that we all tend to avoid the present moment until the social or emotional consequences compel us to behave differently—or to seek help from a counselor. It's only through applying the cognitive processing and appraisal mechanisms of general intelligence that regulation and behavioral integration of these nonverbal experiences is achieved. The problem ACT therapists face is that these same verbal processes have been socially reinforced to encourage clients to avoid, suppress, or ignore nonverbal experiences, leaving them bundled and undifferentiated in clients' awareness.

Clinical Relevance

Developments in the scientific study of emotion processing and emotion regulation clearly suggest that the ability to interact verbally with nonverbal experiences is the linchpin for successful psychological outcomes. People who can verbally discriminate between pleasant and unpleasant experiences, and also discriminate between distinct types of nonverbal events, tend to score higher on tasks requiring emotional intelligence—such as the ability to alter behaviors based upon social and emotional inputs—and on emotion regulation, meaning the ability to process the personal meaning of emotions and regulate behavioral impulses according to social norms (Smieja, Mrozowicz, & Kobylinska, 2011). From a clinical perspective, applying verbal labels supports three core processes thought to be essential to successful emotion processing:

- Matching the category of emotional event to the appropriate class of verbal labels (for example, using an anger-related word when the feeling of anger is the emotion that's present)

- Discriminative use of verbal labels to identify discrete emotional experiences with different feeling tones lodged within the same experience (for example, the ability to distinguish, via words, the difference between being angry and being hurt in the same interaction)

- Gradation in the use of verbal labels to reflect different intensity levels of a specific emotion state (for example, with anger, using "irritated" versus "livid" depending on the intensity of the emotion)

From an evolutionary science perspective, naming is being able to answer the basic survival question "What is that?" We've focused attention on something; now we need to know what it is. In a modern-day sense, words allow us to answer this basic survival question. After clients first come into contact with an avoided present-moment experience, they often start to act confused. If asked what they're aware of, they may say something like "I don't know; it just seems overwhelming." If asked to pick apart a component of the experience, they frequently hesitate and seem unable to respond. For example, if clients are asked to name physical sensations in their body, they might be able to name only one sensation in one area, and that only with lots of prompting from the clinician. Later in the same clinical conversation, after some processing has occurred, they might report broadly distributed sensations of different types located in multiple areas of the body. In a sense, this phase of present-moment processing can be viewed as a type of discrimination training in which the clinician helps the client identify or develop the lexicon needed to interact with the products of present-moment experience.

In this chapter, we'll address several important features of this discrimination training. First, we'll examine the two central components of naming: finding words, and using direct, descriptive observational labeling instead of evaluations of experience. Then we'll examine the developing neuroscience that shows how emotions and cognitions are integrated within an interactive network involving multiple regions of the brain. Finally, we'll use a case example to demonstrate how you, the clinician, can probe, read, and intervene to facilitate the client's progress in developing these important present-moment processing skills.

Basic Naming Skills

Using words to accurately describe private experiences is absolutely essential if clients are to move on to the more sublime stages of present-moment processing. The metaphor we like to use is learning to write in cursive. The first step is to learn the letters of the alphabet; then you learn how to print the letters and spell basic words correctly; then and only then do you acquire the more advanced skill of writing in cursive. Just as orienting, focusing, and shifting attention are distinct mental skills, the ability to use words in a positive way to process experience is a skill. Because of dysfunctional family or role modeling environments, many clients lack these basic skills. Your job as the clinician is to help clients acquire these important abilities.

Finding Words

Simply put, to bring nonverbal experiences into contact with cognitive processes requires selecting socially congruent labels and attaching them to each relevant component of the experience. For the social functions of language to be useful, there must be a close correspondence between the labels one person would use to describe a particular private experience and those another person would choose in the same basic type of experience. Practically speaking, this means that common human perceptual or somatosensory experiences must share the same labels in people's socially constructed language system. For example, in some Chinese dialects, there is no word for "hope," so speaking of "hopelessness" in a clinical conversation about managing depression will simply draw a look of confusion. This example also highlights another important feature of working with words. Like it or not, you, the clinician, represent society and its conventional ways of talking about private experiences. You are the reality check, so to speak, on how the client is functioning with respect to this important social skill.

Clients might exhibit difficulties with finding words in two important ways. The first is a notable deficiency in their general lexicon such that the words to describe common experiences simply aren't there. Some people, when asked what they're feeling at the moment, will just draw a blank—and not because they're suppressing or avoiding whatever is there. The problem is that they don't have a word in their vocabulary that matches what they're feeling. In this circumstance, a client might say, "I don't know what I'm feeling" or "I'm not feeling anything." Importantly, this doesn't mean the client isn't having a private experience; rather, it means the client can't engage it verbally. Many clients we've worked with exhibit this deficiency, often due to an impoverished emotional environment in childhood. These environments typically value actions over words; therefore, there is no premium on being able to describe one's private experiences. This can result in acting impulsively, without using words to mediate or regulate urges.

The second difficulty, which is related, involves using the same basic word to describe a wide range of experiences within the same somatosensory or perceptual dimension. An example would be someone who uses the word "mad" to describe both a situation involving being stuck in a slow line at the grocery store and a fistfight with a bouncer at a bar. What's lacking is a command of words that might better help the person discriminate between these two distinctly different levels of being mad (for example, "annoyed" versus "ass-kicking angry"). When the same general label is repeatedly used to describe dimensionally discrete levels of an experience, the resulting precognitive emotion tone is likely to be exaggerated in either a negative or positive direction. Returning to that same example, this individual might present with a seeming anger management problem because of a tendency to react violently to even low-level situations involving frustration, annoyance, disagreement, arguing, and so on.

Using Words That Are Descriptive, Not Evaluative

Because avoided private experiences often entail a complex array of perceptual and somatosensory inputs, they must be "unpacked" to allow for healthy processing and integration. The "enemy within" that we referred to at the beginning of this chapter lies in the mind's tendency to apply evaluative rather than descriptive labels to unpleasant experiences. Why might this be? There is an evolutionary advantage to making false positive evaluations of threat in response to the appearance of a vague or uncertain stimulus. Put succinctly, it is much more important to quickly evaluate a threat and activate escape behavior than it is to accurately describe what the threat is. You can do the describing part after you've escaped to safety. Therefore, the evolved human brain is hardwired to produce a negative information processing bias that's instantly magnified if the target of attention is emotionally unpleasant. This process happens within milliseconds of making contact with a stimulus of potential interest. In that brief time, the emotional tone (pleasant, neutral, or unpleasant) and behavioral predisposition (approach versus avoid) are quickly established.

This process can quickly trigger the SNS and recruit the brain resources responsible for bottom-up attention. There is little that can be done to stop this well-honed threat detection pathway in the brain, nor would it be good to abolish it. It's probably essential for survival, even today. However, we can teach clients to use words that slow the immediate urge to avoid or escape a stimulus that has an unpleasant feeling tone. If the clinician doesn't provide this kind of moment-to-moment structure and guidance, clients are likely to inject more evaluative and threat-producing words into their descriptions of their experience, which will amplify the perceived threat level.

The ACT concepts of fusion and rule following apply directly in this situation. In addition to clients having an instinctive urge to avoid or escape the unpleasant feeling tone, their mind will introduce socially transmitted rules about what they should do to protect their health and safety in relation to a potentially noxious experience. These rules are often embodied in evaluations that implicitly trigger escape behavior. For example, a patient with chronic pain who states that the pain feels like being stabbed in the back with a butcher knife is unlikely to be very open to backing up and just describing the physical sensations that are present. As one client wisely noted, "I'm not going to describe much of anything when I'm in the middle of a panic attack!" So during the naming phase, clinicians must also facilitate discrimination training as needed. You are not only teaching clients how to use words, but also teaching them which words are user-friendly and which escalate fear and avoidance behaviors.

Neuroscience Considerations

Whereas older theories tended to view emotion processing as quite distinct from the cognitive functions of the brain, the contemporary perspective is that emotions and cognitions interact within a shared neural network that utilizes fairly diverse regions of the brain (Barbey, Colom, & Grafman, 2014). This network, while broadly distributed, is also surprisingly specialized. On the one hand, it recruits neural resources responsible for somatosensory organization and perceptual processing (think of these as the inputs into the system); on the other hand, it recruits resources related to verbal comprehension and the ability to juggle multiple competing inputs without an excessive drain on brain resources (think of these as the outputs). Indeed, research shows that individuals with higher levels of emotional intelligence, general intelligence, and stable personality traits show widespread, synchronous activity in these brain areas compared to individuals with brain lesions that have resulted in impaired emotional intelligence, reduced general intelligence, and unstable personality traits.

The epicenter of verbally based processing appears to be the orbitofrontal cortex, which is uniquely positioned in the brain to monitor both somatosensory and visceral-motor inputs. The medial and lateral regions of the orbitofrontal cortex seem to be responsible for distinctly different processing responsibilities. The medial region appears to be responsible for monitoring the affective properties and reward value of multimodal and somatosensory stimuli. It is now thought that this medial region also regulates emotional learning and the development of adaptive social and cognitive behaviors associated with emotional intelligence. The lateral orbitofrontal cortex appears to be responsible for processing negative reinforcements and adapting behaviors to minimize negative consequences.

Research into emotional processing provides further evidence indicating an interaction between regions of the brain responsible for emotional and cognitive processing. For example, brain lateralization studies have shown that persistent negative affect is associated with higher levels of activation of core neural pathways in the right hemisphere and proportionately less activation of core structures in the left hemisphere. Feelings of well-being, on the other hand, are strongly associated with high levels of left hemisphere activity compared to right hemisphere activity. These differences have also been correlated with susceptibility to depression, anxiety, rumination, and worry (Lang & Bradley, 2010; Schuyler et al., 2014). Returning to the neural network model just described, one could speculate that deficiencies in verbal comprehension and working memory capacity result in less efficient somatosensory organization and perceptual processing, and this, in turn, results in underactivation of the medial orbitofrontal cortex. One of the more common findings in studies of mindfulness training among depressed people is that it results in a significant decrease in self-reported rumination (van Vugt,

Hitchcock, Shahar, & Britton, 2012). This finding is consistent with our theory that well-targeted mindfulness-based interventions are actually a form of brain training that strengthens previously weak neural pathways.

• Case Example: Anne

Anne is a sixty-two-year-old divorced woman with three adult children. She was referred by her family physician because of long-standing problems with depression, and her doctor didn't know what else she could do to help Anne. Anne describes her life as empty and boring: she goes to work, then comes home and essentially holes up in her house. She reports that she doesn't feel motivated to do anything beyond just surviving. She's tried a variety of antidepressants without much success.

Anne was married to an abusive alcoholic, whom she divorced eighteen years ago after he left her for another woman. Anne never sought another relationship after the divorce. She focused on working to support her family and raising her kids, which she did essentially by herself. Her relationships with her children are fairly strained. She always had to play bad cop with them, especially because her ex-husband set no limits and lavished them with toys and clothes during visitations. According to Anne, her children blamed her for the divorce. Anne presented at the initial interview looking sad but displaying a very limited range of emotion. She responded to questions in a monotone, and when asked what she was seeking, she said, "Well, basically, my doctor told me to come in to see you and that she doesn't know how to help me."

Probe, Read, and Intervene

Typically, the process of naming unfolds a short while after a client has been able to show up and make contact with a present-moment experience. It's important not to rush into naming interventions until you are quite sure that the client is fully engaged with the clinically relevant experience. This can be frustrating with certain types of clients, particularly those who demonstrate a slower processing style than you're accustomed to. Due to her apathy and disinterest, Anne required quite a bit of prodding to exhibit even slight engagement in the interaction. The topic that finally brought her into the room involved her strained relationships with her adult children. Apparently, her children had been having an ongoing conversation amongst themselves about "what to do about Mom." Her oldest son in particular had made very hurtful comments suggesting that Anne was just seeking attention and acting like a victim. He was obviously annoyed with her ongoing mental health issues and was influencing his siblings to believe she was just a negative person who didn't want to be happy. During this brief exchange, Anne's face began to show signs of animation and she seemed to come out of the fog she was in.

Probe: Dismantling

Once you have clients in contact with a present-moment experience, it's time to help them engage in uncharacteristic ways of processing the moment. Different facets of their experience are typically jumbled together such that there isn't a lot of room to work with discrimination training. This calls for conducting an informal assessment of clients' lexicon for describing different types of private experiences. Can they describe thoughts that are present? Can they generate different types of emotion-specific words and link them accurately to various emotional states? Can they recognize and describe the content of memories? Are they able to describe different physical sensations spread throughout the body? In the interaction that follows, the clinician is probing Anne's ability to do all of these things.

Clinician: It seems like talking about your son and how he's judging you brought you to life a little bit, like there's a sore spot in there somewhere behind that wall of yours. What happened?

Anne: Oh, well, that's just something that… It's an uncomfortable subject for me to talk about. Nothing ever comes of it. [Read: Anne is providing a rather vague, general answer that doesn't really move the conversation forward, suggesting that this may be a good point of entry.]

Clinician: So, it sounds like this is something you've thought about and maybe even discussed with someone before. Would you say you think about this issue quite a bit when you're alone?

Anne: Yes, I think about it quite often.

Clinician: So, when you think about it, what reactions do you notice yourself having?

Anne: (*In an irritated tone of voice.*) What do you mean by "reactions"? Whether I get bothered by it? [Read: Anne is pushing back again, probably in an effort to avoid the painful experience. She needs a little more guidance and structure to help increase her engagement.]

Clinician: Well, by "reactions," I mean what goes on inside you when this topic comes up for you. That could be thoughts you have, feelings that show up inside, memories that are triggered, or physical sensations you experience. Are any of those things going on right now as we talk about your son?

Anne: Well, is not caring about what he thinks or tries to convince the other kids of a reaction? [Read: This response has a rather weak quality, focusing on a single aspect of the experience to the exclusion of all others. It suggests that Anne is struggling to actually engage the range of reactions that are probably present. More guidance will be needed.]

Clinician: I guess that would be an example of a thought you have when this topic shows up: that you don't care what your son says about you and you don't care about whether the other kids believe him. I'm curious about other reactions that might be there. For example, what feelings go along with telling yourself not to care? Are there memories that his actions stimulate? What does your body feel like as you go to this place of not caring what your son thinks or says?

Anne: I'm not aware of having any feelings at all. I guess I should have some emotions about this, but mostly I don't know what I feel. Yet there is a memory I have, now that you mention it. It's of my ex saying the same kind of disrespectful, insulting things to me when he was drinking and then threatening to hurt me if I opened my mouth. Sometimes he followed through on that threat. And whenever I remember those things—and they happened year after year—I start feeling all knotted up in my stomach, just like I did when he'd push me around or punch me. [Read: This is a very interesting response, both because of the absence of any emotion words and because of the depth and specificity of Anne's memories linked to her domestic abuse.]

In this brief vignette, the clinician has located a specific experience that might yield therapeutic benefits and has begun to dismantle it, unpacking it piece by piece. The clinician helped Anne begin to put names on certain aspects of her present-moment experience and, at the same time, tested Anne's ability to attach words to her experience that correspond accurately with it.

Read: Formulating a Clinical Impression

Based upon brief but revealing probes, as illustrated in the previous section, clinicians can begin to formulate an impression of clients' relative strengths and weaknesses with naming skills. These impressions are dynamic and will continue to evolve as a function of repeated opportunities to probe deeper and deeper into their naming skills. At this stage, clinicians are basically interested in trying to determine which naming skill is in need of immediate support. Is the task at hand to help the client develop more verbal labels to better describe and discriminate among various facets of an experience? Or is it helping the client recognize and step back from self-defeating evaluations that disrupt the natural neural feedback loops that are activated when an experiential state is simply described in a self-referential fashion ("I'm feeling humiliated right now" versus "I'm feeling humiliated and that isn't good for me"). Sometimes both of these skill areas require further development.

Often, it's helpful for clinicians to silently consider the following questions before starting to intervene:

- Is the client able to spontaneously produce emotion words?

- Does the client use emotion words that roughly match the emotion that's probably present?

- Does the client exhibit the ability to use a wide range of emotion words to describe inner experiences?

- Can the client discriminate between lower- and higher-intensity experiences involving the same emotion?

- Does the client show some self-recognition in the four categories of private experience (thoughts, feelings, memories, and physical sensations)?

- Does the client demonstrate an awareness of the difference between evaluations and objective descriptions of emotionally relevant experiences?

- How often does the client insert evaluations into descriptions of present-moment experiences?

Intervene: Putting Names on Things

In Anne's case, her lack of basic emotion vocabulary is so significant that the clinician is going to have trouble even getting a glimpse of hidden evaluations until some simple emotion-word discrimination training has been completed. This isn't an unusual situation, particularly for clients who come from dysfunctional families. Perhaps, in childhood, toxic and prohibitive attitudes about expressing emotions suppressed the emotional interactions needed to allow such clients to develop an emotion lexicon. Whatever the cause may be, the clinician needs to both intervene and continue probing.

Clinician: Okay, that sounds like a load of different stuff coming at you. And some of it sounds pretty painful to remember. What do you make of the emotion thing? You mentioned you think you probably should be having some emotional reactions, but you drew a blank.

Anne: Frankly, I don't want to open that door, because whatever is in there isn't going to be good for me. But you know, honestly, even though there is something in there, I don't know what it is. My father and mother taught me to keep my feelings to myself—that sharing them with others makes you seem weak and foolish. [Read: This response suggests that Anne has a heavy load of negative rules about the meaning of unpleasant, unwanted emotions. Rather than push her too hard too fast, which might have the effect of reactivating her withdrawal strategies, the clinician will do a bit of an end run.]

Clinician: Okay, so let me see if I can make this a bit easier to do. Let's imagine you're someone else who hears that her son has called her a whiner, a victim, and a high-maintenance train wreck. What kind of feelings do you imagine might show up for that person?

Anne: Well, the person would feel cut off at the knees. I mean, I guess she would feel worthless and ashamed. [Read: Two of her three descriptions aren't actually emotions, but they are closely tied to some type of emotional experience. However, being ashamed is an emotional experience, and the clinician will try to dismantle it.]

Clinician: Okay, so it's feeling cut off at the knees. What feeling would go along with being cut off at the knees?

Anne: Well, being humiliated and like you're ashamed to be seen.

Clinician: Okay, and what about being worthless? What feelings or emotions might go along with thinking you're worthless?

Anne: I guess that's mainly just sad… You know, no one is going to love you or care about you.

Clinician: Okay, and then what about being "high-maintenance"?

Anne: That's just about the cruelest thing someone can say. I mean, it would hurt, and you'd be really furious about such a cruel joke. [Read: Anne is actually doing pretty well handling this set of probes. There are some indications of negative rules about emotions, but none are really intruding into the interaction. For example, she isn't refusing to play along because of the rule that talking about emotions makes you vulnerable to being seen as weak and foolish.]

Clinician: So would it be fair to say that this type of situation would actually produce a lot of different reactions, including those negative thoughts you described and then some painful emotions? If you looked at your life situation and peeked inside for just a second, do some of those reactions show up?

Anne: I think some of them have to be there.

Clinician: So would you agree that at least some of your bottled-up reactions involve being sad, feeling shame, and feeling punished by your son's cruel comments? That you have some very negative thoughts and memories about all this—being humiliated in front of your children, remembering your husband messing with your mind and beating you, and then you being punished for being the "good guy" and leaving the marriage to protect your children? I mean, you did what you felt would protect you and your children, right?

Anne: Yeah, and I got totally thrown under the bus by everyone. Even my father made snide comments that I would never find another man who would put up with me. [Read: This is a genuine statement that suggests positive movement is happening.]

Clinician: That must have really hurt. I could almost imagine that kind of comment going straight to your heart and leaving you feeling defeated. I can't help but notice the sadness in your eyes.

Anne: Feeling defeated is a perfect way to describe how I'm feeling. *(Tears up.)* [Read: Anne is showing the ability to verbally connect with her feeling state; she's displaying some interest in making contact, even though it's painful.]

Clinician: And feeling defeated involves this sense of inner sadness and shame, and sort of a "What did I do to deserve this?" disbelief in what has happened: the abuse, being blamed for leaving to protect yourself and your children, having people suggest that maybe you're the one who has the problem. It must be like, "Am I just having a bad dream, and when am I going to wake up?"

Anne: You said it. That's it. For years, my life has been a nightmare.

At this point in the interaction, the clinician has helped Anne begin to put names on certain facets of her present-moment experience and, at the same time, is developing her ability to select words that correspond accurately with her experience. There are definite signs of psychological movement erupting inside the interaction. Anne has gone from being withdrawn and rather noncommunicative to being actively engaged, and she's actually volunteering information that's widening the scope of the conversation.

Intervene: Witnessing Rather Than Evaluating

At this point in the interaction, the clinician wants to better understand the factors that contribute to Anne's limited ability to process emotional experience. They are likely to involve learned evaluations of emotional experience that Anne has been carrying around since childhood. The goal of this intervention will be to help Anne stand in the presence of her painful experience and simply describe it, rather than evaluate it. The term we like to use with clients is "witnessing," because most clients are familiar with what's required of a witness in a court hearing: to tell the truth, the whole truth, and nothing but the truth.

Clinician: So let's just say, for the sake of our work here today, that when you opened that door you were talking about, out leapt three emotions: humiliation, sadness, and furiousness. What's the first thing that would show up for you when you notice these emotions?

Anne: Push them back in the room and close the door because they'll destroy you if you don't.

Clinician: So your immediate reaction would be to treat those reactions as dangerous to you, perhaps to your sanity.

Anne: Well, that's what I learned—that those types of feelings are just going to drag you down and make you miserable inside. You might end up killing yourself or turn to drinking. And then it's just a downward spiral from there. [Read: This is probably the core rule of the system Anne was trained to follow. It will make it very difficult for her to stay present with painful experiences and will drive emotional numbing. The clinician needs to challenge this rule using Anne's direct experience with applying it. This will be the motivational intervention.]

Clinician: So that would make it nearly impossible for you to be willing to just experience those feelings, because your mind tells you it's the road to hell. It sounds like a heavy judgmental view of your inside experience was pounded into you by your mom and dad. But the problem is, what are you going to do about those experiences when they show up on their own? Because you can't stop them from appearing, right?

Anne: No, but you don't let them take over. I mean, if I just let myself get into my sadness, it wouldn't ever stop.

Clinician: Well, what if you were to take your judgments—actually your parents' judgments—of sadness off the table and just sit with being sad? Because if sad is bad, shame is bad, anger is bad, and so on, you don't have any option but to check out. And being checked out is no fun, right? That's why you're here, right?

Anne: Are you saying just let myself be sad, and that's it?

Clinician: Well, maybe think of it this way: "I'm going to be sad when sadness is called for. I'll resist the temptation to put my judgments about sadness into my experience. Then I could really see what sadness is from an objective point of view, almost like I'm a witness giving testimony." The judge asks you, "What do you feel?" and you say, "I feel sad." You don't say, "Oh, and by the way, Your Honor, did you know that sadness is bad for you and I shouldn't be feeling that way?" If you do, the judge will say, "I didn't ask you what your opinion of sadness is; I asked you to tell me what you're feeling." So, there's a very big difference between just describing what you're experiencing and evaluating it.

Anne: Well, then what am I supposed to do with those reactions? [Read: This response indicates that Anne is engaged enough to be curious about other ways to deal with emotions. The clinician will take advantage of her openness to new ideas.]

Clinician: Notice they are there, use words to describe them as best you can, and leave it at that. Like Joe Friday, the detective in the TV show *Dragnet* would say, "The facts, ma'am—just the facts!"

Anne: This feels weird. It's like I'm disobeying all my lifelong learning. [Read: This is actually a very interesting response in that it shows some perspective taking ability. Anne can compare the new way of coping with how she was taught and see a clear difference, and she can also identify her urge to follow the old rule. The clinician will try to create a pathway to acknowledge the presence of the old rule while following a different one.]

Clinician: There's nothing wrong with disobeying a rule that has just about killed you off. Remember, this basic instruction put you in the hole for the last fifteen years. It led you to feel defeated in life. It led you here, without any sense of hope that anyone can help you. Would you be willing to just focus attention on describing what's going on inside and leaving the heavy-handed self-judgments on the sideline?

Anne: I can try, I guess. It couldn't make things any worse than they already are.

In this brief exchange, the clinician reinforced the discrimination between objective descriptions of experience and personal evaluations of them. And Anne has started to show some real curiosity about handling her painful thoughts and feelings in a different way.

Practical Clinical Tips

In this section, we want to give you some practical tips on how to use naming strategies in clinical practice. As with any present-moment-awareness process, there are important technical issues that, depending on how you handle them, support or undermine the ultimate outcome of the intervention you're trying to implement.

Vocabulary and Grammar

Unlike some aspects of present-moment work where the goal is to let clients discover something important in the experience itself, developing naming abilities often requires clinicians to act as a vocabulary teacher. You give the client words to use, put those words into a meaningful emotional context, and then, using skillful questioning, ask the client to use the word repeatedly. For example, you might ask something like

"Can you give me a word or phrase to describe what you're feeling or experiencing right now?" The intent is to provide clients with words or phrases that allow them to interact verbally with their nonverbal experiences.

Another tactic we often use is to teach words that are qualifiers, to increase clients' ability to distinguish between various levels of an emotional experience. For example, you might ask something like "So, in this situation with your son, would you say your feelings were hurt a little bit, somewhat hurt, or very hurt?" An alternative way to do this is to find unique words for each level of the experience: "Would you say you were irritated, offended, aggravated, or furious?"

For clients who have a reasonably strong emotion lexicon but can't avoid inserting judgments, discrimination training will involve helping them identify and differentiate between evaluative and descriptive words. It's still a vocabulary lesson, but one of a completely different nature. For example, a therapist might engage a client in a game of spontaneous labeling of emotions, situations, and judgments. In orienting the client, the therapist might say, "I'm going to say a word that represents a feeling, like feeling happy, or a situation, like being at your son's house. I want you to respond with the first word that comes to mind. I'll make a list of those, and then we'll sort them into two categories: descriptive and evaluative. This game will give you a chance to notice how quickly evaluations come up and to better discriminate evaluations from descriptions."

Instruct, Don't Invade

It's important to differentiate between teaching emotion words and telling clients what they feel. Telling clients what they're feeling is very invasive and contrary to good clinical practice. There is a high likelihood that you're telling the client what you're feeling and mistaking it for what the client is feeling. Similarly, don't argue or disagree with a particular emotion word that a client uses (for example, "I don't think you're feeling sad here; you're just feeling guilty"). So, to approach training in the lexicon of emotions, you need to employ skillful questioning: "In addition to feeling sad about this, can you imagine or think of any other feelings that might go along for the ride here?" Really good clinicians are really good at asking questions rather than making directive statements.

Focus, Focus, Focus

Entering into the naming phase often requires clinicians to narrow the scope from initial awareness of a broad set of present-moment experiences to a focus on a single experience that seems like it will yield a lot of fruit. It's better to basically stay with a single experience and work it for all the detail you can, rather than shifting from topic to topic. Many clinicians fail to stay with a single topic long enough to really capitalize on the richness of private experience it contains. Using the TEAMS acronym (Robinson, Gould, & Strosahl, 2010) will give you a mental template to follow when you establish the focus of the discussion. Within any given present-moment experience, there are going to be five aspects, each of which can be explored with the intent of developing vocabulary or detecting toxic evaluations clients are inserting into their experience:

- **T**houghts
- **E**motions
- **A**ssociations
- **M**emories
- **S**ensations

The take-home message is to let yourself and the client linger within an experience, snooping around and locating constituent parts, and then applying verbal labels accordingly.

Gentle Reminders

In this chapter, we've examined naming, the second phase of present-moment processing. Most clients cannot effectively integrate nonverbal experiences like emotions, memories, and sensations without interacting symbolically with them. Learning to apply verbal labels to nonverbal experiences allows clients to bring these experiences into cognitive awareness, allowing higher-order processing to occur. To do so, clients must have a vocabulary sufficient to put unique verbal labels on unique experiences. In addition, they must be able to refrain from using evaluative verbal labels and instead use simple, descriptive terms. This often requires the clinician to function as a teacher of words, and to view this phase of present-moment processing as a kind of discrimination training in which clients learn to use specific words that promote clinical movement.

As Anne's case clearly demonstrates, getting clients to apply verbal labels to nonverbal present-moment experiences sets the stage for more advanced mental processing of the meaning of those experiences. So while attaching verbal labels helps clients get emotionally located, location itself isn't sufficient to carry the day. The clinician next needs to teach clients how to interact with their verbal representations of private experience in ways that promote psychological growth. In the next chapter, we'll address the first of these more advanced strategies: the process of detaching from potentially harmful and self-destructive products of the mind. In this book, we refer to this phase as letting go.

CHAPTER 6

Let Go

He who would be serene and pure needs but one thing: detachment.

—Meister Eckhart

Learning to notice what is present, and then learning to give it a name, orients and focuses clients' attention within a present-moment-awareness intervention (orienting functions, as described in chapter 2). After those two phases are established, the next step is to neutralize the predictable interfering activities of busy mind. Left unchecked, these activities will inhibit clients' abilities to emotionally process and integrate material that's showing up in their present-moment awareness. Adopting a detached, accepting stance toward the provocative messages of busy mind thus functions as a counter-inhibitory process and is truly the linchpin of present-moment-awareness interventions.

The reality of being human is to live with a busy mind that never eases its grip on us. We have to interact with it continually and in highly flexible ways. And, as mentioned, sometimes it pays handsome dividends to listen closely to busy mind and follow its directives. If you try to walk across a busy intersection without steadfastly following busy mind's instructions, you do so at your own peril. But busy mind isn't good at everything; and to compound the problem, it doesn't seem to have a self-regulatory feature that automatically disqualifies it from giving us advice when we're dealing with material it simply knows nothing about. The areas of life where the usefulness of busy mind breaks down happen to be exactly the same areas that cause the most suffering when clients enter into present-moment awareness. One key area where this arises involves making evaluations of self and others in terms of the mind's favorite evaluative polarities: good-bad, right-wrong, fair-unfair, and responsibility-blame. The mind further delights in projecting such polarities forward and backward in time as part of its ongoing sense-making operations.

Furthermore, as we'll discuss in detail in this chapter, this feature of busy mind appears to exist within the default mode network. Practicing detachment activates the executive control network, which then recruits attention resources away from the default mode network and reallocates them to the task-positive network. Detachment can thus be thought of as a mental task that involves redirecting attention away from the content of mental activities and toward the context in which those activities take place.

Clinical Relevance

The Latin root of the word "detachment" means to be physically apart or separate from objects or circumstances. The Latin root of the word "attachment," on the other hand, means to be literally appended or bound to an object or circumstance. When clients become attached to a present-moment experience, they overidentify with it. The psychological space between them and what they contact inside of present-moment awareness vanishes. Figuratively speaking, clients are being led around by the nose by the ever-changing content within their present-moment awareness. Going back to the discussion of levels of observational awareness in chapter 4, attachment pulls clients into the participant mode of observation. The goal is to help clients establish fluid movement between the participant-observer and observer levels of awareness.

Experiences that elicit a high degree of attachment generally have a high emotional salience and valence for clients: distressing and unwanted emotions, provocative and negative self-evaluations, painful memories of the past, catastrophic images of the future, and unpleasant physical states. When clients have these private experiences in a completely fused state, the experiences typically become unbearable and trigger a full array of escape and avoidance behaviors. Indeed, some of the self-evaluations clients overidentify with might be socially inculcated rules that encourage experiential avoidance in the service of protecting personal health and well-being. In such circumstances, clients' attention resources will be predominantly self-focused and bottom-up in nature, with motives like being right, showing others up, getting revenge, or being a victim prevailing over attempts to simply accept present-moment experience for what it is.

From an evolutionary science perspective, detachment is part of an appraisal process that must answer the critical question that comes up after attention has been focused on a target and the target has been named: "Is it safe or dangerous for me to be near this target?" Viewed from this perspective, detachment is the result of an instantaneous cognitive appraisal in which the object of attention has been determined to pose no particular threat or danger; it's safe for the client to be in proximity to the experience without any need to pay a lot of attention to it. In a detached state of awareness, few events, situations, or interactions are worth fighting over, trying to get revenge for, or feeling victimized about. So detachment involves not only the ability to step back and create some psychological distance from an experience, but also the ability to evaluate the experience as not deserving so much attention. This results in a dramatic reduction in the emotional valence of whatever is contacted in present-moment awareness, with a resulting decrease in the likelihood that clients will attach to or fuse with whatever is in the moment.

In this chapter, we'll examine several important aspects of using detachment to facilitate present-moment processing. First, we'll describe two core components of detachment. Next, we'll discuss some very intriguing findings from neuroscientific investigations into cognitive appraisal, wandering mind, and detachment—findings that suggest several specific ways to intervene in order to strengthen clients' detachment skills. We will then use a case example to demonstrate how to probe for specific detachment skills, formulate an overall clinical impression to inform treatment planning, and intervene to help clients build skills in letting go.

Basic Detachment Skills

There are two central components of detachment that are the focus of clinical assessments and interventions during therapy: nonreactivity and disengagement. Each is fundamental, and the absence of one essentially negates the benefits of the other. In practice, these two processes occur at nearly the same point in time, so you won't have to do two separate types of probing to activate them.

Nonreactivity

Within a matter of seconds of coming into contact with a potentially threatening stimulus, the brain launches a sentinel program designed to appraise the nature and degree of threat present. The sentinel program makes a precognitive, or implicit, evaluation that immediately establishes the feeling tone of the stimulus. The feeling tone can be pleasant, unpleasant, or neutral in emotional valence. Depending upon the appraised valence, the brain will immediately motivate instinctual approach or avoidance behaviors via activation of either the parasympathetic or sympathetic nervous system. In the case of unpleasant emotion tone, the immediate urge will be to avoid or escape if doing so is possible. Thus, a key detachment skill is to resist the knee-jerk urge to escape from or avoid contact with a present-moment experience that has an unpleasant emotion tone. In mindfulness terms, being nonreactive requires accepting what has shown up in the present moment and holding still, figuratively speaking.

Disengagement

A second core feature of detachment is the ability to maintain a state of emotional neutrality with respect to whatever has shown up in awareness, be it a provocative thought, a disturbing memory, an unpleasant physical sensation, or a negative emotion. Disengagement allows people to separate from their experience—even if it's uncomfortable in feeling tone—based upon an appraisal that denies the perceived personal relevance of that experience.

It's easy to get confused about what goes into denying the personal relevance of certain aspects of a present-moment experience, so some clarification is in order. Yes, the experiences clients have in the present moment are personal, but are they relevant to what clients are seeking in the moment? The relevance of any aspect of a present-moment experience is determined within a functional contextual framework. Does allocating attention resources to any particular thought, feeling, memory, or sensation serve the client's best interests or promote what the client is seeking at this exact moment in time? Even though a present-moment experience may have a strong negative feeling tone, that doesn't mean it's relevant to what the client is currently seeking. To put it in meditation terms, if you're seeking oneness, then even the most provocative experiences are irrelevant if they lead you away from oneness.

Many clients habitually get thrown off track by paying attention to aspects of their immediate experience that are basically useless in promoting positive outcomes. For example, ruminating about past failures is a total nonstarter unless it results in radical and functionally positive changes in present behaviors. Thus, when memories of past failures show up for clients, they might learn to see that those memories may not have a particular bearing on how to live life from now into the future. From a clinical perspective, the appraisal that an experience isn't personally relevant frees up attention resources that can then be applied to other purposes that are more functionally useful.

Neuroscience Considerations

Detachment appears to recruit the executive control network, resulting in rapid down-regulation of the limbic system and particularly the amygdala. One study compared detachment to cognitive reappraisal strategies in an anticipatory pain task and found that, although both coping strategies initially recruit a common set of brain resources, over time each results in unique patterns of brain activation. Detachment recruits brain regions that have been implicated in the executive control network, whereas cognitive appraisal recruits left-hemisphere semantic processing areas (Kalisch et al., 2005). In terms of emotion regulation, cognitive reappraisal is considered to be a late-stage strategy, whereas detachment is regarded as an early-stage strategy. Interestingly, recent studies have shown that detachment has a more powerful impact on emotion regulation when applied to more intense and negative emotional stimuli (Shiota & Levenson, 2012; Sheppes, Brady, & Samson, 2014). Another recent study examined experienced meditators matched with naive control subjects who were asked to perform three different types of meditation. The results suggested that, for experienced meditators, each type of meditation resulted in reduced activity in the default network and increased activity among and between several brain structures thought to be associated with the executive control network (Brewer et al., 2011).

The result is that conscious detachment not only activates the task-positive network to compete for resources with the default network (thus increasing somatosensory and perceptual awareness), but also recruits the executive control network to enact its gatekeeper function, thus downregulating the brain's sentinel programs (and the bottom-up attention and SNS activation they produce). The result? Clients literally come to their senses! Individuals in a detached state aren't lost in reverie; they are, in fact, exquisitely aware of what's going on both inside and outside the skin. This creates opportunities to engage in higher-order learning and cognitive integration.

•   Case Example: Gail

Gail is a thirty-two-year-old lesbian female who currently lives by herself in her sister's basement. She's an accomplished and well-respected artist but has stopped producing art due to her steadily worsening depression and social anxiety. She's alternatingly angry and depressed. Her anger outbursts are directed primarily at her sister, and she feels very bad about these afterward. She spends most of her time in her room and feels anxious when she gets into social settings.

She reports being sexually abused by an uncle during her childhood, from age seven to age thirteen. She continues to have flashbacks and nightmares. Her moods are up and down a lot. She used to be a heavy drinker and smoked a lot of pot until she decided to stop in an effort to promote her artistic side. During her dark periods, she ruminates about all of the disappointments and traumas in her life. She worries that she has no future and will ultimately end up killing herself. Previously, when she was a heavy drinker, she attempted suicide on two different occasions. Gail is very articulate, and possesses a fair amount of emotional self-awareness and word-finding ability. Her problems seem to center around her inability to extract herself from ruminations about her past and worries about her future, leaving her feeling depressed, anxious, and paralyzed in life.

Probe, Read, and Intervene

When clients' attention is focused on the present moment and they can supply names for the core experiences that are showing up, it's time to begin probing to assess how reactive they are to their content and whether they can discriminate between relevant and irrelevant emotional information. At this stage of a present-moment-awareness intervention, probes are often sequential, meaning that the clinician tests the client each step of the way during the interaction. This is also a good time to begin shifting the way language is used, as demonstrated in the following section.

Probe: Asking Clients What the Mind Is Saying

During the earliest moments of the detachment phase, it's important to manipulate your use of language to subtly alter the client's view of the basic problem. The client typically sees the content of distressing and unwanted private experiences as the problem (for example, "I can't stop thinking about my mistakes"), whereas for the clinician, the problem is the client's tendency to attach to and overidentify with these experiences. So the clinician can begin to insert odd and unusual uses of language that promote detachment. As you'll see in the following dialogue, asking questions that imply the mind is a separate entity from the client is a powerful way to begin injecting detachment into the mix, even before launching a more formal intervention.

Clinician: Gail, I'm curious about how this process of being a prisoner in your sister's basement works, sort of from the inside out. I mean, can you walk me through what this looks like so I can get my arms around it?

Gail: Sure. Yesterday, my sister made a comment that I didn't seem happy and that she wished I would try to get out of the house more. I went ballistic and started yelling at her, then she told me to go downstairs and pull myself together. I just lie on my bed for hours thinking about what I've become. I used to be strong. I could do things in life, like making ceramics, and I could overcome my negative attitudes. Now I'm almost unable to go out of my house. My personal strength is just gone.

Clinician: So, let me make sure I understand. This is the type of stuff you think when you're on the bed, right? Your mind tells you that you're weak; it tells you that you don't have the strength of character to do things anymore. It tells you that you've lost the ability to do things.

Gail: Right, that's what I do, and I go through it for a long time. I don't know how long it really lasts, but it seems like hours.

Clinician: So, what else does your mind tell you when you're lying on the bed?

Gail: You mean, like, my mind is telling me things? [Read: This response suggests Gail is at least willing to entertain the idea that her mind is separate from her. The clinician will attempt to expand this idea a bit and then dive back into deconstructing Gail's rumination experience.]

Clinician: Well, I guess what I was saying is that each of us has a mind. I mean, my mind is talking to me all the time. Have you ever talked to yourself in the shower? (Gail nods.) Well, one day I was talking to myself in the shower and it dawned on me that if there's only one of us in here, then who's talking to who? I mean, if someone is speaking, then there has to be someone listening.

Gail: (Laughs and smiles.) That's kind of cool. I've never really thought about it that way.

Clinician: So, to make this easy, let's just say that your mind is there on the bed with you and is talking to you about how you're doing in life up to now and what the future holds for you. What else does your mind say?

Gail: It tells me that I'm broken inside. That I'm never going to have a life partner—that I'll keep screwing up my relationships like I have in the past. That I don't fit in. That eventually I'll be entirely unable to produce my art. [Read: Gail's use of the term "it" when describing her mind's activities suggests that she's accepted the distinction between herself and her mind.]

Clinician: So, I'm just checking: Was it your mind that just told me that, or was it you the human being reporting to me on what you're hearing your mind saying?

Gail: Both. When I was first telling you, it was just my mind and I was actually starting to feel myself going down. Then I had this image of my mind telling me this stuff, which it does all the time, and then I remembered that this means there must be two of us here. From there, it didn't feel nearly as bad to talk about it. [Read: This suggests that Gail is able to adopt a nonreactive stance if she has the appropriate cues to remind her.]

Clinician: I'm guessing that there are a lot of emotions that get stirred up when this is going on. Probably some memories too?

Gail: Oh, yeah. My memories are the hardest to deal with because I have vivid pictures in my mind of what my uncle did to me. I'm a very visual person. I used to paint the pictures on canvas, like I was trying to bleed myself to be free of them. My emotions are all over the place. I'm hopeless. I'm afraid. I feel abandoned and alone and that no one will ever understand me. It depresses me. Sometimes it's so hard to breathe that it feels like someone is sitting on my chest. When I'm at the worst spot, it feels like I'm going to disappear into nothingness.

Clinician: Wow, your mind is really playing a number on you. I don't know how you can swim in that soup without getting sucked under.

Gail: It's definitely not pretty.

In this vignette, the clinician has gone inside Gail's ruminative experiences and, figuratively speaking, is beginning to comment on them from Gail's point of view. This shift of perspective typically disarms clients' defense mechanisms and makes it easier to inject new ways of talking about their present-moment experience.

Probe: Workability

Now that the clinician has a sense of Gail's ability to separate herself from her mind and be at least somewhat nonreactive, the next goal is to see if she's able to pick up the idea that it's okay to disengage from narrative mental experience that isn't useful in promoting her life goals. This will make it easier for her to disengage from the literal meaning of her private experiences.

Clinician: Okay, I think I have a feel for what this looks like from the inside out. Can you tell me what the promise is if you just go along with your mind and repeatedly have the same thoughts and worries, day in and day out? What's supposed to happen if you do this?

Gail: I'm not sure what you're asking me. Can you ask it another way?

Clinician: Well, I mean, your mind is telling you to pay attention to all these messages. By paying attention to them, what's supposed to happen to you so that your life goes better?

Gail: You mean, does ruminating and worrying help me live my life as an artist or help me socially? No, it definitely doesn't. Now that you asked it that way, it's probably the opposite. [Read: Gail seems to be tracking the built-in paradox of rumination and worry: they don't help you get better as a person, and they don't protect you from the future.]

Clinician: So, what you're saying is that ruminating about the past, ruminating about your flaws and failure and traumas, worrying about the catastrophes that are coming your way, none of that has given you a new angle in life? I mean, have you had a sudden burst of "aha!" insight into how to live life better, something like "Now I know the secret of how to live a vital life?"

Gail: (Tears up and looks down.) I've wasted years of my life doing this with nothing to show for it. I'm even a bigger loser than I thought I was. [Read: Gail is backsliding a little bit into attachment, so the clinician will reinstill the separation between Gail and her mind.]

Clinician: You mean your mind just told you that, right? Maybe this is another part of how it works. You get close to finding the exit door, and your mind says you should have known where the door was all along. But if we could, let's come back to this issue of how ruminating and worrying is working for you and whether it's helping you discover a better way to live. What were you going to tell me before your mind sideswiped you?

Gail: That I haven't really learned anything new about myself that would help me grow. In fact, doing this is keeping me down. I mean, I'm not producing artwork, which is my passion. It's also my only way of being financially independent so I don't have to mooch off my sister. [Read: Gail is ready, at least intellectually, to disavow the relevance of rumination and worry to pursuing her best interests in life.]

Clinician: Would you agree, then, that taking this approach to understanding how to respond to the challenges of your life isn't working, and that, in fact, relying on rumination and worry might even be the problem?

Gail: Now that you put it that way, I suppose it doesn't work.

In this brief exchange, the clinician has helped Gail make experiential contact with the chronic self-defeating impact of identifying with her mind's negative evaluations and predictions. This has been accomplished by gently but persistently looking at the real-life results of her mind's advice on how to live her life.

Read: Formulating a Clinical Impression

There are two basic goals to strive for in assessing skills in letting go. The first is to get a very clear read on the client's ability to be nonreactive at first contact with aspects of present-moment experience that might detract from active learning and integration. The second is to assess whether the client can disengage with this content in a matter of seconds or minutes.

There are a number of ways you can both probe for and promote actively taking a nonreactive stance, again by using well-designed questions, such as the following:

- "Can you just hold still here and not do anything about what's coming into your awareness, even if the messages seem powerful and compelling?"

- "Would you be willing to just let this stuff be here, without trying to control it in any way?"

- "Can you just see what happens if you don't take any action, either toward or away from what's in front of you right now?"

You may need to use these prompts repeatedly as a client transitions from one aspect of a present-moment experience to the next.

Probing and assessing clients' abilities to become and stay disengaged often involves an ongoing interaction between the clinician, the client, and the provocative features of any present-moment experience. With some specific coaching, is the client able to demonstrate disengagement in the moment? What are the aspects of present-moment experience that tend to draw the client back into overidentifying with private content? Often, the feeling tone of sequential present-moment experiences varies, as does the perceived impact on the client's present-moment processing abilities. You can respond to disengagement, as well as shifts in disengagement levels, with strategic questions or even suggestions:

- "I noticed that you picked up that feeling and started to wrestle with it. Could you put it down again and just let it be there?"

- "When your programming starts running, can you just notice that it's running and choose to do nothing?"

- "Can you get behind the idea that even though your mind has very powerful opinions about this part of your life, they are just opinions and you don't have to obey your mind if doing so doesn't help you?"

Because disengagement is a task-positive processing activity, you may have the sense that you're both probing and intervening with a client's abilities in a back-and-forth way. The key is to have a clear idea of what you want the client to be able to do so you can assess whether the client is practicing disengagement. This will allow you to use the present-moment-awareness intervention to continuously shape disengagement skills in a moment-to-moment way.

Intervene: Dealing with the Bully

The ultimate goal of interventions during the letting go phase is to teach clients how to maintain control over their attention in the presence of provocative personal experience. Creating and maintaining space between the self and private experience is an ongoing activity within present-moment experience. The clinician needs to watch for positive examples of the client creating this space and quickly reinforce the actions that created it. When the space begins to shrink, the clinician needs to quickly intervene to help the client learn to recognize fusion and then use it as a signal to practice specific detachment skills.

Continuing with our example, the clinician wants to help Gail identify both rumination and worry as classes of responding that are irrelevant to her quest to achieve her stated life goals, leading to the following interchange.

Clinician: Gail, it seems like your mind is kind of bullying you—pushing you around and getting you to focus on things that don't really give you a new angle in life. It keeps coming at you with these alarming images and warning messages that are hard to keep your hands off of. I'm just wondering… Instead of lunging in and trying to wrestle with the bully, can you think of another way to deal with the taunting mind?

Gail: Well, I try to ignore it as long as I can. I suppose I'm hoping it will stop. But it never does. [Read: This is just another form of avoidance: pretend it isn't there and maybe it won't be. The clinician will try to help Gail see the unworkability of this move.]

Clinician: And is that what you're doing right now? Because you seem to be focusing on being here, yet it seems like you get pulled away. Even though you try to ignore your mind, you can hear it chattering at you, can't you?

Gail: Yeah, I've been thinking… I mean, I'm hearing thoughts that this isn't going to make any difference. It will be just like all the other counseling I've tried. It may work for a while, and then I'll be right back where I always end up. [Read: Now Gail is responding to the content of her rumination. The clinician wants to take her back to seeing the context of the message and then to return to its workability.]

Clinician: Okay, so right now the bully is telling you that you don't have what it takes to change and live your life based upon what matters to you. So, let me ask you, is this message in any way going to help you in your quest to become the artist you want to be?

Gail: No, it will probably make me avoid taking any risks.

Clinician: Is this message going to help you forge positive relationships with friends and a life partner, which you've said is a basic life goal for you?

Gail: No, I'll avoid people because I'll be thinking it won't work out somehow.

Clinician: So one way to deal with a bully is to try to ignore what's being said— the taunting, insults, and name-calling. Secretly though, you have rabbit ears: you hear everything that's being said, and the bully knows you're listening, even if you pretend not to be. What should we do with the idea that nothing your mind is saying is really useful to your life journey? That it isn't going to help you get to where you want to go? What would you do if you took that stance?

Gail: Well, I wouldn't have to ignore it then. I could just discount it. It wouldn't mean anything in particular about me. I could hear it and then just move on and do my thing. I have an image of this gnarly bully who wants to get me to fight. Instead, I just turn around and walk away as the bully tells me that I'm a coward and curses at me. The bully is really trying to get my goat, but I'm not taking the bait. [Read: This is a powerful, self-generated image that has definite carrying power. The clinician will reinforce this physical analogy and try to enlarge upon it.]

Clinician: That's a very cool picture. Now that you have that, can we return to the set of ideas the bully gave you a few minutes ago, about nothing ever being different?

Gail: Oh, I won't have to look far; it's always nearby.

Clinician: Okay. So are you aware of any urge to take action, like wanting to run away from or fight with the bully? If you notice any urge to act, just let the urge be there and don't do anything with it. See beyond any urge to act. What kind of stuff shows up when you just hold still?

Gail: (*Starts to cry.*) It's been around so long. I don't know how to get rid of it or make it stop. I just feel so sad and so alone. I don't want to go there. [Read: Gail is having trouble with fusion, so the clinician will do some minute-to-minute coaching to teach her what it feels like to detach from a fused state.]

Clinician: Consider this: Maybe you don't need to do anything to stop or get rid of sadness or aloneness. The question is, does the bully have anything to tell you that's important for your life journey? If not, you don't have to get into a shoving match. You can let it be there and leave it alone.

Gail: There's nothing here that will help me live my life better. It only makes things worse. (*Pauses and seems to be distracted by something.*) [Read: Gail just disappeared back into her content, so this is another opportunity to give her discrimination training so that she can better recognize when she is or isn't controlling her attention.]

Clinician: So, right now, at this exact moment, who's winning the battle for your attention? You, or the bully?

Gail: Wow! Just as you said that, I was getting lost in those images. So I suppose the bully is winning. Now I can see how I was getting drawn in. [Read: This is a positive sign that Gail has integrated some of the discrimination training, which the clinician will reinforce.]

Clinician: Okay. So now that you've recognized what it feels like to be pulled into your mind, can you pull back now and just keep that stance of not getting into a shoving match?

In this brief exchange, the clinician has helped Gail increase her ability to notice the process of fusion as it unfolds in the moment and then use it as a cue to redirect her attention to the task at hand. That task is to step back from her provocative content and let go of the urge to struggle with, manipulate, or control it. To achieve this outcome, the clinician used present-moment lapses in attention as opportunities to train specific skills.

Practical Clinical Tips

The letting go phase of present-moment processing can be very challenging for both clinician and client. This is because clinicians are operating at ground zero, and there's no place to hide—for either you or the client. We sometimes call this phase "the lion's mouth." All of the client's avoidance behaviors are going to appear, in both obvious and not so obvious forms. If you can help clients stay with their present-moment experience during this phase, there's an excellent chance that you'll promote a radical transformation in how they relate to their experience. The following sections offer some practical advice about how to optimize the effectiveness of your detachment interventions.

Detachment and Attachment Are Bookends

It's easy to get drawn into the belief that detachment is somehow a miracle drug that guarantees freedom from suffering, and that the goal is for clients to practice detachment for detachment's sake. Not so. No one lives life free from attachments. In fact, attachments are actually a good thing. For example, try to experience an orgasm in a detached state of mind! Some things in life are designed for us to experience in an attached, or fused, state; some are not. The main clinical principle is to help clients learn to discriminate when attachment helps and when detachment helps. We sometimes tell clients that if they're going to attach to something, make sure it's fun, because we'd rather have them experience a fun illusion than a painful one. Since everything we mentally construct is an illusion, it's okay to pick the illusions that feel good and to dump those that cause suffering.

Detachment Is a Dynamic, Ongoing Process

In our outcome-obsessed culture, it's often difficult for clients to treat detachment as a process, not an outcome. When they find themselves caught in attaching to some negative content yet again, this can launch a counterproductive inner dialogue that ultimately triggers even more attachment. So teach clients that detachment is a dynamic state of mind that's continually shifting. We often joke with clients that life isn't going to give them a "certificate of detachment" so that they never again have to worry about getting attached. The mind is far too tricky for such an approach to work. As we pointed out at the beginning of this chapter, the goal is to learn to relate to the mind along a continuum from attachment to detachment. We are all always located somewhere along that continuum. The dynamic is so pervasive that, as the dialogues in this chapter demonstrate, detachment levels can ebb and flow over a matter of seconds. So be a keen observer of these ebbs and flows and point them out to clients if there is something they can learn in the moment by doing so.

Second-to-Second Coaching

Because of the dynamic nature of the detachment-attachment dialectic, the clinician must be aware on a second-by-second basis of what the client is doing with feared content. It isn't unusual for clients to require almost second-by-second coaching in the mental skills required to produce a nonreactive, disengaged stance toward feared content. It's often helpful to generate placeholder verbal labels you can instantly use to reconnect a client with the ongoing dynamic of attachment and detachment. For example, in the dialogue just presented, the clinician asked Gail whether she or the bully was winning the battle for supremacy. This is a shorthand way to instantly coach Gail back into a disengaged, nonreactive state if she appears to be slipping. The goal of this second-to-second coaching is to give clients repeated chances to practice the mental skills that produce a detached, disengaged state.

Create Space the Size of a Postage Stamp

Many clinicians have trouble maintaining their focus on a single useful clinical topic and tend to follow clients to other topics if clients make that move. A young clinician once commented that our approach seems to be to create a very tiny space where the majority of the client's pain is located and then to circle around it again and again. Once you lock in on an area of feared content, it's important to stay there and milk it for all it has to offer the client. This might mean coming back to the same area after the client has managed to avoid contact by changing the topic. Circle around and bring the client back into contact with that tiny space where the salient pain is located. That said, there's a fine line between maintaining a minute focus on a topic and falling into a pattern of being right and trying to push clients into believing you know what they're avoiding. A better image is that you and the client are working together to keep the client in direct contact with something that is both painful and incredibly informative. However, the information cannot be extracted without first going through the pain.

Gentle Reminders

In this chapter, we've examined the first of three pivotal voluntary actions clients must learn to take to successfully navigate the present-moment landscape. This step involves learning to let go of attachments to provocative messages that originate in busy mind and make their appearance once the present moment is contacted. Two critical skills that support letting go are being nonreactive when unpleasant content appears, and then specifically disavowing the self-perceived relevance of the messages that busy mind is conveying. It's important to remember that letting go is an ongoing process, much like pursuing life values. When coaching clients, this requires a second-to-second awareness of what's unfolding in the moment, along with an understanding that levels of letting go naturally ebb and flow. Sometimes this fluctuation occurs in response to painful and provocative content that shows up in awareness, and other times it happens all on its own, as this is the nature of mind.

Once clients are holding ground on this front—letting go—clinicians are in position to help them take the next step in moving through the moment: softening in the face of harsh, critical self-narratives. This is the topic we'll examine in detail in the next chapter.

CHAPTER 7

Soften

You, yourself, as much as anybody in the entire universe,
deserve your love and affection.

—Buddha

Try as we might, there are certain aspects of private experience that stick to us like glue when they show up in present-moment awareness. We like to call these unsavory bits of personal history "warts." Warts might involve things we've done to others that we aren't proud of: lying, cheating, having an affair, stealing, violating an agreement, exploiting someone, and so forth. Warts also include events that can leave us scarred for life: being sexually molested, losing a child to sudden infant death syndrome, being rejected by a life partner, and so forth. You'll know you're in the vicinity of a wart if you wince when the memory of that event comes to mind.

Most of us don't know what to do with our warts, so we're naturally inclined to push them out of awareness and pretend they aren't there. But because warts carry pain that's a direct reflection of what matters the most to us, they don't disappear easily. It's difficult to take a detached stance with warts because, the truth is, they must somehow be integrated into the personal narrative that busy mind constructs to help us make sense of our life journey up to the present moment. Thus, another major inhibitory process that must be dealt with in present-moment-awareness interventions is the harsh, self-critical narratives that tend to show up. These are the targets of softening. Note that softening isn't just a counter-inhibitory process; it's actually an act of mental judo in which you not only accept yourself, warts and all, but also use the pain of having flaws to foster compassion toward others and acceptance of their flaws. Thus, softening serves both counter-inhibitory and generative functions.

A further defining issue is that we seem to be much better at practicing compassion for others than we are at practicing compassion for ourselves. At least in Western civilization, we're typically taught to be kind to others but unkind to ourselves. This is a derivative of our social training, in which self-control actions are among the most heavily shaped social behaviors. We're taught to control our emotions, words, and actions from the time we begin to acquire language. When we fail at self-control, the consequence is generally either punishment or negative reinforcement. Over time, through advanced language activities, we learn to control ourselves by internalizing the aversive consequences of failing. We no longer need someone else to correct a flaw through external reinforcements because we've been trained to do the same things symbolically. Simply put, our relationship to self-control behaviors has been conditioned to be negative. Meanwhile, we're positively reinforced for other-directed kindness, respect, and compassion because these are essential features of prosocial culture. Thus, our relationship to compassion toward others is conditioned to be appetitive. Just asking clients why they can't show the same level of compassion toward themselves as they do toward others isn't likely to promote change. This isn't an intellectual issue; it's a social conditioning issue.

The desire for sense making is so ubiquitous that it has become one of the main evaluative activities of busy mind. Sense making and the self-rejection it often contains have become the sine qua non for how we relate with others, almost as if we were explaining ourselves to ourselves. Regardless of whether a wart is something we've done to others or something others have done to us, the drive to make sense of what has happened is irrepressible. Thus, we not only have warts, but we also carry stories about how those warts came to be in the first place and what they might mean for us presently and into the future. Because sense making itself is a basic operation that helps us organize the world, the narratives it leads to are likely to capture our attention whenever they appear. While it *is* possible to detach from personal narratives, there's an even more powerful place to stand as we stare directly at our imperfections: self-acceptance.

Clinical Relevance

Clients typically deal with warts in one of two ways. They either push them out of awareness entirely or they become preoccupied with them. Neither strategy is likely to work in the long run. Ignoring warts results in intrusive rebound events in which thoughts and emotions seem to come from out of the blue. These events are quite traumatizing for people who are convinced that out of sight really is out of mind. Quashing these intrusive experiences can be quite a task and may lead to emotional exhaustion. Clients who take this approach often have chronic problems with low-grade anxiety, apprehensiveness, and dysthymia. In the back of their awareness, they know their issues are simmering, and they don't know when or where those issues will make an unwanted appearance. They live life waiting for the proverbial other shoe to drop.

At the other end of the continuum, people overidentify with their warts. The resulting wart-oriented self-narrative creates a life in which their flaws and shortcomings become the major organizing principle. Such clients believe they're broken and that it's highly unlikely that anything can be done to fix their numerous shortcomings. Consequently, they engage in a lot of behavioral avoidance of meaningful life situations where their self-perceived flaws are likely to be seen by others. Their narratives are designed to give good reasons for why they must avoid doing what matters to them. Until they somehow fix their flaws, they have no chance of succeeding at important life undertakings. Their narratives often lead to rumination about what's wrong with them and why they can't seem to fix these flaws.

As clients work on detaching from some aspect of a present-moment experience, you might notice that they suddenly get hooked by a self-narrative that brings up the basic self-related questions we all grapple with: "Am I okay just the way I am, or am I not?" "Can I look my warts squarely in the eye and be okay with them?" "Is it okay to simply acknowledge that I have flaws and that I don't always do the right thing?" The power of any particular present-moment-awareness intervention resides in both how the clinician frames these questions and how the client responds to them. The reality is that we can acknowledge our flaws and imperfections without having to beat ourselves to death for having them. However, the social conditioning of busy mind very much wants to pair these two separate processes (acknowledgment and self-criticism). If clients are allowed to unleash all the negative evaluative powers of busy mind in such moments, the outcome is likely to be traumatic. On the other hand, if the clinician is able to elicit a softer, self-accepting stance and keep the mental processes of acknowledgment and self-criticism separated, clients might walk through a door into new perspectives on themselves and on life.

In this chapter, we'll discuss how to elicit awareness of self-narratives that arise in the present moment, and how to then generate a self-accepting stance toward the real or imagined warts that show up in clients' awareness. We'll examine two principle skills that combine to create a stance of softening: perspective taking and self-compassion. We will then review recent advances in the neuroscience of meditation that bear directly on the kinds of clinical interventions that are useful for building softening skills. Then, as in all the chapters in part 2 of the book, we'll use a case example to demonstrate practical clinical strategies for probing, reading, and intervening with softening and self-acceptance during present-moment experiences.

Basic Softening Skills

Unlike detachment, which is clearly a self-focused form of attention, softening involves shifting clients' attention outward and making it more expansive. Interestingly, this contrast between intense, inwardly focused and expansive, outwardly focused attention is also mirrored in meditative traditions. Both types of focused attention have the capacity to bring us into the present moment but probably do so via different neural pathways. Present-moment-awareness interventions during this phase definitely have a meditative feel to them. The questions being raised are universal, and the door we're asking clients to walk through is definitely one that opens onto peace of mind and self-enlightenment.

Perspective Taking

Perspective taking involves shifting the position from which a particular event is viewed and processed. Indeed, the Latin root of the word "perspective" literally means to look closely at or through an optical event from different positions or lines of sight. Similarly, in this phase of present-moment-awareness work, we're asking clients to look at what has shown up in the present moment in a different way: to look at it more closely and examine it from different angles so that it can be known in a different way. Often, the change of angle might involve having clients step back from the seeming reality of a personal narrative and begin talking about it as a process of mind. The ACT approach is full of perspective shifts, many of which can be used to address overidentification with a negative, arbitrary self-narrative. Simply having clients accept that what's present is a narrative about their life is itself a perspective shift. Instead of the narrative being reality, it is now being talked about as a story or movie that the mind is giving them. Once this division is solidified, it's easy to have clients look at their narratives from other points of view.

Self-Compassion

The Latin root of the word "compassion" means to suffer with someone. Compassion involves having empathy for the pain of others and the ability to experience that pain as if it were your own. This deep sense of identification with the suffering of others creates a desire to alleviate their suffering. Self-compassion can be thought of as compassion extended in the opposite direction: you identify your suffering with the suffering of others, and this deep sense of connectedness creates a strong desire to alleviate your own suffering, just as you'd alleviate the suffering of others. The resulting intention is to heal your suffering rather than create more suffering.

Neff (2003) proposed that there are three principle features of self-compassion: self-kindness, common humanity, and mindfulness. Neff cites numerous research studies showing that we tend to be far more critical of our own shortcomings than we are of the shortcomings of others. Self-kindness is treating yourself the way you would be likely to treat another person with the same problem you have. Common humanity involves the recognition that suffering is ubiquitous, and that when you suffer, you are not alone. Rather than seeing your imperfections or flaws as unique and feeling cut off from humanity, you recognize that everyone has imperfections, and that other people have some of the same imperfections you have. Mindfulness, as Neff describes it, is really practicing detachment in the face of harsh mental narratives. You take a balanced, nonreactive approach to busy mind's evaluative chatter and self-critical narratives. These features of self-compassion directly convert into specific clinical strategies that we'll describe in detail later in this chapter. The take-home message is that self-compassion isn't an intellectual event; it's a transcendent process that originates in quiet mind. Busy mind, on the other hand, is incapable of self-compassion due to its heavy grounding aversive reinforcement as the primary mechanism of self-control.

Neuroscience Considerations

Neuroscience research shows that perspective taking is a complex brain activity that helps regulate emotional arousal while also stimulating the brain circuitry responsible for motivation and personal agency. In particular, self-perspective taking (for example, imagining you're receiving a painful electric shock) and other-perspective taking (imagining someone you know is receiving a painful electric shock) appear to originate in different areas of the parietal cortex. Self-perspective taking activates the left parietal cortical region, whereas other-perspective taking is supported by activation of the right inferior parietal cortex. Interestingly, the inferior parietal cortex is a multisensory integration area that's ideally suited to detect distinctions between self-generated and externally generated stimuli. We speculate that perspective taking is a prerequisite condition for self-compassion. If you are able to both take perspective on your own internal events and imagine these same circumstances in someone else, greater overall activation of the parietal regions will occur, thus strengthening the underlying brain network responsible for compassionate and self-compassionate responding. Thus, practicing self-compassion ought to stimulate both the left and right parietal regions and the associated networks responsible for agency.

Indeed, recent research suggests that compassion-based mindfulness practice increases the density of gray matter in certain areas of the brain and is associated with increased electrical activity in the gamma wave band. This type of activity is thought to be associated with highly focused attention, as well as reports of transcendent mental clarity often associated with meditative peak experience (Lutz et al., 2004). Further research has demonstrated that long-term meditators exhibited gamma wave amplitudes thirty times greater than ever recorded in nonclinical populations (Brefczynski-Lewis, Lutz, Schaefer, Levinson, & Davidson, 2007). Even student meditators exposed to just three months of meditation training showed significant changes in gamma wave activity (Lutz et al., 2008). These areas of the brain are involved in learning and memory processes, as well as emotion control, self-awareness, and perspective taking (Hölzel et al., 2011).

Interestingly, social self-awareness (that is, seeing yourself as affiliated with others, which is part of the process of self-compassion) appears to be supported by an overlapping but distinctly different set of neural circuitry associated with empathy and also with the ability to mentally visualize and compare different problem-solving approaches (Quirk & Beer, 2006). In addition, it appears that the experience of compassion for self and others reduces activation of the amygdala, the brain center involved in producing negative emotions (Schuyler et al., 2014). In other words, the practice of compassion toward oneself upregulates associated brain networks responsible for emotion regulation. When you help clients engage in perspective taking behaviors and practice being empathic and compassionate toward themselves and others, you are, in effect, strengthening neural circuitry that supports activation of quiet mind.

• Case Example: Joanne

Joanne is a twenty-four-year-old married woman with a five-year-old son. She was referred by her family physician for evaluation and management of depression. She's twenty-two weeks pregnant and has become increasingly morose with each passing week of her pregnancy. About two years ago, her second child, Laura, died in her crib at home from heart failure. Shortly after Laura's birth, Joanne discovered her blue and unresponsive in her crib but was able to revive her with CPR. At the hospital, Laura was diagnosed with a severe congenital heart defect that required radical surgery and repeated visits to specialists. The prognosis was that she wouldn't live more than a month, even with the surgery. To everyone's surprise, Laura didn't die. She was eventually stabilized and discharged to the family home, where she was kept alive with life-support equipment. Joanne reports that she was monitoring Laura continuously to make sure her life-support equipment was operating properly.

Laura actually began to show signs of social and cognitive development. Joanne remembers that the night Laura died, she was cooing in her crib, smiling, and making eye contact. That night, Joanne woke up suddenly in the middle of the night and realized she couldn't hear the life-support equipment running. She ran to Laura's crib and found her blue. She tried CPR, but she was so panicky she couldn't focus on what she was doing. Laura died before the medics arrived. Now, ever since Joanne found out she's pregnant, she's been unable to regulate her sadness and seems to cry for no reason. She openly states to her husband that she's unfit to be a mother because she allowed her daughter to die. At the same time, her religious beliefs led her not to seek an abortion. Concerned, her husband urged her to seek help.

Probe, Read, and Intervene

It's often necessary to let clients sit with a deeply painful experience for a while to tease out harmful narratives that may be floating beneath the surface. In general, the clinician's goal is to keep the client in contact with the pain while offering gentle reflections that insert different perspectives into the conversation. This type of reflective insertion really functions as a probe of the client's ability to make even small changes in perspective. Usually, the less responsive clients are to these insertions, the more limited their perspective taking skills.

Probe: Perspective Taking

Initially, the clinician wants to get a better feel for Joanne's level of cognitive flexibility in regard to any underlying narrative that's present. Obviously, if she's able to shift from one perspective to another, the clinician will have many more opportunities to help her disidentify with the literal meaning of her self-narrative.

Clinician: Wow, Joanne, I can hardly imagine the pain of your loss. It's something you'll carry with you forever. I can only imagine the horror of that moment when you saw Laura lying there unconscious.

Joanne: (*Cries softly.*) I can't even bear to think about it. I don't let myself think about it. I'm responsible for her dying. I shouldn't have fallen asleep. I slept with one eye open for weeks after she came home. I don't know how to even begin to accept that I went to sleep. I can't. [Read: Joanne is pretty clearly stating her agenda for how she's going to cope: using avoidance and suppression. But she isn't running from the present-moment experience, and the clinician wants to take advantage of that to probe for Joanne's narrative.]

Clinician: So, one thing that shows up with the pain is that you are to blame for her death?

Joanne: Yes. I should have been able to revive her like I did the first time she almost died. I was able to do it that time, but I failed the second time. Because of me, she's dead.

Clinician: Assuming you might have been able to revive her, how do you deal with the fact that she didn't revive like she did the first time?

Joanne: It was my fault. I panicked. I should have known what to do. I mean, I tried to revive her, but I don't think I did it right. I was screaming for someone to help me—someone to call 911.

Clinician: So because you panicked, you may have missed a few breaths or chest compressions. Can you imagine what someone else might have gone through if they were in your position?

Joanne: (*Cries with her head in her hands.*) My husband has said that too. He says anyone would panic in that situation. But I knew better. I had revived her once before. I knew how to do it, and the second time I didn't do it right; otherwise she would still be here. [Read: This isn't a promising response to a perspective taking probe. Joanne seems to be unable to imagine what others would experience upon finding their baby unconscious. The clinician is going to uncover the rest of the narrative that Joanne is carrying.]

Clinician: Okay. What does that mean for the future, given the fact that you feel responsible for her death and now you're pregnant again? Where do we go with that?

Joanne: I don't think I'm capable of being a good mother. I'm afraid that I won't be able to bond to my baby because of the pain it causes me. What if she has the same problem Laura had? I mean, my son asks me where his sister is almost every day. I've never told him his sister isn't going to come back. If I can't handle his questions, how am I going to handle having a baby who's totally helpless and needs me?

As this exchange demonstrates, Joanne is totally identified with the narrative that she's an unfit mother and that bad things are likely to happen when she gives birth to her new baby. She has the powerful emotional event of Laura's death, and her attributions that she fell asleep and then panicked are actually true. As painful as her narrative is, it does help her make sense of this terrible event in her life. Challenging her narrative directly, such as by asking her whether there are any other potential interpretations of how and why her baby died, will go nowhere, given the level of Joanne's identification with her story of being responsible.

Probe: Self-Compassion

Given the harsh, negative, and self-rejecting quality of Joanne's narrative, the clinician is going to probe to see if Joanne can activate a compassionate response to her tragedy.

Clinician: I can hear that you're being very, very hard on yourself about what happened. And I can understand that this type of overwhelmingly painful stress makes you want to make sense of what happened. So let's say you had a friend who lost her child in the same way you lost yours and she came to you asking for help. What would you do to help her?

Joanne: I would tell her that it was God's will. That as terrible as this is for her, she needs to put it behind her and move on and live her life as best she can. [Read: This is actually a better response than any of her previous responses to probes. There's an image of moving forward in life that isn't present in her current narrative. The clinician is going to test this image a bit.]

Clinician: What if she's convinced she killed her baby, like you? How would you help her with that?

Joanne: I'd tell her to pray for forgiveness. That's what I do. That's really all you can do. [Read: Although this might just be a product of her religious upbringing and not a deeply held personal belief, her use of the word "forgiveness" puts her in the neighborhood of self-compassion. Therefore, the clinician wants to create a little more depth in this area.]

Clinician: What form would forgiveness take if God granted it?

Joanne: I don't know.

Clinician: Well, let's imagine that there's a pie chart of blame here, so that 100 percent points have to be distributed between "I'm to blame" and "It's God's will and nothing I did or didn't do would have made a difference." How much of the pie goes to you and how much goes to God's will?

Joanne: I'd say 95 percent is my fault.

Clinician: Okay, now let's imagine that God has forgiven you. God is walking the walk with you, telling you that you are forgiven and to move forward with your life. How would that change the pie chart?

Joanne: (Cries.) I can't ever forgive myself. [Read: Her narrative showed up in spades during this little exchange. She comes to the edge of practicing forgiveness and self-compassion, and then her narrative pulls her back.]

In this brief exchange, the clinician has managed to help Joanne unlock from her nonnegotiable self-punitive stance and at least consider other possibilities. Since Joanne is so overidentified with her negative self-narrative, the clinician enacted an end run that required Joanne to practice compassion for the suffering of someone else as a prelude to practicing self-compassion.

Read: Formulating a Clinical Impression

As Joanne's case demonstrates, forming a clinical impression about a client's ability to take perspective and adopt a self-compassionate stance is an ongoing process that involves probing and testing the client's moment-to-moment reactions. This requires the clinician to be tuned in to how the client is reacting to questions and then to gear each successive question to move the conversation one level deeper. Effective probes during this phase of present-moment processing can prepare the ground for a subsequent intervention. For example, if Joanne had responded with more compassion in her comments to the hypothetical friend who had lost a child, this could then be incorporated into an intervention (for example, "It sounds like you'd tell your bereaved friend to be kind to herself and to let herself off the hook. Would you be willing to extend that same gift to yourself?").

There are a number of generic ways to initiate probes that stimulate perspective taking behavior. Of course, you'll want to tailor the exact language of the questions to fit the client's circumstances:

- "If you were looking at your life situation from behind my eyes, how would you describe it?"

- "I know that you have your narrative that helps you make sense of this situation, like I do to make sense of my life. Can you imagine another narrative that might fit this same situation?"

- "What would your narrative tell you to do in this situation? Would it help you succeed with what matters to you in life?"

- "Give me a totally irrational and nonsensical story about these events in your life and how they affected you."

There are two main ways to initiate clinical conversations about self-compassion. One is to go the transpersonal route and focus the client's attention on suffering in the broader world of humans. The other is to directly target the flaws and imperfections that the client has mentioned or come into contact with during a present-moment experience. In addition to customizing the language to fit the client's situation, it's also important to word questions in a way that makes it clear that the client doesn't have to like a particular wart in order to accept the fact that it's there. The following generic questions are good ways to initiate a discussion about self-compassion:

- "I'd like for you to widen your horizons for a few minutes. Can you imagine a world in which other people struggle with the same fears and anxieties as you do? We have about seven billion people on this planet right now. How many people out there do you think might be dealing with the same issues you are?"

- "Can you feel compassion for other people in the world who are suffering like you and open yourself to their compassion for you?"

- "Would you be willing to embrace everything about yourself—the stuff you like about yourself, the stuff you don't like, the good memories, and the bad? Could you just let them all be a part of you?"

- "Would it be possible to just accept yourself, flaws and all, even though your mind wants you to excise all of your flaws?"

Intervene: The Eyes of a Child

The magic of perspective taking and self-compassion resides in the fact that they create an opportunity for clients to completely redefine the meaning of their pain. Clients often present with emotional pain that has a harsh, self-critical narrative attached to it. As Joanne's case demonstrates, this type of narrative, with its exaggerated qualities, further traumatizes the client and makes avoidance behavior almost a necessity. When you can't bear to look at something because of the pain it creates, it makes a lot of sense to avoid it altogether. Joanne's responses in the early stages of this present-moment-awareness intervention suggested that she couldn't find any workable position from which to integrate her sense of grief, loss, anger, and self-blame. In such cases, you can often create leverage by going right to the source of the pain.

Clinician: I'm going to ask you to do something that could hurt, and I want you to know that you can stop this exercise at any time, okay? (*Joanne nods.*) Okay. I'm sure you remember almost every second of the night Laura died. I want you to take yourself back in time to early that evening. You told me she was playing with her rattle, smiling, and cooing at you. Can you put yourself into that place and imagine you're standing there looking at Laura as she coos and smiles at you?

Joanne: (*Cries.*) I've been in that scene more times than you can imagine. It's so painful.

Clinician: Take a minute to just hold that scene in your mind. And as Laura looks in your eyes, what does she see?

Joanne: She sees her mother.

Clinician: Tell me about her mother. What does her mother have in her heart?

Joanne: She loves her daughter like no one else on earth. She wants her daughter to live a good life. She wants her daughter to have the life experiences other people take for granted. She will protect her daughter from anything that threatens her. Her mother is just full of love.

Clinician: (*Tears up.*) So, Laura brought out in you the power of love, the power of attachment, the power of persistence, and the power to lose everything and grieve to the depths of your heart. It sounds like in her short journey here on earth, Laura taught you a lot about yourself.

Joanne: I haven't really thought about her death like that, but I guess it's true. I am a loving mother and wife, and I have goodness in my heart. I don't like to see people suffer or be the one who makes them suffer.

Clinician: And no one wants to lose a child. It's the one thing every parent fears more than anything in the world. There's no making sense of it. You don't get to pick whether your child will die young or not; it's just part of your contract with life.

Joanne: Sometimes I think that way, and it actually makes the situation a little less overwhelming. But then I remember my mistakes that night and it starts over again.

Clinician: I guess we could say that Laura gave you some very powerful gifts, and those gifts don't go away just because Laura went away. Those gifts stay with you, and you can pass them on to others. That's your walk, Joanne. Laura's walk is over, but your journey has just begun. You have another life inside of you, and your child will need all of those powerful gifts Laura gave to you.

Joanne: This is hard for me to put into words, but it seems like you're saying that I didn't just lose Laura. I also gained something very precious from her.

Clinician: If Laura were here right now and had something magical to say to you that would let you move on, what would she tell you?

Joanne: That it's going to be okay. (*Tears up.*) To take good care of her brother and the new baby. That she will miss us but will be looking over us. To be the mother I have the ability to be in my heart.

Clinician: So, to do that, would you be willing to take the gifts she gave you, as well as the intense grief, the regrets, and the certain knowledge that you will never forget Laura? Because you have a son and another life-force inside of you that will benefit from all of your experiences with Laura—the good ones and the hard ones.

Joanne: For sure. I look at my son differently every day. I realize he's alive; that's not to be taken for granted. Every day with my child is precious.

Clinician: Even the days when sadness and loss are around are precious.

In this exchange, the clinician succeeded in creating a new perspective that Joanne could adopt to soften the impact of her harsh self-critical narrative about Laura's death. The clinician helped Joanne create a self-compassionate message that can transcend the harsh self-narrative of her busy mind and bring her into a state of quiet mind. The clinician allows for the possibility that one narrative does not have to win out or vanquish the other; the painful narrative and the self-compassionate narrative can coexist. By doing so, the clinician effectively paired the two messages so that when Joanne starts to descend into her dark narrative, the self-compassionate narrative will be triggered.

Practical Clinical Tips

The softening phase of present-moment experience can be a very emotional yet transcendent experience for both clinician and client. After all, we are often dealing with universal themes that everyone must come to grips with in life. There's nothing quite like the feeling of hitting the "sweet spot" in a client's life experience and seeing that client's sense of self-empowerment grow exponentially. Naturally, such an important clinical event must be approached within a specific framework that allows the clinician's artistry and creativity to reign. In this section, we'll discuss some important guidelines to follow when doing this type of clinical work.

Go Inside the Pain

Rather than talking about the client's emotional pain, the clinician's verbal behavior should be oriented toward having the client experience the pain directly while maintaining ongoing contact with the clinician. Clients typically bounce off their pain in the present moment. When this happens, gently steer them back toward whatever they're avoiding. Your demeanor should be calm and relaxed, with a soft focus. Some clinicians feel that they're being mean or intrusive in such circumstances; however, the purpose is to create an opportunity for clients to see their pain from a different point of view that might allow a transcendent, self-compassionate stance to emerge. If there's any concern about the pain being too much for the client to handle, as was the case with Joanne, it's okay to tell the client that the plug can be pulled at any time. In our experience, clients don't take advantage of this escape hatch very often because they're in therapy to find a different way to handle their personal pain.

Don't Intellectualize

Concepts like self- and other-perspective taking, self-compassion, and transcendent awareness are pretty cerebral, which can lead to clinicians lecturing about the virtues of these mental skills. The paradox is that the more you talk about perspective taking and self-compassion, the less sense they make to clients. We've seen many therapeutic encounters where clinicians intellectualize, realize that they've lost contact with the client, and then lecture even more as the client slowly drifts out of the interaction. The key thing to remember is that the kind of perspective taking needed involves action, not words. We're trying to build skills, not intellectual muscle. Give clients experiential tasks that require perspective taking, and then help them discover what the act of shifting perspective feels like from the inside out.

That said, self-compassion can be tricky to introduce without some type of intellectual explanation. It's pretty risky to just go straight at clients and ask whether they can accept their flaws and imperfections without providing any grounding. Based on our experience, we recommend that, when introducing self-compassion skills, you first talk about the paradox of self-kindness. For example, you might mention that people are generally kinder to others than they are to themselves, and tend to forgive mistakes in others but not the same mistakes in themselves. Offer some humorous examples of limited self-kindness in your own life, then ask the client to provide similar examples. Gradually turn the conversation to the idea that most people struggle with many of the same problems as part of their contract with life. Consequently, it's easier to practice self-kindness when you realize that you are not alone and that others struggle with the same issues you're struggling with.

Be Authentic

As mentioned, the softening phase of present-moment-awareness interventions is a very powerful, emotional experience. Something about being in the presence of another person's carefully protected pain makes it hard to protect your own self from that pain. Some clinicians are reluctant to enter into this type of emotional intimacy for fear that they'll make a mistake or, worse yet, that they'll lose control of their boundaries. Our experience is that it's okay to be emotional with the client—to cry with the client when that response arises, and to engage in cheerleading when cheerleading is called for. This is quite possibly the most important moment in the client's life, and it isn't the time for the clinician to hold back.

The clinician's life experiences and the perspectives generated from those experiences are half of the therapeutic conversation. If clients already had these perspectives available, they wouldn't be coming in for help. Like it or not, clients are expecting clinicians to come to the table with different perspectives and beliefs that might help them get unstuck. As the clinician, you have to come into the interaction knowing you have something to offer that's going to help. You have to be willing to talk about spiritual issues, bigger life themes, the nature of life itself, and other transcendent concepts as they arise.

At the same time, resist the urge to force-feed clients your life beliefs as if they were the only alternative. The philosophies that allowed you to succeed with a particular issue in your life may not apply to a client's life. So offer your ideas, beliefs, and spiritual perspectives to clients with open, clean hands. You don't have to be right to help clients; you only have to be authentic and to stimulate thinking about and contemplating different approaches to the same problem.

Gentle Reminders

In this chapter, we discussed an essential phase of present-moment processing: teaching clients to soften into their experience while in the middle of it. This involves teaching them to shift perspectives on key life experiences and the self-narratives they generate. It also requires that they practice some degree of self-compassion for real or imagined flaws and imperfections. This phase requires clinicians to show up and share the emotional intensity of the moment with clients.

Assuming that all of this goes according to plan, there's still one more phase of present-moment processing to be accomplished: empowering clients with a new sense of life purpose that will lead to powerful and more effective behaviors. We refer to this phase as expanding, and it's the topic we'll turn to in the next chapter.

CHAPTER 8

Expand

Vision without action is a daydream. Action without vision is a nightmare.

—Japanese proverb

In ACT, we're in the business of behavior change. Generally speaking, if a present-moment-awareness intervention doesn't lead to a perceptible shift in the client's behavior in life situations that matter, then it isn't effective. In other words, the underlying purpose of any present-moment-awareness intervention is to change the way the client is behaving outside of the therapy setting. To use a baseball analogy, we aren't going into the present moment to draw a walk or scratch out a bunt single to reach first base; we're trying to hit a home run that completely redefines the client's life mission. Often, clients have been living an avoidance-based lifestyle dominated by rule following and attachment to a self-defeating personal narrative. They aren't living vitally; rather, they're trying to steer clear of emotionally salient life situations that might trigger more emotional pain. Helping clients expand their sense of purpose and life trajectory is the ultimate generative function associated with present-moment-awareness interventions.

In a general sense, the multitude of private experiences that populate present-moment awareness are interesting only to the extent that they function as barriers to the client engaging in effective action. By deliberately provoking these private experiences using a present-moment-awareness intervention, we get a much clearer view of which experiences actually function as barriers and which don't. Obviously, those that function as barriers must be taken on. The remaining experiences, however interesting they might be on any number of fronts, aren't targets for present-moment processing unless they show themselves as relevant down the line.

By processing the barriers posed by busy mind in an intense, focused way, clinicians are trying to neutralize their functional impacts on clients' lives. Sometimes neutralization occurs because clients learn to recognize private experiences for what they really are, not what they advertise themselves to be. Other times it involves clients learning to see their discomfort within the present moment in an entirely different light, with personal pain that was previously experienced as traumatic transformed into a reflection of a deeply held value that dignifies the individual's discomfort and makes it purposeful.

Regardless of its positioning in the therapy process, the desired end result of all present-moment-awareness interventions is expanding clients' behavioral repertoires. On the mental front, the repertoire changes from believing that the goal is to avoid or minimize personal discomfort to being willing to embrace and accept discomfort in the service of important personal values. On the behavioral front, the repertoire changes from responses largely governed by escape and avoidance to active approach behaviors based in personal values. Is all of this possible within a five-minute present-moment-awareness intervention? We think it is!

Clinical Relevance

We often refer to the expansion phase of present-moment processing as "the ribbon cutting." Like the ceremonial dedication of a bridge or building that's being put into service, the expansion phase involves devoting everything the client has learned in the previous few minutes to a completely new purpose. Assuming clients have successfully navigated the previous four phases (noticing, naming, letting go, and softening), they're in an ideal position to do something really powerful in their lives. There is often a light, airy, almost playful feeling that accompanies this phase. It frequently feels as though clients are celebrating their newfound personal freedom now that they can stay detached from the negative and self-critical rants of busy mind. Once they've made firsthand contact with the important realization that they are just fine, there's no need to get absorbed in personal narratives that lead nowhere. At this point, clients are truly in a position to play the game of life with a full bag of tools, instead of with both hands tied behind their back.

In this chapter, we'll discuss this final, exciting phase of present-moment-awareness interventions in detail. First, we'll examine the two defining features of expansion: repurposing and agency. Next, we'll look at recent findings from neuroscience that have a direct bearing on which clinical interventions to choose to improve clients' expansion skills. Then, once again, we'll use a case example to demonstrate how to probe, read, and intervene to improve clients' expansion skills.

Basic Expansion Skills

For clients to leave a present-moment-awareness intervention with a newfound sense of purpose requires that they effectively discard the old purpose and feel empowered to act on the new purpose. As their location in the final phase of present-moment processing suggests, these two important clinical events tend to occur near the end of a present-moment-awareness intervention. From an evolutionary science viewpoint, this phase answers the important organizational question "Now that we can relax around whatever is present, what should we do with it from here on out? Are there generalizations that can be made about this kind of experience that can be carried forward?" In other words, important learning has taken place within the experience. How is the client going to carry that learning forward into the next minute, hour, day, week, or year?

Repurposing

Clients invariably come into therapy with an already established frame of reference that helps them make sense of their "problem." Indeed, from the very beginning of the initial interview, the clinician is typically seeking to understand what this frame of reference entails and the degree to which the client is fused with it. Typically, the frame of reference contains some explanation of what the problem is and what must happen for the problem to be solved. This part of the frame of reference is heavily conditioned by the social training our culture gives us about such matters—namely, that these distressing, unwanted private experiences are highly problematic and must be controlled or eliminated. Experienced ACT therapists might recognize this part of the frame of reference by another name: the client's change agenda.

However, there are other important components of the client's frame of reference—for example, relevant historical events and associated subjective reactions to them, including evaluative thoughts, painful emotions, disturbing memories, or unpleasant physical sensations. There are the client's previous experiences with trying to solve the "problem" and the emotional and cognitive reactions that those problem-solving efforts have provoked. There is the self-reflective narrative that speaks to the client's relationship with the problem as it's evolved over time. Together, all of these components create an often cluttered and rigid frame of reference that can leave clients at a loss as to what to do.

Repurposing occurs when the original frame of reference is broken so that the components can be sorted into a new frame of reference that isn't as cluttered and provides clients with more psychological freedom of movement. Most clients are unsure what the purpose of a present-moment-awareness intervention is even as they enter into it. The purpose gradually unfolds as they learn to just notice whatever is there, give it a name, detach from provocative details, soften in the face of a harsh self-critical narrative, and then redefine their life mission. And if the mission is not to organize life so as to control the pain, then what is it? This is the question repurposing answers.

Agency

Agency, simply put, is learning to act mindfully in situations that previously might have triggered mindless avoidance or escape behaviors. It's a motivated state of mind in which clients intend to behave in a different way—one in alignment with a newly discovered purpose. They adopt an action orientation toward a particular behavior that was previously avoided or done incompletely or conditionally. Another popular term we hear used to describe this motivated state of mind is "self-efficacy." In this terminology, clients come to believe that previously ineffective behaviors can be changed to be more effective. Whatever the terminology, clients approach behavior change with positive affect in tow, even though any specific behavior change might trigger distressing, unwanted private experiences. Because they have learned, experientially, that such difficulties are part and parcel of being human and pose no threat to personal welfare, they are willing to engage in new behaviors even when distressing private content is present.

Often, clients who are approaching agency within a present-moment-awareness intervention are surprised to find that they know exactly what they need to do in life to promote valued outcomes. The burden of barriers imposed by busy mind gives way to the serene self-assurance of quiet mind. Quite often, the conversation during this phase of present-moment processing is lofty and broad, rather than restricted in scope. Clients are busy generalizing the lessons of the present-moment-awareness intervention to other similar situations they may encounter as they move along the path of life.

Neuroscience Considerations

All of the client's learning is brought from the past into the present. After all, without the client's recollections being available to muse upon, there would be nothing to talk about. Working with recollections, brought onstage in the present moment, is what therapy is all about. When you intervene in the present moment, you're effectively calling up stored memories the client is carrying, and reprocessing them with the goal of putting them back into memory, this time with a revised emotional meaning. Thus, when that memory is retrieved again, it will have a different functional impact on the client's private and public behaviors. One could argue that all psychotherapeutic interventions work this way at the neural level. The client brings in an experience that's stored with one type of meaning and emotional tone and, by means of the intervention, learns to carry the same memory with a different meaning and emotional tone.

The problem clients face initially is that negative emotional information is given preferential access to the brain's finite memory resources (see LaBar & Cabeza, 2006, for a review). To put it simply, we're evolutionarily primed to process and store negative information much more readily than positive information. The two main factors that mediate access to emotional memory are the degree of arousal and the emotional valence of an event (Lang & Bradley, 2010). *Arousal* describes how powerful the emotional experience is, apart from its positive or negative tone. *Valence* describes whether the experience is negative, neutral, or positive in emotional tone. Events or private experiences with high intensity and high negative valence are given preferential access to brain processing resources, are stored in memory much more quickly, and will be recalled more accurately and powerfully than other memories. Interestingly, different regions of the brain are activated in response to these two qualities of experience. Arousal depends on a neural network supported by the amygdala and hippocampus, whereas valence originates in a prefrontal cortex–hippocampal network that supports factual recall and semantic processing (Kensinger & Corkin, 2004). Some defining features of emotional memory include vivid recollections and a focus on central emotional details to the exclusion of peripheral nonemotional details. Typically, the most powerful forms of present-moment experience involve emotional memories that have been stimulated by the therapeutic conversation.

To combat the brain's built-in negativity bias, clinicians need to help clients strengthen neural pathways that compete for the brain's higher-order, finite processing resources. This is achieved by leading clients to engage in three distinct forms of learning. First, the client must get the facts straight. The problem is that emotional memories, by their very nature, omit many important details that could very well change the arousal level or valence associated with the memory. And indeed, the goal is to change both of these qualities to allow clients' recollection and understanding of their recollection to deepen. Clinicians use repeated probing of the present-moment experience with the goal of stimulating recognition of events and reactions that have previously lain outside the memory. This helps clients recognize potentially relevant patterns, concepts, or features of their personal experience that they previously may not have included in the emotional memory.

Having clients notice and describe different and seemingly unimportant physical or mental experiences within the present-moment-awareness intervention is, in effect, a way of expanding the frame of an emotional memory. This type of learning is often called *declaratory knowledge* because it involves objective, real-world data that can be consciously retrieved. Declaratory knowledge is supported by activation of the medial temporal lobe and the hippocampus and consists of two types of information processing: semantic knowledge and episodic knowledge. *Semantic knowledge* incorporates verbally constructed rules that guide behavior. *Episodic knowledge* includes recollection of specific events in terms of concrete details, personal reactions, and so forth.

After getting the facts straight, clients must learn from direct experience that different responses are possible and must acquire the know-how to try different things. This type of experience-based learning is called *procedural knowledge*. It originates in anterior parts of the brain (the prefrontal medial cortex) that are specialized to help us learn how to do things, ranging from low-level motor skills to higher-level executive function skills. One of those core procedural skills is the ability to redirect the brain's memory processing functions away from negative, affective information and toward information that's positive or neutral in emotion tone and valence.

Finally, executive level learning occurs when clients appreciate why something is important. In ACT, this often involves talking about clients' values and what their desired outcome is relative to their expressed values. This clinical activity stimulates and strengthens neural pathways that underlie the ability to evoke interest, organize attention, motivate sustained effort, and form behavioral intentions. Such learning involves a complex interaction between primitive brain structures, including the amygdala and limbic system, which establish the emotional valence of a behavior, and the anterior insular cortex, which seems to be responsible for evaluating imagined responses and their consequences and then exerting executive control toward a preferred action (Brass & Haggard, 2010).

• Case Example: Rick

Rick is a forty-eight-year-old divorced man who presents for help with depression, panic attacks, and pot use. He works in the IT department in a city government agency. He recently relapsed into pot use after being clean and sober for six years. Prior to getting sober, his preferred drugs were narcotics and alcohol, which he had been using since leaving college at age twenty-three. He entered treatment in an effort to save his marriage and felt very betrayed when his wife divorced him about six months later after getting into an affair with a mutual friend.

Rick has two teenage sons who live with their mother, and he complains that they don't really want to spend time with him. Rick isn't involved in many activities outside of work. He tries to engage himself in recreational or leisure pursuits but feels he always stalls out after a short period of time. He smokes pot almost every night after getting home from work and then watches reruns on TV. Although he's been divorced for five years, he doesn't date, and he tends to make excuses for not going to social events where he might meet women or make new friends. His panic attacks tend to be worst when he's home by himself. They usually arise during distracting activities like surfing the Internet or playing video games, or during lapses into prolonged periods of daydreaming.

Probe, Read, and Intervene

Clients who spend inordinate amounts of time and energy doing nothing in particular aren't just engaging in experiential avoidance. The function of these distracting behaviors is often to keep them out of contact with the more thorny issue of lacking a sense of life direction. The anxiety that results is a signal that, even though the client may profess to be lost and lack a sense of direction in life, aimlessness is, in fact, a life direction. Not acting with a sense of life purpose *is* a life purpose. There is no such thing as behavior that doesn't have a purpose, and ultimately, life doesn't allow clients to hide from the consequences. The depression often seen with this behavior pattern is due to the fact that these clients aren't getting any rewards from life; therefore, their motivation to initiate new behavior gradually decreases and may even disappear entirely. In technical terms, they're out of contact with positive reinforcements that could function to stabilize their mood, so slowly but surely they experience increasing levels of depressed affect. Often clinicians need to jolt such clients back into awareness by bringing up the issue of felt self-purpose and clients' sense of being the owner and operator of their human vehicle. The key questions to be explored in the present-moment-awareness intervention are what the client's destination is and what will happen upon the client's arrival at that destination.

Probe: Repurposing

Probes into self-felt purpose often require clients like Rick to first show up out of their haze of mindless distraction and get anchored into the moment. This immediately puts them in contact with issues related to sense of life direction. In this case, the clinician wants to see if Rick can make contact with his lack of self-felt purpose and how this feeds into his mindless approach to daily routines.

Clinician: Rick, I've been having this gut reaction to how you describe your routines at home. It feels kind of empty to me…almost like it's oppressive just to be in your skin. I mean, to me it feels like—and tell me if I'm wrong—that you're trying to kill time. Each day, it's like drudgery for you just to make it from morning until bedtime. I don't want to put words in your mouth here. Can you relate to what I'm saying, or am I way off base?

Rick: I'd say you pretty much hit the nail on the head. I feel lost and like I don't know how to find my way out. [Read: This is a promising response. Rick isn't running away from the emotional content of the probe, and his answer indicates that he's looking for another way to live in the moment.]

Clinician: So, you just diddle around and try to kill the hours by doing nothing in particular, just keeping yourself involved enough in something that you don't go stir-crazy. I'm wondering if being bored and empty on the inside serves some kind of purpose here? Sort of like you're saying, "My purpose in life is to have no purpose. So at least when people ask me what I'm doing with my life, I have an answer for them." When you get into that space, what's it like in there?

Rick: Well, it feels like I'm lost in some kind of haze, and no matter what I do, I can't seem to get clear of it. I feel like it's hopeless to even try anymore.

Clinician: And if you just stare at the haze and don't distract yourself from it, what happens next? What shows up emotionally for you when you just stand there with your feet on the ground looking at the haze?

Rick: You know, it's funny because I just had the same reaction now that I get when I'm at home. It's actually painful when I snap out of a daydream or suddenly realize that I'm here and I've lost my marriage, my children, and my social world. What usually comes up right away is this sense of emptiness and feeling lost. Then I get very frustrated with myself and try to find something else to do, like watching TV or playing video games. [Read: This response shows quite a bit of self-perspective taking and emotional awareness. Rick is able to differentiate between the experience of daydreaming or engaging in mindless distracting behaviors and coming back into his senses. He's able to recognize boredom and lack of involvement as an unpleasant experience.]

Clinician: Okay, so right now you aren't judging yourself; you're running off and doing something to distract yourself. Can you imagine having a different purpose than just running from this stuff?

Rick: I guess it would be to confront my losses and try to make something of my life. But when I go there, I start to feel overwhelmed. It will require so much energy and effort, and I'm not sure I have what it takes to succeed.

In this brief exchange, the clinician has used Rick's present-moment experiences of indifference, emptiness, and boredom to reveal their opposites: caring about things, passion, and engagement. Rick has been reasonably open to exploring options in response to each of the clinician's probes, a positive sign that he might be ready to develop a new sense of life purpose.

Probe: Agency

Probes for agency typically involve getting a feel for the client's degree of self-efficacy in the quest to change important behaviors. As alluded to earlier, self-efficacy is can-do energy. When clients are strong in this area, they're prepared to take on emotional obstacles to implementing new behaviors and are confident in their ability to persevere and succeed in the long run. Agency also involves recognizing that although emotional reactions triggered by approach behaviors are painful, they aren't harmful, and they can't stop clients from doing what matters. Rick doesn't seem to be there yet, so the clinician follows up on Rick's statement that change seems like too much effort or feels too overwhelming to contemplate.

Clinician: So, when you say it feels like so much effort to start over again, what does that bring up for you?

Rick: Well, I'm sure you can appreciate this. I've tried to do this before on my own, just get back to living the way I used to. But it seems to sap my energy, so I eventually give up and say what the hell... [Read: Rick is directly presenting agency as a core problem for him. The clinician will probe further to see what barriers are responsible for blocking his sense of agency.]

Clinician: So, what's the "it" that saps your energy so completely? What is "it"?

Rick: Trying to stay positive all the time and not letting rejection or failure get me down. But it does get me down. When my kids make up an excuse for not coming over for their visitation, it gets me down. So I don't feel like I have what it takes to keep going. [Read: This response is fairly common among clients who have been stuck for quite some time. Following rules that require them to stay positive all the time doesn't work, and over time it damages their self-efficacy. The clinician will probe further to see if Rick can take some perspective on the futility of trying to stay positive when painful things happen.]

Clinician: Okay, so your mind tells you that to succeed at getting back on track in your life, you must always stay positive and chipper, no matter what happens. I mean, it sounds like even when you're disappointed by something like your kids blowing you off, you're supposed to put on a happy face and just keep going. Does that strike you as even a slightly realistic approach to something as complicated as starting your life up again?

Rick: *(Laughs softly.)* No. When you put it that way, it doesn't make any sense to me. [Read: This is a nice, clinically useful response that the clinician will try to amplify using some hyperbole.]

Clinician: I mean, my god, we're already nearly suffocating in here from the draining effect of boredom, emptiness, and indifference. The last thing we need now is some rule that you can't be a human being and respond to sad events with sad feelings and to happy events with happy feelings. I mean, let's get some air in here!

Rick: Okay, so I don't have to be positive all the time. I get it. [Read: Rick is showing some flexibility in his outlook, along with a willingness to try new tactics. The question is whether he has a different tactic in mind that can be substituted for the tactic that doesn't work.]

In this brief exchange, the clinician engaged Rick about his sense of agency in making a potentially major shift in his approach to life. Probes revealed that his self-efficacy is low due to following an unworkable rule about maintaining an artificially positive state of mind regardless of the type of life event he encounters. The clinician then intervened to see if Rick's rule could be disrupted and restructured, with surprisingly positive results.

Read: Formulating a Clinical Impression

Formulating an overall impression of clients' self-felt purpose and sense of agency requires clinicians to think outside the box. Clients' stated purpose is often to find ways to avoid making contact with painful issues, past or present. Yet this pain is just one side of a coin. The other side contains the things that matter to clients in life, like relationships, parenting, friendships, career, spiritual growth, and protecting their health. It's easy to get caught up in the pain and emotional turmoil that surrounds clients' ostensible purpose; however, the leverage for radical change lies in shifting the conversation to focus on the other side of the coin.

This phase of present-moment processing often evokes discussion of clients' values and overall sense of life purpose, which can feel like the traditional ACT focus on values and committed action. However, the present-moment version of discussion about values and committed action is far less structured and much more likely to happen in the spur of the moment. There are a variety of highly adaptable ways to initiate and further conversations about repurposing and agency. Here are a few:

- "If you could describe your life purpose right now as though it were the title of a chapter in the novel of your life, what would the title be?"

- "Thinking about your current approach to this situation, if I asked you to describe the exact opposite of it, what would that look like?"

- "It sounds like your main focus is on the pain you're feeling about how your life is going. Yet if you didn't care about anything in life, you wouldn't be in any pain. What is it that matters to you here, such that you suffer for it?"

- "Would you be willing to take both what matters to you and your emotional pain into this situation and do what you need to do?"

- "The reality is that even if your mind tells you that you aren't going anywhere or have no purpose, that itself is a purpose. The important question is whether this is the purpose you want to have define your life."

As the previous exchanges with Rick demonstrate, he's living in a rather aimless way, with lots of avoidance behaviors populating his daily routine. He's been doing this for so long that he's fallen out of contact with important life purposes. Although he's apparently made previous efforts to restart his life, he's always collapsed inward due to trying to maintain an unrealistic degree of emotional control. On the other hand, Rick shows quite a bit of perspective taking ability and flexibility in his responses, especially once he receives feedback that suggests an alternative approach. He definitely seems to be open to trying something new.

Intervene: Life Path

For clients like Rick, what's missing in the bigger equation is what matters to them in life. What are they here to do, and are they aware that they're here to do it? The clinician is going to explore this important aspect of Rick's present-moment experience using a physical exercise called the Life Path (see Strosahl et al., 2012, for more explanation of how to conduct this exercise).

Clinician: Let's assume for the moment that you're on a life journey that began when you were born and ends when you die. One direction you can take on your life path is to go toward being bored, empty, and indifferent about it. So over at this end of the life path is living alone and isolated, and maybe being depressed and anxious about it. (*Extends one arm and points out with that hand.*) Now, what I'm curious about is the end of the other life path. How would it look if you could have anything you want in life? What about this direction over here? (*Extends the other arm and points out with that hand.*) What would that look like?

Rick: Well, I would definitely like to be in my boys' lives more. I guess I would want another life partner. I would take better care of myself—quit eating junk food, cut down on or even stop smoking pot, and start getting more exercise. I would get back to hanging out with my friends. I guess I know what to do, but I just can't get myself to do it.

Clinician: Let's not worry about what your mind says regarding whether you can do this or not; let's just look at it as if anything were possible. We can come back to the barriers later. What I'm hearing you say is that you'd like to be a more involved father, maybe to be a life partner to someone, to practice better health habits, and to have more social connections. What shows up inside when you imagine living life in that direction? (Points to the second outstretched hand.) And where would you put yourself in terms of living one or the other of these life paths right now? Just point to or touch where you think you are right at this second. (Rick points to an area about 75 percent down the line toward living with emptiness.) So as you put yourself at this point on your life path, what shows up as you just stay aware that this is you doing this, right here, right now?

Rick: I feel excited, scared, and sad, all at the same time. I'd like to live that way, but I'm scared that I'll collapse again. And then, when I think I can never have that life, this heavy sadness comes in.

Clinician: And as you feel these feelings, both good and bad, which way do you see yourself moving on your life path? (Stretching out both arms again.) Just point in the direction that you think you're headed in at this moment in time.

Rick: (Points in the direction of valued living.) I guess just talking about this is me taking a step toward that direction.

Clinician: Interesting… You'd think that if the whole idea is to avoid feeling things, then talking about your emotions would be a step in the wrong direction. Yet now you're telling me that it's a step in the right direction. So could you see yourself moving in this direction even if sadness, emptiness, anxiety, boredom, or depression shows up and tries to stop you? Could you carry these feelings along with you on the journey?

Rick: I'm pretty sure I could do that, but it might bring new problems with it too. Like what if my boys really don't want me to play a bigger role in their lives? What happens if I meet the wrong lady or can't meet anyone I want to spend my life with?

Clinician: So if it isn't about having to stay positive and pretend you don't have any painful feelings inside you, can you think of a different way to approach the complicated and difficult task of starting life up again?

Rick: Maybe just go ahead and try and let the cards land where they may?

Clinician: And feel what is there to be felt?

Rick: Yeah, I guess. Just let it roll.

In this brief exchange, the clinician has succeeded in redefining Rick's self-felt purpose by directly connecting him to the things in life that matter most to him. The clinician has also gotten Rick to buy into the idea that his private reactions don't have to function as barriers to living the life he wants to live. In doing so, the clinician has helped Rick mentally accept that his life journey will, of necessity, involve experiencing both pain and pleasure.

Practical Clinical Tips

In many important ways, the expansion phase of present-moment processing is where radical, transformational change happens. The clinician must be able to juggle many balls at once to make this happen. In this section, we'll offer some practical guidance about how to succeed at this juggling act.

Guide, Don't Define

Because of the developing emotional intensity that occurs as present-moment-awareness interventions unfold, clinicians sometimes freak out, so to speak, and become too directive and intellectual about what the client should learn from this experience. It's very important to maintain a soft, receptive, and measured stance in response to this emotional intensity. After all, the client's intensity is usually what's filling up the room, with the clinician in the role of staying present and responsive to what's happening. There isn't any single take-home message that the client must get; the clinician's role is to let the client roll around in the present-moment experience while continuing to ask questions that have the function of gently guiding the client into salient areas of personal experience. Personal discovery always trumps clinician-directed learning.

Seal the Deal

As mentioned earlier, the main reason we implement present-moment-awareness interventions with clients is to help stimulate radical change. Ultimately, we want the experience to culminate with clients making a commitment to behaviors that reflect a newly found life purpose and an associated sense of agency. In training, we've noticed that clinicians sometimes stall out at this very important moment. It's as if they become tongue-tied and can't think of a way to culminate the present-moment experience. An easy way to avoid this problem is to think ahead in the interaction. Based on what the client has been discussing with you, what areas present opportunities for the client to choose new behaviors that might make a difference? Also be sure to follow these brief therapy rules: Think small and accumulate positives. And if you can't count it, it doesn't count. It isn't necessary to get the client to engage in some type of heroic, brand-new life action. Sometimes just entering a common situation with a plan to respond a little differently can have a huge impact on the client's sense of purpose and agency. Just remember that the end result of this process should be coming to an agreement that the client will try a specific new behavior in defined life situations. Attitude change isn't what you're seeking; you're trying to help the client initiate new, more workable behaviors in daily life.

Anticipate Failures and Protect the Client from Them

The last thing most clients need is another failure experience to go along with all their other real or perceived failures. Don't mistake clients' enthusiasm for preparedness. You must protect clients from picking too grandiose a behavior change and then failing. If a client fails at some specific behavioral commitment, it's because the clinician didn't set it up well. And the magnitude of the behavior change doesn't matter nearly as much as that clients succeed in making a behavioral change. This builds self-efficacy and makes it more likely that they will be motivated to try other new behaviors. One protective strategy is to ask clients to give you a rating of their confidence, on a scale of 1 to 10, regarding whether they think they can succeed in the specific behavior change that's been proposed. Ratings of 6 or below are problematic and indicate the need to revise goals for behavior change so that clients are more likely to follow through with them.

Another strategy is to frame new behaviors as experiments and to be circumspect about what the experiment might reveal. The goal here is to get clients to acknowledge that they're trying something new, and that because it's a new behavior, they can't know in advance what the results will be. They must just be willing to try something different and see what happens. You can even build into the discussion the idea that these types of experiments are no guarantee that problems will immediately evaporate or be solved. Rather, the experiment provides clients with an opportunity to begin collecting information about the viability of different responses to the same problematic situation.

Gentle Reminders

In this chapter, we examined the last and arguably the most important phase of present-moment processing: expanding. This involves getting clients to redefine the problem in a new way that creates a different life purpose. Further, it means helping clients experientially realize that distressing, unwanted private experiences are an important part of living and need not be barriers to engaging in behaviors that matter. This is often the phase of an interaction where clients walk through the proverbial door that the clinician has helped open. This is the moment we all live for as clinicians!

Next, in part 3 of the book, we'll discuss how to use the present-moment processing approach with common problems seen in clinical practice. We will specifically address depression, anxiety and panic, trauma, substance abuse, and self-destructive behaviors, as well as how to use this approach to promote positive lifestyle changes.

PART 3

Using the Present Moment with Common Clinical Problems

CHAPTER 9

Using the Present Moment with Depression

> Do you not see how necessary a world of pains and
> troubles is to school an intelligence and make it a soul?
>
> —John Keats

Depression, in all of its many forms, is arguably the most frequent complaint therapists see in clinical practice. Despite decades of research, it is also one of the least understood and is consistently misrepresented in the media. Collectively, the mental health community has been inundated with messages (generated by big pharma and biological psychiatry) that depression is a disease, a "mood disorder" with specific signs and symptoms, and that you'll know a client's depression is "better" when these symptoms disappear. Entire treatment models have been developed based upon this misguided assumption, and although they have garnered a good deal of publicity, the reality is that these modalities are less than 50 percent effective when you consider the number of clients who drop out of treatment, fail to respond to treatment, or relapse after initially responding to treatment (Gortner, Gollan, Dobson, & Jacobson, 1998; Shea et al., 1992). Meanwhile, the contextual approach to depression (for example, Zettle, 2007; Strosahl & Robinson, 2008) has only recently been gaining some traction in the research community.

The phenomenology of depression is a good place to start in the quest to gain a better understanding of what it is—and what it isn't. Contrary to common belief, depression isn't a "feeling" in the sense of being an emotional experience. A person doesn't feel depressed, although this is frequently how we talk about depression. It's better to think of depression as the *absence of feeling*. It's characterized by an experience of numbness and apathy toward self, others, and the world. The functions of depression (and there are many) are tied directly to this experience of emotional numbness. Specifically, it allows clients to avoid painful emotions, disturbing memories, and other unwanted experiences. Viewed from this perspective, depression is actually a form of experiential avoidance. When you're in the haze of depression, you don't have to deal with all of the complex feelings generated by difficult life situations. Depressed clients have made a deal with the devil. In return for not having to feel painful feelings that might spur them to take difficult but necessary actions, they just drift through life without any sense of direction or connection. This is why depressed clients often report displaced emotional experiences, such as crying for apparently no reason. Their emotions have become disconnected from the ongoing flow of their daily existence.

Depressed clients tend to be vaguely aware that life isn't working very well, but clinicians often get the sense that these clients aren't truly in touch mentally with how bad things actually are. From a neuroscience perspective, depression is a manifestation of the dominance of the brain's default network, with its characteristic lack of somatosensory input (including emotional experience) and ruminative, mind wandering quality. Depressed clients are essentially cut off from the executive control network, making it hard for them to engage in task-positive network activities such as personal problem solving or goal setting. The result is a lot of useless, unanchored cognitive activity: rumination, self-critical thinking, and various cognitive errors. This cognitive activity is what depression theorists and researchers have focused on, and it is at the heart of cognitive behavioral treatments for depression. Yet research hasn't clearly established that cognitive treatments actually change the negative cognitive characteristics of depression, which suggests that these processes may be secondary in importance to what's really driving the depression.

In sum, experiential avoidance and emotional suppression, not cognitive distortions, are what contributes most heavily to depressive states. Therefore, it is no surprise that interventions that promote engagement with difficult and previously avoided private experiences, such as ACT and mindfulness-based cognitive therapy (MBCT; Segal, Teasdale, & Williams, 2013) have proven to be particularly effective interventions for depression. For example, the MBCT treatment protocol involves engaging in a formal daily meditation practice for several weeks, led by a therapist who is an experienced meditation instructor. We believe that a prerequisite for this type of intensive, mindfulness-based approach is that clients must be willing to make contact with whatever shows up in the mind, including distressing and unwanted private experiences they have carefully avoided. We would argue that the active mechanism of MBCT is that it undermines experiential avoidance and, in so doing, neutralizes the secondary cognitive activities, such as rumination, that are stimulated by the persistence of depressed affect.

In this chapter, we'll examine in detail how to use present-moment processing to help depressed clients unlock the shackles of their experiential avoidance and create a life worth living. We'll use a detailed case example to show how each phase of present-moment processing plays out when working with a depressed client.

Guiding Clinical Principles

The overarching goal when working with depressed clients is to get their avoided emotional experiences "in the room." This pulls them out of being dominated by the default network mode, activates the more grounded, higher-order attention of the executive control network, and allows clients to engage in task-positive behavior. The influence of the task-positive network involves, among other things, reconnecting the individual with important sources of somatosensory information, particularly those related to emotional processing. This initiates a process that allows clients to reconnect with avoided private experiences and bring them into fully conscious awareness, without the deadening effect of mind wandering. We'll discuss particular clinical strategies for achieving this important goal in detail in this chapter, but the immediate take-home message is to seek out the client's pain. The primary aim isn't to help these clients feel better, per se; it's to help them feel whatever is there to be felt. Of course, this can be done in a compassionate, humane way, even though it will be painful for clients.

The longer clients have been avoiding painful private experiences, the more likely it is that they'll be fused with rules about the necessity of not making contact with painful emotions. Ironically, one of these rules is that facing unpleasant emotions will make the client's depression worse, not better. For example, a client who's avoiding sadness about the lack of an emotional connection in her marriage may argue that if she lets that emotion in the room, she'll have to do something about her marriage, and that could make things much worse. For example, she might need to make decisions about where to live and how to care for her children with minimal support from her husband. Thus, avoidance of emotions is often done in the service of protecting clients from the feared outcome of developing a much worse mood state.

As a result, an important way of facilitating radical change and helping clients cement a new understanding of their battles with depression is to have them assess their depression in a before-and-after way once the present-moment-awareness intervention is completed. You might do so by asking something like "Compared to the way your depression felt before you got in touch with your sadness about feeling cut off from your husband, how does it feel now?" It isn't unusual for such clients to say they're aware of a variety of feelings. In the example just given, these might include being worried and anxious about how they would support themselves, being sad about the prospect of having a failed relationship, and being lonely inside the relationship in its present form. What is conspicuously absent in such descriptions is "being depressed." When the veil of depression is lifted from their life situation, all of the very appropriate feeling responses clients are having come into view. These feeling responses are directly tied to clients' values and reflect what matters to them. In that sense, these emotions are powerful motivational forces that can help clients expand into the world with a new sense of perspective and self-felt purpose.

• Case Example: Jolene

Jolene is a married fifty-five-year-old postal worker who was referred by her family physician for help with depression. She lives with her husband of thirty-seven years. She has two adult children who live in the area, and both of them have significant behavioral and developmental problems that have kept Jolene in a basic parenting role with them. She hates her job and is angry that she's been passed over for a couple of promotions, which were given instead to workers far less qualified than she. She also feels totally cut off from her husband, who spends most of his free time working on a vintage car in their garage. When Jolene tries to talk to him about their relationship problems, he tells her that he's doing all he can to make her happy and she just doesn't want to be happy. This infuriates Jolene, and they then descend into an icy silence. They last had sexual intimacy about two years ago, and Jolene often sleeps on the couch because her husband snores. Jolene has had several episodes of depression since her early twenties. She freely admits that she's never really been happy and says, "My life stinks." On many occasions, she's thought she'd be better off dead, but she would never consider suicide because she is, as she puts it, "stuck here" having to fend for her two disabled adult children.

During the second session with Jolene, about two weeks after the first, she looks despondent, frustrated, and angry all at the same time. She makes several comments expressing skepticism about "any of this helping" as she's escorted to the therapy room. A bit into the session, she throws her hands up in the air and states that her husband doesn't care about her, and she doesn't think she can tolerate being around him any longer. Then she launches into a diatribe about all of the ways that he's been a disappointment as a life partner.

Notice

The absolutely essential first goal of conducting present-moment-awareness interventions with depressed clients is to get inside their skin. This can involve repackaging what they've said and reflecting it back with an additional comment or two about how they must be feeling in the moment. This is done in an attempt to awaken them from the stupor of depressive mind wandering. Sometimes repeated probes along these lines are necessary before you see the light go on in a client's eyes.

Clinician: Wow, Jolene. It sounds like you've had to put up with so many disappointments in your marriage. I mean, no one gets married thinking they'll have nothing but broken hopes and dreams to show for it. That must feel just awful inside.

Jolene: Well, at least I got this off my chest by telling you how I feel about him. [Read: This response is a little off point and suggests that Jolene is deflecting attention away from her negative emotions. The clinician will need to make a more pointed probe.]

Clinician: So, as you hear yourself telling me this stuff about your marriage, what shows up inside for you? What are you aware of as you say this to me?

Jolene: It's no use talking about this, because nothing is going to change. I've told my husband that I feel like I'm alone in my own house, and he tells me I'm just depressed again and to try to get some help. [Read: Again,

Jolene's response isn't really taking on the question the clinician has directly asked. The clinician will have to further refine the probe.]

Clinician: So you've approached your husband and told him how unhappy you are, and even that move hasn't made a dent in the situation. You feel alone at home and you've asked him to help out, and he didn't help. What feelings go along with that? What's going on inside as you share this with me?

Jolene: *(Puts her head in her hands and silently cries.)* I don't know what to do. I'm stuck, and I don't know how to get out of this. [Read: Jolene is starting to wake up, but she's still bouncing off of her immediate emotional experience.]

Clinician: It sounds like you feel let down in so many ways. You feel alone and feel like your husband doesn't understand you or even want to understand you. You feel trapped in this situation and don't have any clue about how to deal with it. What else goes along with all these thoughts?

In this brief exchange, the clinician hasn't moved away from the topic of Jolene's avoided or suppressed private experiences. When Jolene makes an avoidance move, the clinician gently redirects the conversation back to what Jolene is experiencing in the present moment.

Name

At some point in the present-moment process, clinicians need to shift depressed clients from excessive default network dominance and low executive control into a task-positive mode that requires more participation from the executive control network. The best way to accomplish this important task is to have depressed clients begin to generate and attach verbal labels to various suppressed or avoided private experiences that start showing up during the present-moment-awareness intervention. Because the clients' defenses are going to be set up to suppress emotions and negative thoughts, a good entry point is to help them focus on bodily sensations first, and then gradually work back toward memories, emotions, and thoughts that show up in the same space with physical sensations. The following dialogue, which picks up where the previous one left off, demonstrates this approach.

Jolene: I don't know what shows up; it just feels like a big clump of pain. I have no idea what's in there. [Read: Jolene is staying present with the pain, and the clinician is going to help her stay present with it while simultaneously initiating a higher-level processing task.]

Clinician: Can you just keep focusing on the clump? Don't push it away... So, tell me, where do you notice the clump happening in your body? What sensations are you aware of in your body right now?

Jolene: *(Sits hunched over in her chair.)* My chest feels like there's an elephant sitting on it. The back of my neck hurts…all the way down my back. I'm having trouble breathing. *(Takes several forced deep breaths and sort of gasps for air, crying.)* This is really uncomfortable. What's the point of doing this? It's not going to help. [Read: Jolene is sustaining her attention, but her avoidance response is kicking in, so the clinician will try to neutralize it.]

Clinician: Just stay with that clump of pain if you can, okay? I want to help you pull it apart so we can see what's inside of it. It might seem a little less frightening to you that way. So, as you focus on that tightness in your chest, the difficulty breathing, and the pain up and down your back, are you aware of anything else showing up? It could be anything: another physical sensation in your body, a memory of something, a feeling, or some kind of thought that appears.

Jolene: I'm alone. *(Puts her head in her hands and starts crying.)* [Read: This is a good, clean response. The clinician is going to slow down and just let Jolene make contact with the first feeling, knowing that there are more where that came from.]

Clinician: Okay, so loneliness has shown up. Look around and see if anything else is there with loneliness.

Jolene: Well, it's sad too. I feel ripped off by life. [Read: These are two separate private experiences, so the clinician is going to call them out by name. That way Jolene's evaluation of sadness won't be mistaken for the direct emotional experience of sadness.]

Clinician: Okay, so sadness has shown up. Its companion is a thought you carry around that life has screwed you over.

Jolene: And I'm a good person. I don't deserve this.

Clinician: So, two more powerful thoughts show up with sadness: that you have good intentions inside and that you aren't getting what you think you deserve in life.

Jolene: And I, just now—isn't this weird?—I remember my dad telling me that I'm dumb and fat and will never amount to anything. I don't know how many times he said that to me as I was growing up. Even when I got good grades, he would focus on the worst grade on my report card and tell me I could do better. [Read: This type of seemingly out-of-the-blue memory intrusion isn't unusual with depressed clients. It's something the clinician will eventually come back to but not intervene with now. The main goal now is to get the client to attach verbal labels to private experiences.]

Clinician: So, what showed up inside that clump is a cascade of memories of your dad verbally abusing you in your childhood: telling you that you were dumb, calling you fat and unattractive, and telling you that you had no future. Wow! There's a lot of stuff sitting inside that clump. Are any other things showing up?

Jolene: I'm really angry. I'm angry at myself. I'm angry at my husband. I think I'm angry at the world. [Read: This is a different kind of anger, qualitatively speaking, from the anger Jolene walked in with. It's much better situated, and there's more emotional discrimination present. The clinician also notes that Jolene's physical appearance is changing at this point. Even though she's talking about really painful stuff, her face and body are starting to relax and show more alignment.]

Clinician: Yeah, I can imagine that with all of this other stuff swirling around you, it would be pretty natural to want to lash out to protect yourself from all this hurt. Anger is a protective emotion; it's usually the second emotion people experience in response to a painful experience.

In this brief exchange, the clinician has succeeded in getting Jolene to use her higher-level processing abilities to begin to attach verbal labels to discrete, painful, and unwanted private experiences. Jolene has also begun to accurately discriminate between different kinds of private experiences and between experiences from different eras of her life. In addition, the clinician has developed a verbal tag ("the clump") that can be used in successive phases of the present-moment-awareness intervention.

Let Go

Continuing to progress through the phases of a present-moment-awareness intervention requires that clients take a different stance with respect to painful, unwanted private experiences that have been elicited. Getting clients to first notice and then name previously avoided, discrete private experiences is one thing; getting them to carry these experiences in a completely different way is quite another. At this point in a present-moment-awareness intervention, clients often run out of tolerance for being in contact with the moment and begin to exhibit their customary avoidance behaviors. The clinician should use the appearance of these avoidance behaviors as an opportunity to teach a very different way of relating to self-experience, and to the very concept of self.

Jolene: I don't like talking about this. It's too painful to go on. I just don't see how I can go through this anymore. Are we about done? [Read: Jolene is starting to recoil from the clump, and her desire to disengage from the present moment shows up in the form of an interruptive and challenging question. The clinician will validate Jolene's fear and desire to avoid the pain while continuing the present-moment-awareness intervention.]

Clinician: If you can, just stay with me a bit longer. I know this is very painful for you, and I admire your courage in doing this in the first place. It's natural to want to run away from this stuff; that's certainly one way to cope with it. Lots of people do that. The problem is, the clump is still there when you stop running, and when you try to live the life you want to live, it will block you. Isn't that what you've already discovered in your life? No matter what you do to get rid of the clump, the clump is still there.

Jolene: Well, what am I supposed to do? Just pretend it isn't there and act like nothing has happened? [Read: Jolene is beginning to articulate other responses that are consistent with her strategy of avoiding or suppressing painful experiences. The clinician will take these off the table as viable alternatives.]

Clinician: Absolutely not. You don't need to pretend anything. That's just another way of avoiding it. What if we were to sit here with your clump, notice what's in there, and just let it be here, right now, in front of you and me?

Jolene: So is that how I can make it go away—by just staring it down? [Read: Jolene is still fixated on finding a way to either control or eliminate the pain. The clinician will use this opportunity to introduce letting go as an alternative.]

Clinician: Well, I think you've already learned, directly, that nothing makes the clump disappear. It's yours. You own it. You can't change what's in it by force of will. If willpower could work, you would have conquered this thing already and you wouldn't even be here. There's something tricky about learning to live with clumps. You don't have to like them or want them around, but you must accept that they are there. The question is what you do with your clump. Do you despise it, fight it, and spend your life energy trying to stay away from it? Or do you accept that it's yours and just allow it to be here right now, without having to do anything about it?

Jolene: (*Speaks in a disgusted tone.*) Oh that's great! So now I'm just supposed to accept that I'm dumb, fat, and ugly and will never get any good things in life. [Read: Jolene has mistaken acceptance for defeat and resignation, and she's taking her mind's messages literally, instead of seeing them as products of mind. The clinician will correct this impression.]

Clinician: What if, instead of seeing your feelings, memories, thoughts, or sensations as literally defining who you are, you just accept them as part of a clump of mental experiences? You have many clumps inside you. And while you don't like the one we're dealing with now, there are other clumps that are positive, like the desire to be a positive, protective parent for your children. One single clump doesn't define who you are. The goal is to be aware of and accept the presence of clumps when they show up, without getting lost in what's in there. You can be the observer of a clump without having it take over your life and ruin it. Of course, that's hard to do when the messages inside a clump are painful.

Jolene: So it's okay to feel alone, sad, and angry about that? [Read: This is a very solid response that the clinician will reinforce and ground by returning to the present moment.]

Clinician: It's okay to feel sad, alone, and angry. I've never known anyone who died from feeling what they feel, but I know of a lot of people who have died from not letting themselves feel what they feel. If you would, just look at your clump right here, right now… Just try to cozy up to it. Let it be there without trying to struggle with it or change it.

Jolene: (*Sits silently for a while with her eyes closed.*) I'm just trying this for the first time. I don't think I've ever done this before.

In this brief exchange, the clinician has succeeded in getting Jolene to experiment with an alternative to emotional avoidance. To accomplish this, the clinician needs to make sure Jolene isn't misconstruing acceptance as defeat or resignation to living a horrible life, and that she doesn't use acceptance as a stealth avoidance strategy.

Soften

The sine qua non of depression is self-loathing. No matter how clients learned to turn the lens of the critical inner advisor on themselves, this issue will come up in present-moment-awareness interventions. Usually, this occurs when clients exhibit a modicum of detachment from and acceptance of whatever has shown up in present-moment awareness, since private experiences that clients bounce off of are usually the pathway to their self-loathing. Again, this dialogue picks up where the previous one left off.

Clinician: (*Stays silent for a minute or so while Jolene practices sitting with her clump.*) Is there anything in that clump that's really, really hard to leave alone?

Jolene: Oh yeah. That picture of my dad, sort of lecturing me and criticizing me and my appearance. That's a hard one. That's the hardest one. [Read: The fact that Jolene has pulled up a memory she identified earlier suggests that she's succeeding with letting go and has run into an emotional barrier. The clinician suspects that this barrier is tied to many of Jolene's other emotional and cognitive experiences and will probe it further.]

Clinician: So, tell me, what's hard about making contact with that picture?

Jolene: *(Cries softly.)* It's hard because it's true. I never was that smart. I didn't go to college. I never had a boyfriend, while my friends did. I had friends and I was very active physically. I played sports and I went fishing and camping all the time. But men weren't attracted to me. Then I got married to the only man who ever showed any interest in me, and now I'm alone; he isn't interested in me anymore. Every time I've started to do something in life that was important to me, like having children, I got snuffed out. I think my dad was right; I'm basically a loser. And now I have all these health problems, like diabetes and back issues.... [Read: As is often the case, early parental abuse or neglect resulted in the client acquiring mental programming that has probably functioned as a self-fulfilling prophecy. The disappointments and setbacks of the past can't be undone, so the clinician wants to help Jolene find a different way to relate to these negative events.]

Clinician: So, when you cozy up to that picture of your dad lecturing and criticizing you, it conjures up all these other images of your defects, setbacks, and disappointments. I can see why that would be hard to stomach. It would be tempting to just throw in the towel and say, "Screw it! Life is over." The problem is, you're only fifty-five and your life is far from over. Trying to live life after giving up on it isn't going to be pleasant at all.

Jolene: Yeah, I'm not going to stay around for life if this is what it's going to be like. I'll kill myself instead, just to take mercy on myself and my husband and children. [Read: Although the content of this response appears to be high-risk and could easily divert the clinician into a downward spiral of suicide-risk assessment questions, it's actually a positive response from a contextual perspective. Jolene doesn't want to give up, and she doesn't want to feel like she has no future. If she can find a way to carry her past, she might be able to connect with what matters to her and not be governed by her programming.]

Clinician: Yeah, that tells me that living life dead inside is worse than actually being dead. So, we have to find another way for you to carry what you've gone through, without putting on rose-colored glasses and pretending these things didn't happen. At the same time, the way you explain your life journey up to this moment in time seems harsh and self-critical. And it seems like that harsh and self-critical stance toward yourself might set you up for even more setbacks in life. It's almost like the story tells you that you're going to be disappointed in the end. Does it have that feel to you?

Jolene: Oh yeah. That story never stops playing in my mind.

Clinician: That's the one your dad gave you, right? We know what that one is going to read like. We don't even have to go there. The neat thing is, just like there are lots of different clumps inside, there are lots of potential ways to explain your life and make sense of it up to now. Can you think of a different way, maybe a softer and less self-damning way, to describe your life journey up to now and, even more important, your journey into the future?

Jolene: You mean taking a life full of failure and painting it in a different light?

Clinician: Well, your dad is in the grave, but he's reappeared right in front of us. If that's where you want to take your life story, you can. It's your life story at the end of the day, not your dad's.

Jolene: (*Smiles ever so slightly.*) I'm guessing you're going to tell me I don't have to follow my dad's story if I don't want to. [Read: Jolene is already softening without the clinician pushing her, so the clinician will just reinforce her psychological freedom.]

Clinician: You said it, not me.

In this brief exchange, the clinician has succeeded in getting Jolene to reconsider whether her life story, as currently constructed, is helping or hindering her quest for a vital life. The clinician has avoided proposing that a different life story—one that's somehow better—is out there somewhere and should be adopted. The clinician has merely pointed to the existence of a life story that's the product of earlier learning. This implicitly suggests that this story is an arbitrary product of busy mind, not truth with a capital T.

Expand

At the beginning of the expanding phase of a present-moment-awareness intervention, the atmosphere in the room is often light and playful. The client's horizons are beginning to open up. Psychological barriers, while still present, have been recast in ways that make them less potent. At this point, clinicians need to seal the deal by helping clients incorporate their barriers into a new framework that's more expansive and purpose driven. Once again, this dialogue takes up where the previous one left off.

Jolene: Well, yes, I did say it. This means I could possibly not have to live in this dark place I have in my mind. [Read: There's a high level of self-perspective taking in this comment. Jolene appears to be open to creating a new sense of purpose and life direction, and that's what the clinician will address.]

Clinician: You're reading my mind. I've noticed that you're a pretty astute judge of people. You seem to know where I'm going before I go there! Maybe in the second half of your life you should consider doing something that capitalizes on that strength.

Jolene: You know, I've always been good at judging people and helping them with problems. I just don't follow my own advice. (*Smiles.*) I wanted to be a counselor when I was young. Then I got married and had two disabled children, and that goal went out the window. But I've always had this pipe dream of doing something like that. I think I would be good at it. [Read: Jolene is now talking about the future in positive terms, indicating that she's open to a transformation of purpose. The clinician will continue to promote this discussion.]

Clinician: I'm sure you would be, and if you don't let your dad's programming get in the way, this could actually be fun. How would you see yourself moving forward with this pipe dream?

Jolene: I'm coming up on my thirty years and can retire next year if I want. I have a friend who works at a domestic violence center that's looking for volunteers to work as advocates for victims. Maybe I could check that out and see what they're looking for and how it might fit in my schedule. [Read: This is exactly the type of new goal the clinician is looking for: concrete and small in physical scope while large in symbolic scale and immediately attainable. The clinician will amplify Jolene's motivation to follow through with her goal.]

Clinician: You know, your dad is going to turn over in his grave if he learns that his dumb, fat, unattractive daughter ended up living a vital, purposeful life—and freed herself of his bullshit in the process. How cool is that?

Jolene: Oh, that would be sweet.

In this brief exchange, the clinician has succeeded in helping Jolene reconnect with a core self-felt purpose in life, incorporating previously existing and often avoided psychological barriers in the process. Implicitly, Jolene has accepted all of the failures and misfortunes of her life in a new, softer, and highly flexible way. In the process, she's developed the ability to stay connected to what matters to her as she moves into a new era of her life. Interestingly, her marriage is hardly an issue at this point. Her husband will either reengage in the marriage or he won't. Jolene's identity and sense of being complete in life is no longer tied to that issue, as it was at the start of this present-moment-awareness intervention. This will enable her to end the marriage if need be, or to take the risk of making herself vulnerable once again if approached.

Summary

In this chapter, we've explored how to conduct highly effective present-moment-awareness interventions with depressed clients. To achieve this goal requires that clinicians learn to view depression as the natural result of experiential avoidance, rather than a biological illness or a mood disorder. Therefore, the main clinical goal is to get depressed clients out of the fog of depression and into present-moment contact with avoided private experiences. Encouraging depressed clients to engage in active verbal and psychological processing of avoided material decreases the dominance of the brain's default network while activating the task-positive network and bringing higher-order executive control functions to bear. This shift facilitates detachment, self-compassion, and repurposing so that clients can start living life guided by their personal values, rather than experiential avoidance.

CHAPTER 10

Using the Present Moment
with Anxiety and Panic

Anxiety is a deep conscious breath away from dissolving.

—Mike Dolan

From a present-moment-awareness perspective, anxiety results when people lose the battle with the mind over where their attention will be directed. In people predisposed to anxiety, busy mind will broadcast a message that a real or imagined threat to their welfare is present. If they take this message literally, busy mind will then recruit bottom-up attention resources to detect and evaluate potential threats. This results in perceptual narrowing and unstable, constantly shifting attention, along with activation of the SNS. To reverse this process, clients must be able to recruit higher-order executive control over the scanning and evaluative activities of busy mind. We often tell clients that, in order to conquer anxiety, they first need to be able to control their attention. This means being able to direct their attention when and where they want to direct it and sustaining that attention even when busy mind tries to direct it elsewhere.

Although anxiety and depression are often talked about as if they're different sides of the same coin, this is only partially true. Anxious clients often develop secondary depression because of their continuing inability to control their anxiety—which makes sense; it *is* depressing to conclude that you'll have to deal with anxiety for the rest of your life. However, from a neuroscience and clinical perspective, anxiety and depression are quite distinct. Whereas depression is associated with excessive dominance of the brain's default network, anxiety is a task-positive network problem. Anxious clients are constantly engaging in either threat-scanning activities that produce anxiety or in futile attempts to reassure themselves. The fact that these strategies don't work doesn't prevent anxious clients from continuing to use them. The problem is, when task-positive network dominance is combined with bottom-up attention, behavior patterns become fixed, ineffective, and inefficient.

There's something about chronic anxiety that, unlike chronic depression, makes people question their sanity. Anxious clients often make comments to the effect that they believe they're going crazy. You hardly ever hear a depressed person say something like this. We think this is because anxiety is an emotion, whereas depression is not. Anxiety is a powerful motivational state, and when there's nothing you can do to relieve it, the stored-up anxiety itself can easily become the dominant focus of attention. Anxiety is thus a very heavy drain on the brain's finite attention resources. And as attention becomes absorbed in anxiety, more and more somatic and perceptual experiences become linked to it. We often liken anxiety to a magnet: it tends to attach itself to anything and everything that comes near it.

Moreover, efforts to control anxiety exhaust already depleted brain resources while paradoxically ratcheting up anxiety. In the therapy room, clients tend to get anxious just talking about their anxiety. Secondary coping mechanisms, such as chronic worrying or mindless, repetitive activity, can best be thought of as strategies designed to deflect clients' scant remaining attention resources away from the anxiety magnet.

In this chapter, we'll examine in detail how to use present-moment-awareness interventions to help anxious clients win the battle over who will control their attention—them, or their minds—thereby allowing them to engage in loftier life pursuits than constantly scanning for threats in their inner and outer world. We'll do this using a detailed case example that shows how each phase of present-moment processing may play out with a typical anxious client.

Guiding Clinical Principles

The overarching goal with present-moment-awareness interventions for anxiety is to help clients direct, focus, and sustain higher-order attention while being aware of, but not behaviorally regulated by, the mind's provocative threat-oriented messages. Typically, anxious clients engage in anxious behaviors from the first moments of therapy, so it's relatively easy to disrupt their characteristic ways of relating to and coping with anxiety states.

Whereas with depressed clients the goal is to awaken their task-positive network, with anxious clients the goal is to dampen task-positive activation. Practically speaking, clinicians can use present-moment-awareness interventions to help anxious clients slow their rate of cognitive processing, practice mindful awareness of anxiety experiences, make room for threat messages from the mind, practice softening in response to the fear of losing emotional control, and incorporate anxiety to motivate more values-oriented behaviors in daily life. In short, you want to help clients use their anxiety to motivate positive, life-changing actions, rather than continuing their frantic efforts to control their anxiety.

There are several core themes that will show up in present-moment-awareness interventions with anxious clients. First, such clients must experientially learn that anxiety isn't dangerous or toxic in any way. Yes, it's uncomfortable—because it's evolved over eons to get our immediate attention. Anxiety is therefore a normal emotion state, not evidence that clients are abnormal or going crazy. Further, the anxiety might illuminate a genuine threat to a client's health and well-being that the client either isn't aware of or is consciously suppressing, such as a failing marriage, a dead-end job, or loss of a social network. If so, what might that threat be? After all, anxiety seldom shows up out of thin air; therefore the goal is to figure out what's producing it.

Second, clients must experientially discover that the best strategy for handling anxiety is to accept the emotion and then listen to what it's telling them. Instead of focusing attention and energy on trying to control or eliminate anxiety, clients must learn to direct their attention outward and take action to solve life problems. Typically, they must learn to hold still in the presence of anxiety so they can see what information it's carrying. Conversely, clients must appreciate that being unwilling to feel anxious or repeatedly engaging in strategies designed to eliminate anxiety only worsens anxiety. If anxiety is indeed a natural human emotion, trying to suppress it is neither workable nor desirable. Unfortunately, many clients have been practicing avoidance and control strategies for so long that they can't even remember what triggered their anxiety to begin with. The anxiety has come to be self-generated by the avoidance pattern itself and is often disconnected from any real, substantial issue in their life. We call this "dirty anxiety" because it is the direct offshoot of attempts to suppress and control the original anxiety.

Third, anxiety is a powerful motivational force, and the goal isn't to help clients get rid of it, but to teach them how to use it to promote positive problem-solving behavior. However, when anxiety is present, positive problem-solving behavior is possible only if clients can induce the higher-order state of attention characteristic of quiet mind. To that end, clinicians must help clients get out of the rut of trying to detect and eliminate real or perceived threats. The antidote is to practice being aware and mindful in daily life. Thus, present-moment-awareness interventions are used as a platform for teaching clients such mindfulness practices as deep breathing, attention control training, simple awareness, and detachment.

Finally, clients must learn to attach a different meaning to the experience of anxiety—something that will make them be willing to stand in the presence of their anxiety and engage in life-affirming actions. So rather than seeing anxiety as a signal that something is wrong with them, they come to see that it is a signal that something is right with them. For example, if they didn't care about their children, they wouldn't be anxious about their kids' health and safety. Often, anxiety is a signal that we care about something in life, and care enough to be anxious about it. Indeed, there are few important life endeavors that don't carry the risk of failure or loss. So the only way to avoid the experience of anxiety is to opt out of important life endeavors. Most clients, when presented with this choice, will elect to opt in.

• Case Example: Chad

Chad, a twenty-eight-year-old man, has been married for eight years and has two children, ages four and six. His family lives with his wife's parents because he's been unemployed for several years. This situation weighs heavily on him because he feels he isn't carrying his weight financially. He recently completed vocational school to become an IT worker, but he hasn't been able to focus on completing a certification exam that would make him more employable.

Chad reports that he's struggled with social anxiety and panic attacks since early adolescence. He's always been moderately obese and felt like he didn't fit in socially during his school years. He finds it difficult to complete job applications because of his anxiety about how he'll perform in a job interview. He spends a lot of time playing video games, which distract him from his life issues. His panic attacks typically occur in the wee hours of the morning when he starts to think about some type of household or family activity, like arranging a weekend outing for his wife and children. He begins to imagine every little detail and what could go wrong with each detail. Eventually, he gets into a negative feedback loop in which he becomes so anxious that he just opts out of the activity altogether. He then gets down on himself for being a drain on the household. Despite Chad's problems, his relationship with his wife is very positive. In fact, she was the one who suggested that he seek help, due to her concern that he's suffering with so much anxiety.

Notice

Because anxious clients are likely to be anxious about coming in to talk about their anxiety, clinicians have a built-in opportunity to watch how they've been coping with their anxiety as they do it in real time, in session. There's no need to make evaluative comments about what you're observing; rather, just objectively comment on these processes as they occur. The goal is to continuously redirect clients' awareness to how they're handling their attention resources.

Chad: I know that I should be able to stop myself from thinking this stuff over and over again, but I just can't seem to do it. I must be wired differently than other people. I don't know… [Read: Chad's attention is completely absorbed in his mind's evaluative activities, and his voice is flat, almost like he's reading messages off a computer monitor. The clinician wants to penetrate this veneer and get Chad to practice marshaling his attention.]

Clinician: Okay. I'd like you to just sit with those two thoughts: the one that you can't stop yourself from doing this, and the one that you're wired wrong. Just notice whatever shows up around this stuff while keeping your attention steady.

Chad: (*Closes and opens his eyes several times.*) Then, there's my problem with putting stuff off and getting behind on my life goals. I'm putting a financial drain on my wife and her parents because I just can't get myself to study for the certification test. [Read: Chad's attention just shifted and the clinician will simply point this out.]

Clinician: So, I just noticed that your attention got pulled away by another thought—the thought that you're a burden on your wife and her parents. Did you notice your attention shifting just now?

Chad: Now that you mention it, I did jump to another problem, didn't I? I wasn't even aware I was doing that. But I'll tell you, this happens all the time. When I get into one of my negative spirals, I can't control what I'm thinking about, and eventually I panic. [Read: Chad shifted topics again, so the clinician will redirect him.]

Clinician: So, I noticed that you jumped topics again, now to the memory of those awful anxiety spirals you get into. Did you notice that jump happen?

Chad: Did I? I did, didn't I? [Read: There's a look of recognition on his face as he says this, which is a good sign. He's starting to make experiential contact with the battle for his attention resources. The clinician will help him amplify this point of contact by having him practice just paying attention.]

Clinician: Can you bring yourself back into the room with me right now? Just see if you can stay here without shifting orbit. If you notice yourself getting pulled out of right here, right now, just see if you can bring your attention back. You can close your eyes if you want, or you can fix your eyes on something in the room or on me—whatever feels comfortable for you.

Chad: (*Sits silently for a minute or two.*) You know, I understand what you're asking me to do, but my mind is going absolutely crazy. I'm getting really anxious. This is what happens when I freak out. [Read: This is a positive communication, even though the content is negative. Chad is developing awareness of how unstable his attention is and how it feeds his anxiety.]

Clinician: Good. Now you can see what anxiety is from the inside out. You want to do something simple, like to just be here, and your mind wants you to be off in the future chasing your fears. It's like chasing a really fast and tricky dog on a playground. No matter how much you maneuver, the dog is so much faster than you that you'll never catch it.

Chad: That's a great image. That's exactly what it feels like.

In this brief exchange, the clinician has successfully redirected Chad's attention to how he's handling his attention, rather than the anxious messages from busy mind. Given the complex issues involved in Chad's life situation, there's a good chance that some of this jumping around serves an emotional avoidance function.

Name

Anxiety is such a commanding emotion that it tends to drown out other emotional inputs clients may be receiving. After all, many of the catastrophes anxious clients imagine would trigger markedly different emotional experiences than anxiety, such as sadness, grief, loneliness, or shame. Thus, anxiety is a warning signal and is interpreted as meaning that these other negative experiences would be intolerable and must be prevented. In our practice, we often use a strategy of having an anxious client spin out the entire catastrophic story as a way of promoting contact with the feared emotions eliciting the anxiety. In the next exchange, the clinician will take Chad down this path.

Clinician: I've found that it's easier to keep my attention focused on here and now when my mind has a task to perform that I want it to perform, rather than when I'm just letting my mind do its thing. So let's imagine that all of these negative anxiety messages are actually true and accurate, and that all of these things that are supposedly wrong with you *are* actually wrong with you. Tell me a story about what would happen in your life if this was the case.

Chad: Well, that's easy, because I do it all the time.

Clinician: I figured as much. This time I want you to take those scenarios all the way to the end, instead of running away scared halfway through the story. We're just going to sit here and play this movie all the way to the last frame, okay?

Chad: Okay. The start of the story is that my anxiety will get worse and worse and will never go away. [Read: Chad continues to see his anxiety as the problem to be solved, so the clinician will suggest that there's a different problem to be solved.]

Clinician: You certainly have a struggle going on with anxiety, but let me suggest that your anxiety and worry are just warning signals. They're saying that if your images of the future are true, you're going to be in a world of hurt. But in this movie, we're going to the world of hurt, so there's no longer a need for anxiety. The feared reality is here. So what's in that reality?

Chad: I can't get a job and can't support my family. We have to keep living with my wife's parents, and they eventually get tired of us mooching off them and ask us to leave. My wife has to work because of me being unemployed. Eventually she gets tired of me being a drain and either leaves me or just shuts me out. My kids don't want to have anything to do with me; they think I'm a deadbeat and shut me out of their lives. I'm basically alone in life with no one who cares about me. I might even commit suicide because it feels so empty. [Read: Now the clinician is getting somewhere. Next, the clinician will help Chad make experiential contact with the feared emotions he's avoiding by constantly focusing on anxiety and worry.]

Clinician: Cool! That's a gripping melodrama your mind has fired up for you. If that's what's waiting for you out there, I can see why you'd be anxious. Tell me, if you put yourself right in that space you just described, what shows up inside? You're right there, man. The worst has happened and there you are. What next?

Chad: Shame and guilt about being a failure in life. [Read: This is good stuff and the clinician will prompt for more.]

Clinician: So, shame, blame, and...?

Chad: Well, it's sad compared to what I would have wanted from my life.

Clinician: So, shame and sadness. Anything else in there?

Chad: Well, being totally alone and cut off from everything that mattered to me. [Read: Chad has shown up for his most feared, avoided emotions and seems to be holding his ground. He isn't having a panic attack, and he's staying focused on the exercise. He's able to provide verbal labels for his experiences. So now the clinician will move the conversation in a slightly different direction.]

Clinician: Okay, so being alone and almost feeling like you've been left behind to rot. Can you just hold yourself, right here and right now, in that space? Those emotions aren't off in the future, are they? I can see from your face that they're right here in the present.

Chad: *(Tears appearing in his eyes.)* Oh yeah.

In this brief exchange, the clinician has moved Chad from unstable attention to focused attention and has begun the process of attaching verbal labels to the feared emotional outcomes that provoke Chad's anxiety and worry. Unlike in cognitive therapy interventions, the clinician isn't challenging Chad's imagined life catastrophes as distorted thinking and misrepresented probabilities. The clinician is having Chad go inside his imagined reality to make direct, undefended contact with emotions he wants to avoid. Only by doing this can Chad discover an alternative to his pervasive experiential avoidance.

Let Go

Anxious clients typically fight the losing battle of trying to get their mind to stop giving them anxiety-producing thoughts, memories, and images. This futile quest only feeds their narrative of being intellectually and emotionally underpowered and vulnerable to all kinds of threats and setbacks. With anxious clients, the most difficult phase of present-moment processing can be teaching them about nonreactive awareness and acceptance as viable alternatives to controlling the mind. In the next exchange, the clinician will try to help Chad adopt a different stance with respect to his constant mental chatter.

Clinician: I can see that this is alive for you right now. This is the movie your mind creates for you every day. It's almost as though it would be a relief if you could just get it over with and be in this place—in a life totally devoid of meaning.

Chad: I just wish I could stop this. The movie never stops playing. [Read: Chad's attention is focused on the task at hand, and he's definitely making contact with feared emotions. His comment "I just wish I could stop this" is the mantra he's been guided by for years. The clinician will introduce a different mantra.]

Clinician: What if you didn't have to stop the movie in order to live your life?

Chad: Well, I don't know how you can live peacefully when all of your thinking is so full of negatives and anxiety.

Clinician: What if you did something different with your attention, compared to what you do now? Right now, you're chasing that dog on the playground. The more you chase it, the more the dog gets into the game, and the faster and more elusive it becomes. It's playing with you; that's the dog's nature. It's what dogs do. How do you turn that situation around?

Chad: Well, I guess I would stop chasing it—maybe hold still for a while and offer it a treat to see if it will come to me. [Read: Chad's face clearly reveals that he's crossing this metaphor over to his own battles with his mind. The clinician will expand the metaphorical message.]

Clinician: Isn't that cool? You don't have to do anything to turn things around. In fact, the problem started because you reacted. You started the chase. If you don't run, there's no chase. If you just sit there, keeping your attention gathered in and letting the dog do its thing, it will drop down on its front legs and bark at you, trying to get you to start running. It will run around you in circles, trying to get a reaction out of you. You could just go over to a bench, take a seat, and watch the dog do its thing.

Chad: Are you saying to just do nothing about the movie, to pretend it isn't there and ignore it? [Read: Chad is trying to bring nonreactive awareness in as yet another control strategy: if you try really hard to ignore something, maybe it will go away. The clinician therefore works to create even more distance between control and acceptance.]

Clinician: Well, I guess you could try really, really hard to ignore the dog or to pretend there isn't a dog there at all. You could try that for sure. But does the dog disappear, even if you do this really, really well, as in world-class ignoring and pretending?

Chad: *(Laughs.)* No, the dog is still there. It's not going to disappear, no matter what you think. [Read: Metaphorically, Chad has made contact with a pivotal feature of letting go. The clinician will try to elaborate other aspects of acceptance.]

Clinician: And notice something else. When you try really, really hard to do something, all of your attention gets put into that task. You have no attention left over to do anything else. So maybe you could be aware that the movie is there, kind of on the sidelines of your awareness. You don't have to do anything particular with the movie. It's there. What's important is that you dedicate most of your attention to whatever matters to you at that moment.

Chad: So, say I'm getting ready to open the certification exam book and the movie starts blaring that I'm going to fail the exam and never be in the IT business. You're saying, don't try to get it to stop? [Read: Chad is beginning to generalize letting go to practical daily barriers he's been struggling with—a very promising prognostic sign. The clinician will help flesh out the details of this a bit.]

Clinician: Right. If you try to get it to stop, you're back to chasing the dog. It will consume all of your attention and energy, and you'll lose. Go to the park bench and just watch. You have some studying to do, by the way, so you need to get back to what's important here.

In this brief exchange, the clinician helped Chad start the process of radical change by getting him to abandon a well-practiced but ineffective stance with respect to his anxiety experiences. Chad has learned that it's pointless to struggle with mental experiences or try to control or stop them. Rather, he now sees that the issue is how he allocates his attention between disturbing private experiences and important life tasks in the moment.

Soften

Anxious clients tend to use perfectionism as a supposed antidote for their many imagined personal shortcomings and vulnerabilities. In therapy, they often describe themselves as control freaks. The only protection against their real or imagined flaws is to overprepare for and overthink anything that matters. As a result, routine life activities that pose the possibility of failure are likely to become targets for their anxious overcompensation. For example, many of Chad's worst panic attacks started with him worrying himself sick over making some type of mistake. With anxious clients, softening often involves helping them relinquish the need to control the outcomes of even mundane life activities while also becoming more accepting of failure in general.

Chad: Can we talk about that more? Because it's been a year since I completed the IT program, and I still haven't taken the certification exam. I actually haven't even opened the study guide for a couple of months because I can't concentrate on what I'm reading. After I read a page, I close the book and try to remember what I've just read. Then, when I can't remember much, I freak out and the movie starts. [Read: Chad is giving an excellent and practical example of how his need to overprepare actually interferes with his efficiency. The clinician will use this example to introduce the idea of self-compassion and letting go of the need to control every outcome.]

Clinician: God, I wouldn't want to read a single page of a book under those conditions. No wonder you stopped. If I'm understanding you right, the strategy for taking on this really important life goal is to grill yourself after each page you read. And if you don't pass the test, your life is going down the toilet. I'm guessing that it's your mind that's telling you whether you passed or not, right? That sounds like chasing the biggest, fastest dog in the park.

Chad: Well, I have to pass. I can't fail this exam. If I do, it's like I got all those student loans for nothing. I've just set my family up with a bunch of debt, and I can't earn the money to pay it back. [Read: Chad's attention has once again been captured by his mind's warning messages. The clinician will point this out and then reinforce the centrality of the ability to control attention.]

Clinician: It sounds like you're back to chasing the biggest, fastest dog in the park. Your mind wants to suck up your attention with this scenario that you can't fail and your life will be in ruins if you do. What happens to your ability to control your attention when you buy into this?

Chad: I can't pay attention or concentrate on what I'm reading. It's like I blank out. [Read: Chad is starting to make the connection between his perfectionism and his anxiety experiences. The clinician will expand on this idea.]

Clinician: So, isn't this weird? When you approach an important life task with the idea that you can't fail—that you mustn't fail no matter what—you're secretly assuming that you lack what it takes to succeed and you *will* fail. When you buy the thought that you're basically flawed, your mind tells you that you can protect yourself by holding yourself to a higher standard, like you have to remember 90 percent of what you just read. Since you can't pass this test, you get more anxiety, not less. And the more anxiety you get, the more it interferes with your natural abilities, including your ability to focus, concentrate, and process new information. When you see this happening, your anxiety skyrockets, and off you go again. It's almost like the surest way to guarantee a catastrophe with this exam is to buy into the idea that the definition of success is that you didn't fail it.

Chad: You're reading my mind. One of the things I get lost in is that I'm not that smart and kind of lucked out in getting through tech school—that the exam will show me up. I think I get what you're saying. You're saying that my anxiety is controlling the way I'm approaching the test. I'm studying to control my anxiety, not to learn the stuff I need to pass the test. [Read: This is an excellent integration of the paradox that trying to control anxiety actually increases anxiety. The clinician will introduce another way to approach the possibility of failure.]

Clinician: Right on. So another way might be to let yourself off the hook of that higher standard. Maybe it's okay to not remember everything you just read. Maybe that's irrelevant to the task at hand. Maybe you have better things to do with your attention. For example, you could use it to study the material and then let the cards fall where they may.

Chad: That definitely feels better, but, you know, easier said than done.

Clinician: Absolutely. You'll need to practice keeping your attention in hand so that you're studying the way you want to study, not the way your mind wants you to study.

In this brief exchange, the clinician helped Chad explore the paradoxical results of managing anxiety by obeying the message to control and prevent negative life outcomes. The intense anxiety created by such an approach is itself a far more aversive life outcome than any real or imagined personal flaws or failures. By softening into the possibility of failure, as well as redirecting attention away from the mind's constant warnings, Chad is in a position to approach his important life goal, rather than avoiding it.

Expand

Anxious clients tend to live highly constricted lives because the possibilities for disappointment and setbacks in life are ubiquitous. If you have a typical range of personal values, there are hardly any meaningful life activities that don't carry some risk of failure, disappointment, or setback. As Chad's case demonstrates, anxious clients are particularly unwilling to engage in activities that provoke anticipatory anxiety, a strategy that naturally results in a restricted set of life activities. The ultimate goal of present-moment-awareness interventions with such clients is to help them discover a new life purpose, rather than protecting themselves from anxiety.

Clinician: I know we're talking about the exam quite a bit. It's obviously a centerpiece of your anxiety. Yet I can't help but wonder whether this dynamic shows up in other life activities you're struggling with. Perhaps you're so afraid of making a mistake or not being perfect that you hold yourself to a higher standard? Yet even if you manage to achieve that standard, the whole experience has become traumatizing. If the goal in life is to not fail, then failure is always in the room. That just feels oppressive. Do you get what I mean?

Chad: You know, I was just thinking that this message shows up all the time, in all sorts of daily stuff. For example, when I'm spending time with my kids, I get distracted by all kinds of worries. [Read: Chad is already generalizing the self-compassion concept to other areas in his life. The clinician will expand Chad's understanding of where he can take this in his life.]

Clinician: Right. This is a pretty basic formula for broad problems with anxiety because almost anything that matters to you—like being a good father, a loving spouse who pulls his weight, or a productive worker—carries a certain degree of risk. If these things didn't matter to you, you wouldn't have any anxiety whatsoever. So being anxious is a clear signal that you're about to engage in something that's important to you. The question life asks is not whether you're going to have anxiety but how you're going to respond while you have anxiety.

Chad: So, I can't avoid being anxious unless I drop out of my life?

Clinician: You *will* have anxiety because you're human, and humans have anxiety. The question is what kind of anxiety you want to have. Do you want to be hunkered down in your basement at 2 a.m. imagining all the ways you can fail and then dropping out of important activities? Or do you want to approach life goals that matter to you, making room for your anxiety and doing your best? Which would you pick?

Chad: When you put it that way, I guess there's no anxiety-free zone in life. I'd pick going after my goals and seeing what happens next. [Read: Chad is showing a definite readiness to try a different approach to relating to his anxiety. The clinician will help amplify the symbolic importance of deliberately engaging in this new behavior pattern.]

Clinician: You'll get a chance to try on this new set of clothing over and over again in your daily routine. And I'm thinking that the focal point might be to get back to studying for that IT exam and, as you do so, just practicing keeping your attention focused on what matters, not what could go wrong.

Chad: That would be huge for me.

In this brief exchange, the clinician helped Chad appreciate that he can have anxiety and not view it as his enemy. Rather, anxiety is a direct reflection of his personal values. He doesn't have to control it to live a purposeful and meaningful life. He can take his anxiety with him on his life journey.

Summary

In this chapter, we've explored how to conceptualize anxiety from a present-moment-awareness perspective. Anxiety occurs when clients lose the battle for control over their attention resources. Busy mind is preoccupied with controlling all threats, real or perceived, and left unchecked, it gobbles up clients' finite attention resources. Thus, the goal of present-moment-awareness interventions for anxiety is, in large part, to teach clients how to take those resources back. They can achieve this if they make contact with the feared emotional experiences that lie beneath the anxiety, which the anxiety is protecting against. Then they must learn to detach from busy mind's relentless display of threat messages, abandon perfectionism and avoidance as viable strategies for preventing anxiety, and accept anxiety as a legitimate component of living a valued life.

CHAPTER 11

Using the Present Moment with Post-Traumatic Stress

Unlike other forms of psychological disorders, the core issue in trauma is reality.

—Bessel A. van der Kolk

The dilemma facing clients suffering from post-traumatic stress is how to carry negative personal history in the present moment without letting it dictate or control their behavior. This is hard to do when you have a nervous system that has evolved with self-protection as its number one mandate. When severe violations of safety, trust, or vulnerability occur, including outright threats to survival, humans are wired to shut down higher-order neural functions and fight, flee, or freeze in order to survive the threat. Although post-traumatic stress is typically regarded as an anxiety state, the truth is that there are very few traumatized clients who don't manifest high levels of both depression and anxiety, as well as addictive and self-harming behaviors designed to numb or banish distressing and unwanted reminders of traumatic experiences. We view post-traumatic stress as an amalgam of distinctive cognitive, emotional, memory, and somatosensory experiences that tend to show up unpredictably, in piecemeal fashion. These experiences can arise at any time, elicit high levels of emotional distress and seem to be uncontrollable. This explains why such clients are so anxious, depressed, and ready to take any action necessary to avoid situations or activities that might trigger more trauma-related experiences. The other notable feature of post-traumatic stress is that it's timeless once the process begins. It doesn't matter if the trauma is related to recent combat, the result of a rape a decade ago, or linked to sexual abuse as a young child; the clinical presentation tends to be remarkably similar regardless of the type or timing of the traumatic event.

From a neuroscience perspective, post-traumatic stress, like other anxiety states, is a problem involving domination of bottom-up attention resources and overactivation of the task-positive network. Clients who face it are constantly engaged in scanning for threats in their immediate environment, a trademark of the bottom-up attention system.

However, their attention resources are exclusively focused on detecting situations, interactions, or events that might subject them to further trauma, a focus that is unique to trauma. For example, such clients often can't or won't go into grocery stores for more than a few minutes before developing intense urges to escape. They can't go into movie theaters because the darkness interferes with their ability to detect threats. They can't stay out in their backyard for too long for fear that someone will break into their house through the front door. They have to sit in the corner of a restaurant to make sure no one is sitting behind them. They often won't get in their car and drive somewhere without being accompanied. This is what happens when the SNS is chronically overactivated.

Not surprisingly, people with post-traumatic stress disorder (PTSD) have terrible health outcomes. For example, clients with PTSD have a higher risk of developing cardiovascular disease and cancer compared to the general population. In fact, a recent study (Morath et al., 2014) found that trauma exposure was correlated with a higher level of DNA breakage—and also that exposure therapy seemed to reverse that process.

In this chapter, we'll examine in detail how to use present-moment-awareness interventions to help clients who are suffering from post-traumatic stress. The interventions we'll outline can help them learn to approach rather than suppress or avoid trauma symptoms, and also support integration of symptoms into a coherent narrative that's consistent with valued living, rather than fear-based avoidance. Once again, we'll do this using a detailed case example, showing how each phase of present-moment processing plays out with the typical client suffering from post-traumatic stress.

Guiding Clinical Principles

We think of healing from post-traumatic stress as consisting of two distinct, interrelated processes. One is coming to grips with the original traumatic event and making sense of it within the context of a coherent life narrative. This is the pain part of trauma. The second, and more demanding, process is learning to carry the memory of the trauma, and the symptoms it triggers, in a way that doesn't create oppressive life outcomes. This is the trauma part of trauma. Whereas the clock cannot be reversed and the original traumatic event undone, there is much that can be done to change how clients relate to their trauma-based experiences in the present. At one end of the continuum, clients are capable of reconstructing past events with such precision that it can almost seem as though the trauma is happening again in the present. If they relate to these experiences in a fused state, they'll be compelled to seek safety, so emotional and behavioral avoidance will be inevitable. At the other end of the continuum, they can relate to these experiences simply as unpleasant products of human memory, in which case their behavior won't be regulated by the reappearance of these experiences.

The two themes (accepting the trauma and living a valued life in the presence of trauma-related experiences) are intimately related and often indistinguishable within a present-moment-awareness intervention. Even decades after a trauma has occurred, many clients can't accept the reality of the trauma itself; it just seems like a bad dream that never ends. This leads to emotional (and often behavioral) avoidance of any action that will reignite the seemingly raw reality of being traumatized. If people can't accept what has happened to them, they'll avoid doing anything that might require acceptance of what happened. Therefore, they tend to studiously avoid making contact with distressing, unwanted private experiences associated with the original event. Figuratively speaking, clients with trauma histories carry their history in a bag held at arm's length, as if it were a bag of poop. The problem is, carrying a bag of poop this way consumes a tremendous amount of energy yet still doesn't eliminate the possibility of making contact with it. In fact, the person is still in contact with it, despite having this specific way of carrying it. Speaking figuratively once again, as clinicians we want to help clients learn to cradle this bag of poop as if they were holding a baby in their arms. Even if what's in the bag is despicable, they can carry it this way for a very long time without consuming a lot of physical and mental resources.

Thus, the main goal of present-moment-awareness interventions with traumatized clients is to help them accept the reality of their trauma and all of the associated private reactions stored in their memory. Moreover, they need to accept that these experiences will be triggered randomly by events that naturally arise in the course of daily living. The only control they have is over what they do when these private experiences show up. One alternative is to build a life based on avoiding triggers or preventing them from happening, which requires clients to give up on almost every life goal that matters to them. This is the strategy most traumatized clients are following when they come to therapy, and it's the cause of enormous suffering, given that there is no end to the things that could conceivably evoke the trauma or be dangerous to them. Busy mind absolutely feasts on situations like this. The other path involves learning to let go of attachment to the products of memory and soften in response to the trauma narrative, which typically includes shame, blame, guilt, and mistrust. Clients can then focus on what matters in life and move in that direction, accepting the fact that doing so will trigger previously suppressed and avoided trauma-related experiences.

A very important caveat is that clinicians need to bend over backward to avoid appearing to minimize the seriousness of the trauma itself. Most clients suffering from trauma have been advised to just move on from it, suggesting that the way to cope is to just forget about it. They then feel broken and defective because they weren't able to put the trauma behind them. So it's exceedingly important to bore in on the traumatic event itself, to get clients to tell their story, and then to validate every last bit of emotional pain that resulted. Particularly in the case of sexual trauma, part of the client's story may include the reactions of important others in response to the event. If a young sexual abuse victim finally discloses the abuse to a parent and is told she's making it up and will ruin the family if she tells anybody else, that becomes another trauma the child has to contend with. If you don't first validate clients' emotional pain, you'll probably find it quite difficult to get them to follow you into the heart of the hornet's nest.

• Case Example: Becky

Becky, a forty-year-old woman, is married and has two teenage sons. She originally saw her family physician for chronic insomnia. During the exam, she disclosed that she was having nightmares several nights each week but declined to talk about them further. She did, however, agree to see a behavioral clinician to get some advice on how to address her sleep problems. It turned out that insomnia was only one of many problems Becky was experiencing. For many years, dating back to her early twenties, she's struggled with anxiety symptoms when leaving home, whether to go on errands or engage in social activities. Her husband does most of the daily activities that require leaving the house.

Becky also complains about feeling unsafe much of the time she's at home. She checks the windows and door locks a couple of times each evening before going to bed. While she is able to participate in some of her sons' activities outside the home, she does so with great trepidation and feels emotionally exhausted afterward. All of these symptoms worsened after the sudden death of her mother five years ago. Becky describes her mother as a "crazy woman." Her father, a recovering alcoholic, was an active alcoholic the entire time Becky was growing up. Becky has no relationship with her father to speak of. Her marriage is sputtering along, with her husband being basically in a caretaker role. It's hard for them to sustain any kind of intimate connection because he's so busy covering for her.

Notice

The best way to persistently avoid making contact with painful history is to learn to be very inattentive in general. When post-traumatic stress symptoms are triggered by some internal or external stimulus, these clients' attention is so fragmented that they only make contact with vague, overly general memories and a jumbled mess of associated private experiences. Part of this problem is due to the excessive dominance of bottom-up attention in clients with trauma. However, selective, scattered attention also serves an important psychological function: if they can't recall traumatic events with any precision, they may still be distressed when their history shows up, but not as distressed as they'd be if these events were crystal clear in their mind's eye. Thus, the immediate goal with traumatized clients is to make specific demands of their attention that will result in more clinically useful behaviors. To that end, it's important not to bounce from one time period to another and from one painful experience to another; this won't help them integrate and assimilate their trauma history into a coherent self-story. In the following brief dialogue, the clinician will try to help Becky show up and focus her attention on core aspects of her traumatic experiences.

Clinician: From what you're telling me, it sounds like things at home were pretty dysfunctional and abusive, and your mother was sort of at the center of this. So what did your mother's death mean to you, since it seems to have triggered more problems with anxiety?

Becky: I don't know how I feel about my mother. I remember her whipping me with a willow switch because I had a food stain on my blouse after dinner. My whole childhood was a mess, and she was a big part of it. I was actually sad when she died—but you know, I think I've always had issues with self-confidence. I'm sure my husband just sort of puts up with me. He knows I don't really know how to take care of myself. [Read: Becky is jumping all over the place, displaying severely fragmented attention. The clinician will immediately help her dial in her attention and keep it focused.]

Clinician: I know this is very hard for you to talk about, and I appreciate that there are a lot of things going on inside; it must feel like a big emotional jumble. I want to help you work through this jumble. If you try to take the whole thing on all at once, you'll just get lost in it, and that won't feel very good. The best way to keep this from happening while we talk is to focus on just one piece of the jumble at a time. So, let's get back to your mother's death and go on from there. Did you see her before she died and get some closure on whatever issues you had with her?

Becky: I tried to tell her how I was feeling, and she just looked away and said nothing. It was sad. [Read: This response shows much more focused attention. Becky answered the question without rambling and provided useful information, which the clinician will begin to probe further.]

Clinician: Do you mean you felt sad, or that it was sad in a pathetic kind of way?

Becky: I think more the pathetic kind of sad. I could see in how she reacted that she hadn't changed at all. She coped with everything that went on in the family by looking the other way. So I got up and left, figuring she'd never take any responsibility for anything. That was the last time I saw her. [Read: This is a very organized, integrated response, indicating that Becky is already benefiting from being directed to focus. She has also dropped a clue that the clinician will pursue.]

Clinician: So, what were some of the things that went on that your mother turned her head away from?

Becky: My father had several affairs with other women. He would bring them home when Mom was out of the house. We could hear him doing all kinds of things with them. She knew he was unfaithful and just pretended it didn't matter; life was what it was for her. [Read: This is another attentive, well-organized response indicating that Becky is able to produce trauma-specific information if given sufficient structure.]

Clinician: Sometimes when alcohol is involved and the parents are out to lunch, children can be at risk of being abused or molested. Did anything like that ever happen to you or your sisters?

Becky: I've never actually talked about this with anybody. Just so you know, it's… It's very hard for me to do. [Read: Becky is definitely making contact with painful experiences. The clinician will try to create a safe and permissive environment and give Becky control over what she wants to talk about.]

Clinician: Okay, so this part of the jumble is something that's really painful for you. I understand completely if you're not ready to go there. It's very courageous of you to even agree to come talk with me. I really admire you for just showing up here. So, we can go there if you feel ready to do that. If not, we'll move on to another piece of the jumble. This is 100 percent your call.

Becky: Well, thank you for saying those things. I feel ashamed talking about this, so it's hard. (*Pauses, with some tears building.*) My dad molested me off and on for several years. I think he did the same thing to my two older sisters, but we've never talked about it. I think I was seven or eight when he did it the first time. [Read: Now Becky is going to get her story told, and the clinician will help elicit it in a coherent way.]

Clinician: Do you want to share anything about what he did to you when you were little?

Becky: I feel really ashamed right now. What he did to me ruined my life. I'll never forgive him. [Read: Becky's attention is starting to splinter a bit. The clinician will validate the pain she has expressed while bringing her back on topic and getting the remainder of the story out in the open.]

Clinician: I can tell from looking at your eyes that this is very painful for you. No one should ever have to go through what you went through. Let's just come back to the abuse itself for right now. We'll be able to look at how you've coped with this pretty soon. Can you recall what he did to you? You can be as general or specific as you feel comfortable with.

Becky: He would touch me and rub his genitals on my leg. I didn't really understand it then, but later I figured out he was masturbating. He always had alcohol on his breath. He never tried to have sex with me.

Clinician: So, how long did it go on?

Becky: Until I was fourteen.

Clinician: How did it stop?

Becky: He and my mother had a big fight one night and he moved out for several months. I finally told my mother, and she went crazy on me.

Clinician: What did she do?

Becky: She told me I was lying and to keep my mouth shut, or I'd ruin the marriage and our family, and us kids would be put in foster care. I kept it to myself after that. [Read: This is yet another traumatic event, compounding the original abuse. The clinician will bring Becky back in contact with that source of pain.]

Clinician: So, you clearly had some unfinished business with your mom, didn't you? Is that what you were talking to your mom about when she went silent and looked away?

Becky: (*Speaks with tears in her eyes.*) Yeah. That was pretty hard to take.

In this brief exchange, the clinician has succeeded in getting Becky to use focused attention to make direct contact with her childhood sexual trauma while avoiding the trap of getting lost in self-evaluations. The clinician accomplished this by maintaining a gentle but persistent focus on eliciting the objective details of the trauma sequence and creating a safe, permissive, and emotionally validating space for these painful details to be shared.

Name

At this point, the objective details of the trauma have been exposed in a safe, permissive, nonjudgmental atmosphere. The associated emotional pain is in the room, so to speak, but in most cases, due to fragmented attention, very little of this private experience has been brought under verbal regulation. This poses a serious risk to clients; their emotional pain can seem so overwhelming that they're tempted to change the subject or even abruptly leave the session. Thus, it's crucial to quickly transition from telling the story to eliciting and supplying verbal labels for the wide variety of distressing private experiences contained in the story.

Clinician: Becky, I'm just wondering what's showing up inside as you share this terrible story with me. I can see that there are tears in your eyes and you're sort of hunched over in your chair. What's going on inside?

Becky: I don't know. It's like this horrible secret I've been carrying is now out, and what's going to happen next? Will I start to get worse and fall apart? [Read: These are thoughts that are probably associated with an emotion of fear or anxiety. The clinician will supply these labels and see how Becky handles it.]

Clinician: So I guess you could say you're aware of thoughts that you've let the cat out of the bag, so to speak, and that you may have even more symptoms as a result. I'm thinking that would probably connect to a feeling of being afraid or anxious that things could get worse here. Would that fit?

Becky: Yes, I'm definitely feeling anxious that I've opened Pandora's box by talking about this. [Read: This is a great metaphor that the clinician will utilize immediately.]

Clinician: Yeah, the temptation can be to try to close the lid on that box so nothing else gets out. And maybe that's how you tried to keep this at bay over the years. What if we tried something different? Could we just crack the lid open a little bit and peek inside so you can describe what you see? And just like we did before, we'll look at just one experience at a time. So, another thing you mentioned earlier was that you were ashamed to talk about this. Tell me about the shame.

Becky: I guess I should have been able to stop him, and I didn't. I didn't know what it meant. He said it was just a normal, healthy way for him to express his love for me. I was confused. I knew there was something wrong. I felt repulsed when he fondled me. I remember the smell of his cologne. I had this sense of being out of my body when he would touch me. [Read: Becky is holding her attention in focus and isn't being distracted by the distressing content, so the clinician will just supply more verbal labels that Becky can use while normalizing some of her distressing experiences.]

Clinician: So, you experience shame and blame—shame that somehow you were doing something wrong, and blame because you didn't stop it. Does anything else show up in the box?

Becky: Just sadness that this all had to happen to me. It just seems like a bad dream. I keep thinking I'm going to wake up one day and realize I was in a dream.

In this brief exchange, the clinician helped Becky identify and name various private experiences associated with her sexual trauma. This will allow her to bring these experiences into the verbal world so she can process them and integrate them into a coherent self-story.

Let Go

When traumatized clients do make contact with their painful history, one unfortunate result is that it often triggers a very unproductive form of rumination in which they go over the traumatic events again and again because they're trying to make sense of the incomprehensible. The problem is, it's impossible to make sense of the incomprehensible by doing anything other than naming it as an incomprehensible event. It happened, and that's all that can really be said about it. This stance is unacceptable to busy mind, which is absorbed in trying to figure out who's right and who's wrong, who's good and who's bad, who got treated fairly by life and who got screwed, and, lastly, who's to blame. Busy mind tells the human that any narrative lacking these important elements is incomplete and must be gone over again and again. This particular form of sense making is responsible for maintaining post-traumatic stress symptoms over time. Thus, it's essential for clinicians to help these clients learn to recognize this process for what it is, not what it appears to be.

Clinician: You know, I sometimes like to use the saying that all of life is a dream—not in the way you're talking about, like it's just a bad dream, but this idea that we create a story to explain our life journey. That story literally organizes the world for us. We all need to create stories that help us make sense of life. You have your story; I have my story. The key is that there isn't one "true" story out there that organizes life for us; we have to do that for ourselves. Plus, most of us have more than one story to tell. Just to show you what I mean, let's play this little game for a few minutes.

Becky: This is kind of a different way of looking at life than I was taught, so I'm not sure I get it. Maybe the game will help.

Clinician: Let's imagine you're in three different situations, and in each of them, a person asks you to share a little bit about yourself, okay? Here are the three situations: the first is that you're at a job interview, the second is that someone you don't know approaches you at a social gathering trying to get acquainted, and the third is that a person you're interested in forming a deeper relationship with asks you the question out of interest in you. Just think for a few minutes about how you'd respond in each situation. You've been asked exactly the same question, but in three quite different contexts. The question is "Becky, tell me a little bit about yourself."

Becky: (*Takes a minute or so and is obviously processing the exercise.*) Hmm... Well, that's interesting. This is obviously the first time I've ever done this. But I guess you would tell the job interviewer things about yourself that would get you the job. As for the second situation, I'm very anxious in crowds, so if somebody I didn't know came up and was trying to get acquainted, I probably wouldn't say too much about myself. If I did, the person might start asking me more questions. And in the third situation, if a person I was interested in getting close to showed interest in me, I'd probably say things that I think might get that person more interested in me. [Read: Becky's attention is focused and she's engaged in tracking where the clinician will go with this.]

Clinician: So would you tell the job interviewer that you were molested by your father for six years?

Becky: (Laughs.) Oh my goodness, no. That isn't going to get you any job.

Clinician: And when you want to protect yourself socially from feeling invaded by a stranger, you probably have a story you typically use in that situation, right?

Becky: Right. I'd probably come up with a very vanilla answer that wouldn't result in any follow-up questions, and then I'd excuse myself the minute I got the chance. So where are you going with this? [Read: Again, Becky is very focused and engaged. She isn't getting lost in her own emotional material.]

Clinician: When you came in here to see me today, you carried yet another story with you. This one is about your struggles with anxiety, your mother's death, your secret, your abuse, and what it has done to your life. A psychologist asks you to tell him a little more about yourself, and this is what shows up. Is this situation with you and me, here in this room, any different than the situations in the game you just played?

Becky: Well, it is another story, if you put it that way, but this actually happened. It isn't made up. [Read: Becky is engaged and is trying to discriminate the meaning of this exercise in relation to her trauma.]

Clinician: Absolutely correct. This is a story of something that happened to you. We can describe exactly what your dad did over the years. It's all there. But when we construct a life story, we don't stop there. Our minds put in all kinds of additional stuff to help us make sense of what happened, like whose fault it was, who the good guys and bad guys are, what I did to deserve this, why didn't I stop it if I knew it was wrong, how could my mother tell me I was lying, and on and on. Does your mind give you this part of the story?

Becky: All the time. I'm so disappointed in myself for letting this run me down. I think all of those things. So you're saying that's just part of the story?

Clinician: This is what minds do. They try to make sense of things, and they typically do a pretty good job of it when it comes to things in the concrete world. But for things like being molested by your father over and over again, your mind isn't going to be very good at figuring those out. There are going to be too many unanswered questions. If you buy into that story, you're going to feel flawed and incomplete as a person.

Becky: That's exactly how I feel inside. I don't think anyone has ever understood what that feels like until now. [Read: Becky is tracking and processing the emotional material in the room.]

In this brief exchange, the clinician has succeeded at shifting the level of the conversation from the minute details of Becky's abuse and her immediate emotional reactions to a higher-order form of trauma processing. Rather than becoming absorbed in her emotional reactions and self-evaluations, Becky is beginning to transcend them by looking at them in a more mindful way.

Soften

One of the great ironies of being the victim of a traumatizing event is that the person eventually gets to be the one to blame for the event. Because the busy mind is simply unable to generate a full and coherent story to explain an incomprehensible trauma, it adopts a default rule to plug the many holes in the story. The default rule is that the victim's real or perceived flaws, as well as the victim's actions or lack thereof, are ultimately the cause of the traumatic event. Further, the victim's contemporary emotional or functional problems are explained as a direct result of those same real or perceived flaws. So with traumatized clients, the goal of the softening phase of the present-moment-awareness intervention is to call out the mind and reveal the unworkability of the trauma narrative.

Clinician: So what else does your mind give you about the abuse? Is some of that showing up right now?

Becky: Well, yeah—like, what did I do to deserve this? It feels like I lost my belief in the world. I have no confidence in myself. I've always felt like I'm damaged goods, and that somehow people can tell that. Now I've visited this on my own family. I'm not the mother or wife I dreamed of being. I feel like something was taken from me. [Read: Becky is in flow, so to speak. She's disclosing clinically useful material in a coherent way. The clinician will scoop this material up and go to a higher-order level of processing.]

Clinician: Wow, that's the feel-good story of the year, isn't it? Only a human mind could come up with something like this. I mean, the last time I checked, you were an eight-year-old girl with a crazy mother and an alcoholic father. You were just trying to survive—to keep from being violated by one parent and beaten by the other. And then, over the years, your mind kept pounding away and eventually developed this bogus account of who you are. I mean, when you follow this story, does it help you move on and give you a sense of being alive?

Becky: Oh no. It basically tells me I'm broken, ugly, stupid, and a failure.

Clinician: So this is like going to the job interview and blabbering on about being sexually abused as a child. The story has to fit the purpose, right? So if your purpose is to be alive—to be an involved mother, to be independent, to be socially connected, to be intimate—then this story isn't going to fit that purpose. However, since there's no true story about who you are, you don't have to use a story that defeats your purposes. The gold standard for a story is that it must help you achieve your goal.

Becky: So, what you're saying is that I'm defeating myself? [Read: Part of Becky's story just showed up without her recognizing it. Still, she continues to be engaged and demonstrates focused attention.]

Clinician: I'm guessing that line is also part of your mind's story. A better way to convey this is to say that this particular story is self-defeating, so when you pick it up and treat it as if it were literally true, and not a construction of your mind, you'll be defeated. Unless your main life goal is to be confined to your home, full of anxiety and absent from life, I wouldn't pick up that story line. Let's see if there's something a little softer you can carry with you, something that will help you achieve important life goals. What would be in that story?

Becky: That's interesting. You're saying that this story is like a thing. I can pick it up, or I can leave it alone. I've never really thought about it this way before. I guess I could say that I'm a survivor. And there are things I want in life, and I deserve the chance to at least see if I can get some of those things. Also, a survivor doesn't give up even when the situation is dark. [Read: Becky is focusing on and utilizing the present-moment-awareness intervention to generate a new frame of reference. She's looking more relaxed physically, her voice tone is softening, and her rate of speech is slowing. She's starting to get it.]

In this brief exchange, the clinician has succeeded in destabilizing Becky's fusion with her harsh, self-critical, and self-defeating life story without getting drawn into an argument about whether her story is rational or distorted. What matters is that Becky sees the story as a story and recognizes that, because stories are a ubiquitous and necessary part of our mental experience, the gold standard is whether a given story promotes her best interests. If it does, she can use it. If it doesn't, she can dump it.

Expand

The expansion phase of present-moment processing involves helping clients understand that survivors of trauma possess a deep appreciation for what's important in life. In part, this is due to the fact that they've been exposed to the dark side of humanity, yet they still keep coming back, trying to make their lives meaningful and special. This requires a special kind of resilience that, if put in service of seeking valued life outcomes, produces tremendous motivational force. The goal is to convert the dark energy of trauma into the bright energy of using personal values to create a life that matters.

Clinician: You could say that if you choose to pick up another story, that's just the start of the journey, because you have important life goals you want to pursue. Your old story more or less makes those things unachievable so you don't even try. And even with a new story in tow—a story of being a survivor and not a quitter—even that can produce anxiety, because these things in life that you want really matter to you. They're important to you; otherwise you wouldn't have any anxiety at all. And once you make yourself vulnerable to possible setbacks or disappointment, you can bet your history is going to show up in spades. You know that, don't you?

Becky: I'm already having images that I'm going to fail—that somehow my strength of will isn't going to be there.

Clinician: (Extends her left arm and points to her left hand with her other hand.) This is exactly as it should be. To reclaim your life will require all of the survivor energy you have. So let's imagine that this is your life path, and over here in this direction is living life under the control of fear. Over here, you depend on your husband to cover for you, you opt out of important activities with your kids, and you try to control your anxieties—you know, all the stuff we've talked about, like staying holed up in your house, checking and double-checking the windows and doors, and avoiding social connections. (Extends her right arm and points to her right hand with her other hand.) And over here, in this direction, is the life you've said you want to live—a life that involves being more independent, being involved as a spouse and a mother, having social connections, and doing outdoor activities. Where would you put yourself on this life path right now?

Becky: (Points to about halfway down the left arm, toward living under the control of fear.) Right about there, pretty much living life scared. I want to go in that direction, though. (Points to the clinician's right hand.)

Clinician: Okay, it sounds like you want to turn this situation around and move in the direction of living life on purpose. That's cool. Can you think of steps you could take, even if they're small steps, that would tell you, even if in a small way, that you were beginning to walk in that direction?

Becky: Well, obviously there are a lot of things I need to turn around. It will take a while for those things to happen. But the one that keeps gnawing at me is that I want to feel more independent and not so reliant on my husband. I really think that has hurt our marriage over the years. It's about being able to go out and do errands, to do outdoor activities, and to go to family gatherings outside our home—you know, stuff that I've been avoiding or, I guess, now that I think about it, stuff that my story told me I didn't have the ability to do. I mean, these actions make me anxious, so I haven't done them. But I'll have to do them anyway to be more independent. [Read: Becky is exhibiting a strong connection to her value of being independent and more outwardly oriented, and she seems to understand that engaging in these actions are going to trigger anxiety. The clinician will try to expand on this a bit.]

Clinician: You've been hurt many times in your life, Becky, yet here you are. You've survived and you've bounced back. You're about to reclaim your life from that ugly story you got tricked into carrying with you. You're about to disobey your mind's messages that you will somehow fail or be disappointed. Something special is about to happen in your life. I can tell that it's about to happen. You can start your drive for independence by doing something as little or as large as you're ready to do. Remember, this is your life. You've survived a trip to hell, and now you're back. There's no turning back now, is there?

Becky: No turning back at all. Even if I don't succeed at first, I'm not going to go away.

In this brief exchange, the clinician has succeeded in helping Becky develop a new sense of life purpose. No longer is her purpose to avoid anything that might bring her into contact with painful memories. Instead, as a survivor of trauma, she has a keen appreciation for activities other people might take for granted, in part because she's been deprived of them. In this way, the dark energy of trauma can be converted into the motivational fuel needed to reclaim her life.

Summary

In this chapter, we've examined how to use present-moment-awareness interventions when working with traumatized clients. The core dilemma of post-traumatic stress is how to carry painful personal history forward in life. If clients use fragmented attention and avoidance to cope with what has happened, living a vital life is all but impossible. The alternative is to carry the objective reality of the trauma without the all-encompassing negative self-stories that result from the mind's misguided sense-making operations. Most life traumas simply cannot be understood rationally, so the only option is to drop the quest for sense making and just carry the history itself. Present-moment-awareness interventions with traumatized clients proceed through all five phases: disrupting strategies that involve fragmented attention and avoidance (noticing); helping them create an objective story of the trauma (naming); teaching detachment from evaluations that are nestled within the story (letting go), whether those evaluations are derived from the self, others, or the world; holding the sense of being flawed, to blame, and undeserving softly (softening); and using the experience of being a trauma survivor as a powerful motivational force (expanding).

CHAPTER 12

Using the Present Moment
with Addictive Behaviors

Reality is just a crutch for people who can't handle drugs.

—Robin Williams

There are approximately thirty million people in the United States who are unable to regulate their use of alcohol or drugs, not to mention the countless others who are in trouble with emotional eating, bingeing and purging, sex, gambling, and other addictive behaviors (Compton, Thomas, Stinson, & Grant, 2007). If those people were added into the equation, you would be considered abnormal if you didn't have one of those problems! When a particular class of behaviors becomes so ubiquitous, there must be a correlated underlying sociopsychological mechanism at work.

Addictive behaviors promise safety and security from emotional catastrophes, but with time they become a major problem in their own right. People who are drinkers or drug users eventually become physically and mentally dependent on these substances and experience highly distressing withdrawal symptoms if they try to stop. When people binge and purge, their neurochemistry becomes so disordered that they eventually start having health and dental problems. When people engage in emotional eating, they eventually develop serious problems with obesity and the terrifying prospect of not only needing to control their eating behavior but also having to lose a lot of weight to reduce their risk of developing diabetes or cardiovascular disease. Unfortunately, the emotional distress triggered by these secondary problems amplifies the negatively charged mental urge to repeat the addictive behavior. The result is a vicious downward spiral in which people increasingly turn to addictive behaviors to manage the distress caused by their addictive behaviors. Thus, another key goal is to reveal this paradox of addictive behaviors in a nonjudgmental way. Addictive behaviors don't really provide any safety at all; they only provide the appearance of safety, and after a while, even the appearance of safety evaporates.

From a contextual perspective, the spiral of addictive behavior starts with a negatively charged, mental urge to perform the behavior. Initially, people try to control the urge; then, when control fails, they capitulate to the urge. The urge consists of mental messages that they will feel better, which is defined as removing the individual from proximity to distressing emotions, thoughts, memories, or physical sensations. Messages promoting this definition of "better" are ubiquitous in contemporary society, yet there are very few behaviors that provide enduring emotional relief without any price tag. The paradox is that almost every behavior that provides quick-acting relief can easily become addictive because the relief is only temporary. Depending on the type of addictive behavior, distressing private experiences usually reappear within minutes or hours of engaging in the behavior. People generally know the behavior is unworkable, but they perform it repeatedly, despite a growing pattern of negative consequences. The behavior is also self-reinforcing, in part because it removes the aversive state created by the urge to perform it; however, due to bidirectional conditioning, the frequency of negatively charged mental urges is increased. Pretty soon, most of the aversive private experiences that are being managed through the addictive behavior are actually the result of the futile struggle to resist urges. These persistent failures undermine people's confidence in their self-control and decision-making abilities.

Since many painful present-moment experiences are triggered by unpleasant external events, addictive behaviors also serve a behavioral avoidance function. People caught in the cycle of addictive behaviors reorganize their key life contexts to enable them to practice addictive behaviors. In addition, practicing these behaviors helps them emotionally cope with the pain in those contexts. By cutting ties with the reality of the moment, they get a temporary reprieve from the emotional pain of the moment. The problem is that the reprieve is very temporary, so the addictive behavior must be practiced repeatedly to maintain a state of numbness.

To further complicate matters, people who start practicing addictive behaviors early in adolescence miss many chances to experience distressing and unwanted private experiences directly and don't learn how to cope with them. Therefore, they generally develop severe deficits in emotional intelligence. Thus, if people who are already prone to avoiding their emotions manage to stop their addictive behaviors, they're faced with the daunting task of dealing with emotions that seem overwhelming and uncontrollable. We believe this is why so many people return to addictive behaviors after brief forays into sobriety. They can't handle their emotional landscape without resorting to numbing and avoidance strategies.

In this chapter, we'll examine how to intervene with addictive behaviors and help clients escape self-destructive patterns of numbing out and behavioral avoidance. This requires that they make contact with something bigger and more important than avoiding emotional pain. The principles we'll discuss apply to intervening with all addictive behaviors, not just drug and alcohol problems. These are all birds of a feather. First, we'll go through some basic guiding principles for constructing present-moment-awareness interventions for addictive behaviors. Then we'll work through a detailed case example to show you how to address the five phases of present-moment processing in session when working with these clients.

Guiding Clinical Principles

We believe that neuroscience will eventually demonstrate that the roots of addictive behavior reside in an imbalance in the brain's default mode network, particularly those parts with close connections to the executive control network, such as the anterior and posterior cingulate cortices. These are the structures responsible for paying attention (versus numbing out), decision making, and self-control. Does this mean addictive behaviors are disease entities? Not at all; it could easily mean that practicing numbing and avoidance behaviors repeatedly over time strengthens the neural circuitry responsible for these behaviors. As these circuits are selectively reinforced, their dominance over competing circuitry grows, and therefore the habit strength of the addictive behavior grows steadily over time. We know from clinical experience that this is exactly how addictions develop. Exceedingly few people with addictive habits start out at the end stage of their problem.

Put simply, escaping the cycle of addictive behavior requires that clients learn to live inside their skin, rather than trying to get out of their skin. Clients suffering from unworkable addictive behaviors are emotional avoidance machines. They're scared to death of having feelings and do everything they can to keep them from showing up. So from the outset, the main goal of the intervention is to bring these clients into full, direct, and sustained contact with feared and avoided emotional experiences. Remember that clients suffering from addictive behaviors, particularly if they have been practicing them for a long time, lack the direct emotional learning needed to self-regulate their emotional experience. Therefore, clinicians must function as both coach and cheerleader in this endeavor.

In your coach role, you'll educate these clients about different emotions and how they're linked to different external cues. You'll probably need to teach them how to use emotion words in productive ways that allow them to better discriminate their own experience and then use their emotions to guide their behavior. When you function as a cheerleader, you praise clients for being courageous and taking on the addictive behavior even amidst emotional discomfort. Express your sincere confidence and belief in the client and acknowledge that this is hard work—and that, with persistence, hard work pays off. Also reinforce clients in choosing to stop using the addictive behavior as a cure for emotional pain. Finally, you'll have to be the one to tell these clients the really bad news about stepping outside the cycle of addictive behavior: that the reward for stopping is coming into direct contact with the stuff they've been running from. Their pain will be there to greet them at the doorway to sobriety and a new life.

• Case Example: Rick

Rick is a thirty-eight-year-old man who presents for care after being kicked out of a thirty-day residential treatment program. He was discharged after getting into a physical altercation with another resident in which he punched the guy out. Since his discharge, he's returned to his apartment at a local Oxford House. Rick has been a polysubstance user since early adolescence. He describes his favorite substance as anything that will get him high at that exact moment; it doesn't matter what it is. His drug of choice is alcohol, but he will use pot, meth, oxycodone, or heroin if any of these drugs are available.

Rick describes his upbringing as dysfunctional. He hates his father, whom he describes as a sadist. Rick's father repeatedly told him he was a loser, sabotaged his attempts to succeed, and then physically punished him for failing. As a result, Rick failed academically, athletically, and socially. He quickly fell into drug and alcohol use and, at age fifteen, left home after decking his father in a fist fight. Rick got married at seventeen and had three children by the time he was twenty-two. He has worked at a variety of low-paying manual labor jobs. He either left or was fired from all of his previous jobs because of absenteeism due to drinking or drug use or because of getting into disagreements with supervisors and just walking off the job. His drug and alcohol use also ruined his marriage. He hasn't had any real contact with his ex-wife or children in ten years. His affect during his first session, described below, is clearly agitated, anxious, and hostile.

Notice

Clients suffering from addictive behaviors are in a living hell, and they know it. The problem is, they think their emotional pain is the problem, whereas the problem is, in fact, that they don't know how to utilize the wisdom inside their emotional pain. When such clients first present for therapy, it isn't difficult to see that they're near the breaking point. Their avoidance strategies are no longer working, and their distress is often palpable. This sometimes leads clinicians to avoid pushing too hard out of a desire to protect these clients from experiencing too much pain. In contrast, we like to push very hard in the first meeting to bring clients into full, direct, and sustained contact with distressing material.

Clinician: Hey, Rick, I just can't help but notice that you look really, really wound up and uncomfortable. Is that because you're still withdrawing from chemicals, or is it something emotional? Can you tell me what's going on?

Rick: What? Oh, it isn't that bad, man. I'm just feeling a bit on edge. I have a lot of things on my mind—a lot of issues, you know? [Read: This somewhat superficial response is probably a sign of emotional avoidance. The clinician will dig into this a little more.]

Clinician: So, tell me, what do you notice going on in your body when you're on edge? What does that feel like?

Rick: I don't know what this has to do with helping me with my drug problem, but okay. Let's see—my neck and head are so tight they hurt. In fact, it's really hard to just sit here. Do you mind if I get up and stand? [Read: This last response in particular suggests that Rick is working very hard to avoid making contact with his interior landscape. The clinician will try to integrate this into the conversation.]

Clinician: Sure, no problem. You know, sometimes when I'm really upset I have to get up and walk around too. It's like I'm trying to gain control of my feelings by doing something else. Is that how it works for you?

Rick: It helps me calm down so I can think clearer. Is that what you mean?

Clinician: Well, anything that helps you think clearer is something we want to use in here, so I don't care if you stand the entire time.

Rick: (*Smirks.*) So, what do I need to think more clearly about? [Read: Although the tone is challenging, Rick is starting to engage the clinician, albeit in a very defended way. That's okay. Engagement is engagement, and the clinician will try to build on this foundation.]

Clinician: Well, clarity of thought is important when you try to take on difficult problems, like feeling on edge, being worried about life problems, or trying to gain control over drug and alcohol use. Is there something about being on edge that ties into your use of alcohol or drugs?

Rick: Man, you don't get it. My life is in shambles and I'm not supposed to be on edge? What the hell would you feel like if you were in my situation? [Read: This is an important self-disclosure, even though it's couched in challenging terms. The clinician will use it to start an exploration of Rick's avoided emotional responses.]

Clinician: Well, I guess I would be pretty wound up and on edge if I thought the walls were crashing down on me. Is that what it feels like to you—that the walls are crashing down on you?

Rick: They have crashed and burned. I'm an addict looking at rock bottom. I even got kicked out of treatment when I wanted to clean up my act. I've got no job, no family, no girlfriend, and no future. [Read: This is another important self-disclosure about Rick's level of distress, and it's less defensively disclosed. The clinician will use this information to go after Rick's avoided emotions.]

Clinician: So, as you look at the wreckage, what feelings or other reactions show up?

Rick: This is what they tried to do at the treatment program. They were always getting in my face trying to get me to talk about my feelings. I told them I keep my feelings to myself and it's none of their business. They kept saying I wasn't working the program. [Read: This is a complex, interesting response that appears to be off topic, but Rick is

175

actually disclosing his mental rule about how to deal with emotions. The clinician will try to expand on his use of the rule and the consequences.]

Clinician: So, it's probably safe to say there are a lot of feelings in there, right? One way to deal with them is to just put a lid on them. Maybe they won't keep bothering you that way.

Rick: Well, they aren't going to go away because I talk about them. [Read: This is another iteration of Rick's rule about controlling feelings. The clinician will pose an alternative: just noticing that feelings are present.]

Clinician: Absolutely. They aren't going to go away, and maybe that's part of the problem here. I mean, let's face it, your life isn't going in the direction you'd like, and it would be bizarre if you didn't have a ton of feelings about what's happening to you. Last time I checked, you're a human being, and humans have feelings in response to all kinds of things. You don't have to rub your nose in them; you just have to be willing to acknowledge that they're here.

Rick: I won't go there, man. There's nothing but darkness in there. I'd rather go back to using than have to deal with that stuff. [Read: Rick is engaged and tracking the issues that are arising, and he's showing a bit of self-perspective. What Rick says is actually a nice restatement of the dilemma he's faced his entire life. The clinician will amplify this truth.]

Clinician: So, one way to deal with this is to go back to using. That's a path you've been down before. If that's the path you want to pick—and you do get to pick your life path—then we've accomplished our mission here.

Rick: What the hell do you mean by that? [Read: Despite the challenging tone, Rick is seeking more information, which suggests that he's considering the alternative.]

Clinician: My job here is to help you consider the alternatives. You're the one who will make the choice. There isn't much else to talk about if you choose to go back to using. And who knows, even just allowing your feelings to come out in the open may not help either. Things could actually get worse if you did that too. There are just no guarantees here. I don't think that life is going to give you a hall pass either way.

Rick: Well, I haven't walked out yet. But I'm not promising I won't either.

In this brief exchange, the clinician has succeeded in getting Rick to begin to show up and make contact with his emotional avoidance behaviors. Although Rick has a lot of fears about what will happen if he shows up in the presence of his distressing private experiences, he's continuing the conversation with the clinician instead of leaving the session or just checking out mentally.

Name

Clients battling addictive behaviors are scared to death of feeling what they feel because, at least in part, they lack the verbal lexicon required to process their emotional experience. Rick's statement that there's only darkness inside suggests that he can't discriminate between various feelings, memories, thoughts, and physical sensations. In this undifferentiated state, his private experiences are overwhelming to him. The clinician will try to engage Rick in the process of peeking inside the pressure cooker and beginning to apply discrete verbal labels to what he sees.

Clinician: Let's say you choose a new path here. You try to create a life worth living, and to do that you have to look inside a bit and see what the lay of the land is. Would you be willing to experiment for a second, peeking inside and just picking one thing at a time to look at? Pull it out from behind the curtain and look at it, one feeling at a time.

Rick: (*Speaks in a wry tone of voice.*) You're still trying to get me to talk about my feelings, aren't you? You're tricky. So, what's in the shark tank? Let's see… Well, I have a real problem with anger. I've been angry since I can remember. [Read: Although Rick is cooperating, his first response is somewhat superficial and probably something he's put out in therapy before. The probable function of bringing his "problem with anger" up is to divert the conversation away from more fundamentally painful experiences. The clinician will probe in this direction.]

Clinician: I like to think of anger as always being the second feeling we have. We get hurt or damaged in some way, and then we display anger to neutralize the offender. So let's back up the chain and see if you can find that first feeling—the one you use anger to defend against. And you said anger has been around a long time, probably ever since you were young. Maybe you can peek back into time for that one. What is it that hurts?

Rick: That's easy, man. My father was a prick and basically screwed me to the wall before I had a chance. I was damaged goods by the time I was thirteen. [Read: Rick is inserting an evaluation of what happened, rather than the emotional basis of what happened. This gives him an off-ramp into just being angry again. The clinician will push him back into contact with his emotional experience.]

Clinician: Okay, Rick, so I know you have some real hard feelings about your dad. I get that. What I'm wondering is, can you make contact with what it felt like to be around your dad?

Rick: I was just madder than hell. I was mad at anyone and everything. [Read: Rick is cooperating yet is still resisting making contact with more threatening emotional experience. This tells the clinician that

> those avoided feelings are going to be the crux of the present-moment-awareness intervention.]

Clinician: So, peek behind the anger. See if you can clear the smoke of anger away and look at what's left. Can you do that just for a second? Then you can go back into anger if you want to.

Rick: (*Looks very sad, starts to tear up, then turns away.*) I don't want to go there. [Read: Rick is doing the work, but he's really struggling with emotional avoidance. The clinician doesn't want to make this into a traumatic experience for Rick by shoving him into his darkness, and will therefore try to give Rick a voice by naming some feelings that might be circulating in the moment.]

Clinician: It's okay, Rick. You don't have to go there if you're not ready. I understand completely how dark and scary this must be. I can only imagine how sad, lonely, and cut off you must have felt, with no hope that anyone was going to rescue you or help you.

Rick: Yeah, you pretty much nailed it: sad, alone, and left to rot, and no one gave a crap.

In this brief exchange, the clinician has succeeded in helping Rick begin to apply some rudimentary verbal labels to his painful private experiences. Doing so required the clinician to keep Rick from falling into his evaluations of his experience, which basically enable his avoidance responses, including using drugs and alcohol.

Let Go

The sine qua non of addictive behavior patterns is people's unquestioned faith in the belief that the best way, and really the only way, to relate to emotional pain is to avoid it by any means necessary. The alternative of simply allowing pain to be there, accepting it nonjudgmentally, and doing nothing to change it or control it is nothing short of heresy. The longer clients have been practicing addictive behaviors, the stronger their convictions about the importance of this rule will be. We believe that this rule is the linchpin of addiction and must be directly confronted—experientially, not intellectually—in the present moment.

Clinician: I can see how hard you're trying to keep those feelings at bay. I mean, your jaw is clenched, your body looks tight, and you're hardly breathing. It seems like you're trying to squeeze the life out of those feelings. I'm guessing that eventually it just wears you out.

Rick: After a couple of days, I just say to hell with it and go out and use. [Read: This is a very nice, clinically useful response. Rick is suggesting that he can't think of any alternative other than struggling or using.

The clinician will amplify this unworkable strategy and the paradoxical increase in negative affect.]

Clinician: So, squeeze until you can't squeeze anymore, and then go out and get the hell out of your mind and body. And at the end of the day, your life is in ruins and those feelings are still right there, ready to fight another day. How weird is that?

Rick: Pretty damn weird. So I'm going down a dead-end road? [Read: Rick seems open to considering another approach. The clinician will offer one.]

Clinician: Have you ever used a pressure cooker—you know those pots where you screw the lid on tight so the trapped steam quickly cooks the food inside? If you leave it over the heat too long, the pan will literally blow apart at the bottom, and the lid will still be screwed on the top. The way you prevent a horrible accident is to let some steam vent out. In fact, pressure cookers have a steam vent for this very purpose. Still, the pressure can get too high, so sometimes you have to open a valve to release some steam. To prevent an explosion, you have to do that, even if you're somewhat anxious about getting burned by the escaping steam.

Rick: Are you saying I have to let some of my feelings out so the pressure will go away? [Read: Rick is getting part of the metaphor but is also trying to co-opt it back into his avoidance rule. The clinician will try to undermine this process.]

Clinician: Well, the minute you close the valve on the cooker, the pressure starts to build again. So it's a balancing act between using the steam to cook while keeping the steam from becoming dangerous. You have to pay attention to the pressure on a fairly frequent basis. And if you do it right, you'll end up with some mighty tasty food.

Rick: I guess what I do is leave the kitchen after screwing down the lid and putting the cooker on the stove. Sometimes I even try to get out of the house. [Read: Rick has picked up the metaphor and is beginning to generate his own iterations on it. The clinician will reinforce this.]

Clinician: And then, kablooey! (*Makes an explosive gesture.*) If you're going to cook with this thing, you'd better stay in the kitchen or you're going to get burned!

In this brief exchange, the clinician has succeeded in getting Rick to consider an alternative to his pressure cooker strategy of suppressing and avoiding painful emotional experiences, which ultimately leads to the "nuclear option": using drugs and alcohol to wipe his awareness out altogether. Along the way, the clinician has helped Rick understand that maintaining some type of functional contact with his emotions is a requirement for using them productively.

Soften

Clients trapped in a cycle of addictive behaviors live under the emotional pall of guilt, shame, fear, and a deep sense of self-loathing. In many cases, their long-term pattern of addictive behavior has created significant collateral damage in the form of ruined relationships with friends or family members (including children), damaged careers, decimated finances, compromised health, or a criminal record. In our society, where blame and shame are used excessively to motivate and shape behaviors from an early age, the notion of forgiving oneself is often a hard sell. However, forgiveness doesn't necessarily mean that clients aren't responsible for what happened. Rather, it involves clients being accountable for their actions while absolving themselves of the sentence of self-loathing for the remainder of their lifetime.

Clinician: Rick, I'm guessing one motive for keeping all that steam trapped in the pressure cooker is that some of the stuff in that pot isn't just about what an asshole your dad was. There's also some stuff about what you've done with your life. You kind of said it earlier—that your life is going nowhere, that you're damaged goods. How are you going to let off the pressure of that stuff?

Rick: I really see myself as a loser, just like my dad said I'd be. I don't see that changing even if I get sober. I've lost pretty much everything that mattered to me. [Read: This is a nice, clinically useful response. Now the clinician must avoid getting into an argument about whether Rick's evaluations are accurate. Instead, the clinician will help Rick practice self-compassion in the midst of his self-loathing.]

Clinician: I find it interesting that you hate yourself only to the extent that you've squandered away things that mattered to you in life. It's almost like those losses matter more than any other because you cared about those things. So when you lost them, they hurt the most. Is there any room in there to feel some compassion for the pain of all those losses that you've had?

Rick: What? I mean, I was an addict, and I blew those things off so I could keep using. Why should I feel sorry for myself? I'm to blame. That's all there is to it. I deserve to be where I am in life. [Read: Rick is locked in the shame-and-blame cycle of sense making. The clinician will try to undermine this self-negating stance.]

Clinician: Well, I'm not saying it's necessary to pretend you didn't do what you did. I'm just asking if, knowing full well what you've done, whether there's some room for you to have some compassion for yourself. I mean, right now, just think of the worst thing you've ever done as an addict. Try to zero in on that most horrible thing. Can you extend a soft hand to yourself? See if you can just connect with the fact that you're human, and human beings get lost. We do things we later regret. We aren't gods. Just be silent for a few moments and see if you can reach out to yourself. You're already on an island, and you're the only one who can get back to shore, where your life is waiting for you.

Rick: You're saying to just forgive myself and pretend like none of this happened? What are you saying? I mean, I'm guilty as charged. [Read: This isn't an unusual initial response to the idea of self-forgiveness. It indicates that Rick is trying to incorporate this perspective into a new frame of reference. The clinician will help sharpen the focus.]

Clinician: And that's a very convenient way to deal with this type of situation. Just put yourself on an island of self-hate and live it out. Some people in your life might even say that's what you deserve, so it's not like you're going to be viewed as a weirdo for doing it. I'm just asking if this has to be a life sentence. Is there some point where you can choose to love yourself, warts and all?

Rick: Man, you must be kidding. I mean, this is my fault. I'm responsible. These were my choices, and I deserve what I got. And now you're asking whether I can forgive myself and go out and try to make a life? How the hell would I ever do that? [Read: Rick is tracking the gist of the issues at hand. He can stall his life out forever as part of his punishment for screwing up, or he can choose to be accountable, practice self-compassion, and move forward.]

Clinician: I guess your dad doesn't have to be here to whip you like a dog because you're whipping yourself quite nicely, thank you. I can almost see his presence in here right now, glaring at you and telling you what a loser you are. Hell, forget about having a second chance in life. If you let your dad's programming run your show, you don't deserve a first chance.

Rick: Isn't that pathetic? That asshole is still in my head all the time. [Read: Rick has a distinctly different look on his face—one of self-recognition rather than just repeating his self-story. The clinician will drive this home.]

Clinician: And he programmed you to self-destruct rather than deal with your own weaknesses and limitations. But you know, the cool thing about programming is that's what it is—programming. And you don't have to follow programming if it causes you to suffer. So what will it be? Another decade of obeying the program and flogging yourself? Or daring to disobey the program and accept yourself, flaws and mistakes included?

In this brief exchange, the clinician has succeeded in getting Rick to consider forgiveness and self-compassion as alternatives to a life of self-loathing and, in all likelihood, self-defeating attempts to move on from his past life mistakes. This involves Rick being accountable for his actions while also being willing to make contact with the fact that there are life outcomes out there that matter to him. He isn't a loser; he's a human being who has suffered losses.

Expand

Clients suffering in the throes of addictive behaviors end up walking the path of life with their eyes fixed on their shoes, figuratively speaking. The long-term impact of fighting urges is that clients begin to measure the value of each day based upon their success at resisting urges to use, rather than whether they achieved more personally meaningful outcomes. Meanwhile, the war to live a vital, purposeful existence is being lost, to the point that many such clients can no longer envision a life that they'd like to live. We often tell clients that the rosy promise that they'll have a good life if only they stop engaging in addictive behaviors is basically a cruel lie. The sobering truth is that they need to discover some type of new purpose for living—something different than fighting urges.

Clinician: Okay, let's imagine that you suddenly escaped your dad's programming and didn't have to spend twenty-four hours a day flogging yourself for your mistakes. Just imagine that you were suddenly free to play the game of life. What shows up? What would you like to play?

Rick: Just as you asked, I thought, "I can't do that. I don't have what it takes." [Read: This is an interesting, engaged response, but unclear as to whether Rick is talking about staying sober or finding a life direction. The clinician will probe further.]

Clinician: Do you mean "I can't do that," as in "I can't live my life being a nonuser of substances," or as in "I don't have what it takes to create a life worth living"?

Rick: I was thinking more of living life. But that will increase my difficulties with staying sober. Still, maybe it's more about how I would do that— living differently. I've lived my life battling addiction, trying to live day to day and not using. That's the goal for me. [Read: Rick's sense of a life mission has pretty much been drawn down to just trying to stay sober and avoid inflicting more damage on himself or others. This isn't a sustainable perspective because it has no appetitive features. The clinician will try to expand his perspective and tie it to a message from his father.]

Clinician: Does that sound like part of your father's program, as you hear yourself say it? Doesn't the program say that no one expects much of you, that you're a terrible waste of a human being, and that success in life for you just means you managed to stay sober and didn't hurt anyone anymore? So your gravestone reads, "Here lies Rick. He spent most of his life trying to stay sober." How boring is that?

Rick: That's not much of a life, but it's really what I've been doing all along. [Read: This is an insightful generalization showing self-perspective taking. This suggests that Rick is creating some distance between his self-story and his vision of the future. The clinician will try to amplify this separation.]

Clinician: Okay. So if it isn't "I can't do that" and "I don't have what it takes"—if that's just part of the program and if you separate yourself from it—now you have a clear view of the playing field. It sounds like you want more from your life than just managing to stay clean and sober. So, tell me, where would you like to go with this?

Rick: I've learned a lot about life the hard way. It hurts to think I lost my marriage and have no contact with my children. So, I guess I'd like to try again and maybe make amends with my kids. That will be a tough one because they might blow me off. I'd have to accept that if it happened. [Read: This is a high-quality, present-moment response that the clinician will reinforce.]

Clinician: So, being connected to others, being in that role of a husband or life partner and a parent, is important to you. Well, you never know what will happen if you reach out to your children, but you do know what will happen if you don't. And you're right about having to be willing to accept whatever happens with them. This is the part where you're willing to be accountable.

Rick: It's the darkest part of my life—losing contact with them because I kept choosing to use instead of being their father. [Read: Even though this is a painful conversation, Rick looks engaged and genuine. He's staying on topic and is making direct contact with his values as well as his pain related to his failures as a parent. The clinician will repurpose the goal.]

Clinician: It takes real courage to step into that darkness, Rick. I admire that you're even willing to go there. All you can do is hit the ball over the net and see if they hit it back. I'll tell you this: In my mind, no matter what happens, by just reaching out you're taking a huge step toward that value of being the father you want to be. I mean, in the name of being there for your children, you're willing to be hurt badly.

Rick: What's that old saying? It's always darkest before the dawn. I have to take the mind-set that things are going to change, hopefully for the better.

In this brief exchange, the clinician has succeeded in helping Rick begin to redefine and expand his sense of life purpose, starting from simply trying to stay sober and ending with a values-based commitment to try to create a new relationship with his children. The clinician effectively used the pain of Rick's setbacks in life to shine a new light on his values of being a parent and, ultimately, achieving a long-lasting relationship with a new life partner.

Summary

In this chapter, we've examined how to use present-moment-awareness interventions to help clients who are trapped in a cycle of addictive behaviors. Our perspective is that addictive behaviors are, at heart, emotional avoidance responses. Thus, present-moment-awareness interventions don't really focus on the addictive behavior per se, but rather on its emotional avoidance functions. If the function of addictive behaviors is to get clients out of their skin, then the goal of therapy is to bring them back inside their skin. This involves helping them show up and make contact with their pain. They need to learn to label and discriminate between various sources of pain, to take a detached stance toward distressing experiences instead of struggling with them, and to accept responsibility for the collateral damage caused by the addictive behavior without falling into a habitual pattern of self-loathing. The ultimate aim is to help them discover a new life purpose informed by the pain of previous life failures and setbacks.

CHAPTER 13

Using the Present Moment
with Self-Harming Behaviors

I don't want any more of this try, try again stuff. I just want out.
I've had it. I am so tired. I am twenty and I am already exhausted.

—Elizabeth Wurtzel

Clients presenting with self-harming behaviors present unique challenges that can vex even the most experienced clinician. The prevalence of people with such problems is shockingly high: approximately 10 percent of the general population admit to having made at least one suicide attempt, and another 20 percent report at least one episode of serious, persistent suicidal ideation (Strosahl, Linehan, & Chiles, 1984). Rates of deliberate self-injury appear to be escalating and may function as a stepping-stone to engaging in more lethal suicidal behaviors (Chiles & Strosahl, 2004). In a recent study, approximately 12 percent of ninth-graders and 6 percent of third-graders reported engaging in self-injurious behaviors (Barrocas, Hankin, Young, & Abela, 2012).

Suicidal and self-injurious behaviors can take many forms, and there is no universally agreed upon taxonomic classification system to help guide clinical research. We define the broad class of self-destructive behaviors as discrete acts that the individual or someone else present at the time labels as an attempt at suicide or a deliberate act of self-harm. High-risk behaviors such as repeated suicide attempts, chronic suicidal threats, cutting, or burning are not confined to depression; rather, they are seen across the full spectrum of mental and chemical health conditions. This suggests that such behaviors aren't a symptom of an underlying condition but rather serve a unique functional purpose: they help people control intense emotional pain that they view as intolerable, inescapable, and unending (Chiles & Strosahl, 2004).

Interestingly, clients who engage in self-harm know that their behaviors are destructive in the long run, but they find them highly effective in the short run. These behaviors allow clients to control, shift, decrease, or get rid of unpleasant thoughts, emotions, associations, memories, and sensations that show up in the moment. Deconstructing the history of how self-harming behaviors arise clearly shows that they are learned, shaped, and reinforced by their immediate consequences. Initially, most self-harming clients dabble in these behaviors and quickly experience relief from powerful, aversive, and seemingly uncontrollable emotions. Over time, that reinforcement shapes self-harming behaviors into a recurring habitual response to negative emotional arousal. The problem is, self-harming actions are basically a type of emotion suppression strategy and therefore create an emotion rebound effect, just as thought suppression does. Painful emotion states that clients have avoided and suppressed begin to spontaneously break through more and more frequently, requiring these clients to engage in self-harming behavior more often. This creates an ever-expanding cycle in which they're caught up in chasing their pain with short-term emotion suppression responses. At the far end of the self-harm continuum, they begin to organize their daily routines around winning this battle to control spontaneously erupting emotions. Left in the dust is any sense of living according to long-term values, goals, or principles. Such clients are truly lost souls when they enter therapy, and when asked what they'd be doing in life if their self-harming behavior miraculously disappeared, they usually say, "I don't know."

In this chapter, we'll examine how to use present-moment-awareness interventions to help self-harming clients stop this spiral of emotional avoidance and suppression and learn to stay in contact with feared private experiences. Only by making present-moment contact with these experiences can clients integrate them into a coherent, healthy self-story. We will first examine some guiding clinical principles to follow when assessing, conceptualizing, and intervening with such clients. Then we'll use a detailed case example to demonstrate how to use each phase of present-moment processing to help them come to grips with their personal history, which is often traumatic, and help them rewrite their self-defeating story.

Guiding Clinical Principles

One very obvious function of self-harming behaviors is to control or eliminate noxious emotion states. Clients who habitually engage in self-harm are always on the lookout for any sign of intrusive, unwanted emotions, leading to problems with chronic apprehension and anxiety. Such clients often seem "wired" when they finally seek help. This appears to be the result of excessive activation of the task-positive network, with bottom-up attention in control of the switches. On the flip side, these clients are also capable of suddenly shifting into a state of abject apathy, numbing, and emotional withdrawal, a cardinal sign of excessive activation of the default mode network. This leads self-harming clients into a downward spiral of rumination about past life events and well-rehearsed, negative self-narratives that fuel a lot of sadness, guilt, anger, and shame. Again, the shared common denominator is the predominance of bottom-up attention and lack of input or regulation from the executive control network. In either a depressed or anxious state, these clients have tremendous issues paying attention to what's going on—both inside and outside. Their ability to rapidly shift from highly focused self-harming behavior to being emotionally numb suggests that the overriding clinical issue is lack of executive network involvement that would prevent rapid shifts between domination by the default mode network and by the task-positive network. It isn't unusual to see really severe cutting or other self-destructive behaviors in clients caught in the crossfire of this dysregulated competition for finite brain resources. Naturally, one main goal of present-moment-awareness interventions with such clients is to stimulate and strengthen the executive control network by having them practice shifting their attention, taking the observer role, and engaging in perspective taking activities.

Many of these clients suffer from trauma-based anxiety and respond with anxious fearfulness to a wide range of conditioned cues. What typically happens when such clients encounter an anxiety cue is immediate arousal and a shift of attention from the present moment into the past or the immediate future. These clients often experience a rapid and uncontrollable wave of anxiety, typically correlated with memories of previous similar situations, and at the same time, they predict some type of immediate danger (for example, "This feeling is going to kill me if I don't do something about it"). This is the moment when you're likely to see clients engage in behaviors with rapid effects, such as cutting or burning. These behaviors paradoxically shift attention back to the here and now because of the pain sensations associated with the self-injury. At the same time, the body starts to produce its own painkiller hormones, which also downregulate the aversive emotional state. However, no matter how efficient this process is in regulating emotions, it prevents contingency-based learning, given that the main contingencies circulate within the emotion suppression response. Thus, when intervening with such clients, it's crucial not only to produce aversive emotional states in session, but also to teach them to stay in the here and now as the process of emotion suppression unfolds. You'll need to position yourself so that you can block clients' attempts to suppress aversive emotional states.

While it's obviously important to help clients understand the variable outcomes of self-harming behavior in the long run (being destructive to long-term emotional stability) versus the short run (temporarily providing effective emotion control), it's essential to avoid making this an intellectual concept. In reality, and often within minutes in a session, an event will unfold that triggers avoidance and suppression of emotions. This presents clinicians with an opportunity to have clients make experiential contact with the paradox of short-term gain and long-term pain. A feared, avoided emotion may disappear for five minutes in response to an obvious attempt to suppress it and then reappear in the room just as suddenly. You can bring clients into contact with this as it happens. This allows you to demonstrate the paradoxical effects of emotion suppression. You can simply point out that the client's feared emotions seem to have returned once again, then wonder out loud if this is how it works at other times in the client's life.

The ultimate act of emotional avoidance and suppression is suicide, and it's crucial to bear in mind that self-harming behaviors like cutting, burning, or swallowing razor blades are often associated with future suicidal acts. Thus, the topic of suicidal ideation, including planning or attempting suicide, must be explored with chronically self-harming clients. Even if they don't want to commit suicide, they might accidentally end up dead as a result of their high-risk behaviors. This uncomfortable reality can trigger anxiety in even the most experienced clinician, so the typical response is to try to control and eliminate a client's self-harming behavior in order to assuage the clinician's anxieties. In other words, both clinicians and their self-harming clients can get locked into a reciprocal spiral of emotional avoidance. Thus, it isn't surprising that self-harming clients tend to bring out the worst in therapists. We've seen many examples of even highly experienced clinicians coming unglued in response to suicidal or self-injurious actions and, as a result, devolving into behaviors such as threatening, cajoling, lecturing, arguing, or using pejorative labels (for example, "She's a manipulative borderline"). It is therefore exceedingly important that you, the clinician, accept your own anxiety and fear-producing images of the future without letting them dictate your behavior in session. You already have one person in the room who's crawling with anxiety; you don't need two.

• Case Example: Mia

Mia, a twenty-three-year-old single woman, was referred by a local emergency room physician after being brought in by a friend following a drug overdose. She denied she was trying to kill herself by taking pills. She said she had been drinking and had a panic attack while taking a bath, and that she took the pills because she didn't know how to get rid of the anxiety. She revealed that she has impulsively overdosed on pills on multiple occasions since moving to the city from a rural town at age eighteen. Most of the time she calls someone close by after taking too many pills because she gets scared she might die.

Currently, Mia lives by herself and works at two part-time jobs, one as an assistant in a school, and the other as a bartender. She has superficial friendships and has had multiple casual sex partners since early adolescence. Her parents divorced when she was twelve, and afterward she lived with her mother and brother and had very little contact with her father. Mia feels like her father basically walked out of her life. Her brother fell into drug addiction and ended up in prison, but Mia was well behaved and did well in school. However, she dropped out of college because she couldn't find a subject she cared about. Since leaving school, she hasn't been able to find a direction in life. She compensates for her feeling that her life lacks meaning by staying busy with exercise, online dating, and constantly posting on various social media sites. She admits that lately she's been using alcohol, partying, and casual sex to overcome her chronic sense of boredom.

Notice

We like to say that there's only one place in which you actually can change, and that's in the here and now. With self-harming clients, an immediate goal is to bring them into the present moment, because that's where their feared and avoided private experiences will show up. Most self-harming clients are pretty checked out because they've practiced not being present for a long time. Therefore, clinicians must be aware that bringing these clients into the present can be scary for them and may well trigger a variety of escape behaviors in session. So the first task of a present-moment-awareness intervention with self-harming clients often involves just seeing what they do in response to coming into contact with the present moment. Then the clinician can begin to restrict the client's use of escape behaviors, as demonstrated in the following dialogue.

Clinician: So, Mia, what would you say is the main reason you came in here today?

Mia: (*Looks down and twiddles her fingers.*) Well, you know, they told me to come here because of my overdose. I don't really know other than that one thing. Things haven't been that great for a while, I guess. I've felt kind of withdrawn, and each day seems more like a struggle. I just want to stay in bed instead of going to work or to the gym or seeing someone for lunch or coffee. My schedule is so busy that I hardly have any time to relax or just calm down for a while. [Read: This is a somewhat confusing response. Although Mia seems to be answering the question, her description of the problem—being unmotivated and apathetic— seems inconsistent with her complaint about always being busy, with no time to rest. The clinician will try to clarify this.]

Clinician: What activities fill up your day and keep you so busy?

Mia: I really don't know. I do work a lot of hours, but it just seems like I get less and less time for myself every day. Mostly social stuff, I guess, but it's like it's piling up and not very fun anymore. I've started to cancel things and just watch TV at home, feeling miserable about myself. I used to love to work with the kids at school, but now I dread going to work and count the minutes until I can leave again. I get irritated at the kids for not paying attention in class. But I'm the one who's there to help them with that, so I shouldn't react this way. [Read: This is a rambling response covering a lot of life territory, and Mia displays almost no emotion as she speaks. It almost seems like she's just saying the words mindlessly. The clinician will try to draw Mia into the present moment.]

Clinician: Let's focus on that misery you were talking about. Can you bring that misery into the room right here and now, so we can see what it looks like?

Mia: What do you mean? [Read: This is a fairly straightforward request, so her answer is probably an attempt to stay out of contact with whatever is there.]

Clinician: I mean, can you tell me something about what the misery feels like in your body, and what feelings and thoughts are present right now?

Mia: Oh, okay. Mostly I'm irritated and tired. Things I used to like doing aren't fun anymore. I usually pour a drink and just sit on my couch and watch TV wearing jogging pants. [Read: Mia gave a historical answer, describing her past experience, not the present. The clinician repeats the probe.]

Clinician: So how about right now? What's showing up for you? Are you feeling irritated and tired here? What are you aware of going on inside your body as you talk about this?

Mia: (*Looks away and pauses.*) I'm… I'm not sure what's going on inside. It doesn't feel good, and I don't like to think about what's wrong here. That's when I have anxiety—like when I took the pills. It just gets bigger and bigger, and pretty soon I have to do something or I feel like I'll pass out or go crazy or something. Sometimes I will cut myself if it gets really bad and drinking doesn't help. [Read: Mia is trying to comply with the request, but her emotional avoidance process is still dominant. The clinician will widen the discussion to incorporate other avoidance behaviors and come at the same subject from a different angle.]

Clinician: The ER report mentioned that you were intoxicated when you showed up. Besides cutting and taking pills from time to time, is alcohol another way you keep your unhappiness in check?

Mia: Yes, screwdrivers mostly. I drink too much, I know, but I kind of like to shut everything out and off. It's pretty much the only way I can get any sleep nowadays. When I have the night off from working at the bar, I can lie awake in bed for five to six hours straight, just zoning out. I don't even know what I'm watching on TV. Drinking is the only way I can get to sleep. When I'm drinking, though, I tend to eat junk food. It makes me feel better. But then, in the morning, I have to get up and run even though it's the last thing I want to do, because I'm usually hungover. I guess running is supposed to be a good cure for hangovers, isn't it? (*Giggles.*) Maybe I should change to pot; then I wouldn't have to run off the fat. Hmm… But then I'd probably get the munchies and eat even more. (*Giggles again.*) [Read: Mia is giving the clinician a long list of emotional avoidance behaviors while also changing from topic to topic and giggling uncomfortably, suggesting that emotional avoidance is happening in the present. The clinician will follow up on this.]

Clinician: So, it seems there's something troubling you. And you can get it to shut up for a little while if you just distract yourself or get loaded. If that doesn't work, you can always take pills or cut yourself. I'm wondering—is that thing you're running from sitting in this room, right here, right now? Can you feel it moving inside and around you? Can you just focus your attention really hard on this one thing?

Mia: *(Looks profoundly sad.)* Yeah. It's always there. Whenever I think about it, it's there.

In this brief exchange, the clinician has succeeded at getting Mia in the room with her feared and avoided private experiences. Initially, this involved systematically probing Mia's ability to stay present and then repeatedly bringing her back to the present each time she tried to check out. The next step was using the present-moment-awareness intervention to help Mia make contact with her pain.

Name

Self-harming clients often experience their pain as an undifferentiated mass of negative thoughts, feelings, memories, and unpleasant physical sensations. Years of systematic avoidance have robbed them of the emotional intelligence skills they need to peel their experiences apart and begin to process them individually. As is true for all clients during present-moment-awareness interventions, it is critical to give these discrete negative private experiences verbal labels, which allows the symbolic processing of nonverbal experience to occur, as demonstrated in the following dialogue.

Clinician: So, if something works to shut you down or shut you off, you're all over it. That sounds like almost a full-time job at this point. There must be something knocking on the front door that you really don't want to let in. And as you just said, you know there's something on the front porch. What if we just opened the door and let this shit in? What's the first visitor to walk in the door?

Mia: I don't know… Just the feeling that I'm failing and not getting anywhere in life right now. Actually, I think I'm losing my grip and don't know what to do anymore. [Read: Mia is staying present, as requested, and has offered a surprisingly candid response, given her level of avoidance. The clinician will reinforce Mia's success and implement some emotion discrimination training.]

Clinician: Wow! That didn't take long to bust into the house, did it? It sounds like you have lots of thoughts telling you you're at a dead end. And your face looks really sad right now. I'm guessing that these thoughts, if you take them seriously, create a lot of sadness and even a sense of being ashamed—like you're a bad girl for not making more of your life, like you're a disappointment. I can see the anxiety aspect too, because the message is that you aren't going to succeed in the areas of life that matter to you the most. That would make me plenty anxious, and I'd certainly be tempted to mix a very strong drink to put that stuff to bed.

Mia: Well, god, you just said it better than I could. Those are the things I feel all the time, and I just can't deal with. I don't let myself sit still. I try to stay busy and fill my calendar with stuff. I used to be able to do that, but lately I seem to have run out of gas. Now I feel old and tired, but I'm just twenty-three… Can you believe it? I just can't make myself do the things I used to do any longer. I turn my phone off, pour that screwdriver, and just sit. Sad, isn't it? [Read: Mia is coming into the room with her box full of negative content. She also seems to be connecting with the unworkable nature of her avoidance strategies. There's a tinge of self-critical storytelling present, and the clinician will help her name that too.]

Clinician: It sounds like the second visitor busting in the front door is the thought that you're pathetic and kind of undeserving. Is that what just showed up?

Mia: That's another anxiety producer. When I listen to it, I just want to end the pain. It makes me think I don't deserve to be happy or have a good life.

In this brief exchange, the clinician has succeeded in getting Mia to connect verbal labels to her thoughts and feelings, making them more discrete and differentiated in the conversation—and in Mia's mind. At times, the clinician had to help Mia connect the dots between her negative thoughts and the associated painful emotions. Negative emotional arousal is what's driving Mia's self-harming behaviors, so it's critical that she be able to name her painful thoughts and emotions separately. This will permit other aspects of the present-moment-awareness intervention to unfold.

Let Go

Most self-harming clients impulsively react with avoidance behaviors the minute they make contact with painful material. Even as Mia was attempting to stay in the present moment, noticing what was there and giving it a name, she was also shifting back and forth between being coy (giggling about curing hangovers and smoking pot) and making contact with feared and avoided content. This dance isn't an unusual one among self-harming clients, who typically have layers and layers of avoidance moves. The key in present-moment-awareness interventions with such clients is often getting them to settle into sustained, immediate contact with feared content and helping them learn how to simply let it be there, an approach demonstrated in the following dialogue.

Clinician: Okay, Mia, I'm starting to get a sense of what's going on with your life right now and what you're struggling with. Would you be willing to look at the struggle in a slightly different way?

Mia: (Looks reluctant.) Okay… I'm not sure what you mean by that, but okay.

Clinician: Well, it sounds like your preferred strategies of staying busy, drinking, cutting, or taking pills aren't really keeping your visitors out on the porch. In fact, the more you try to get rid of them, the more they barge into the house and badger you. When this happens over and over again, it wears you down. Your anxiety goes through the ceiling and you feel like the only move left to you is to check out. You know what I mean?

Mia: Yeah. I feel like I'm running away from something I can't get free from, and it keeps pulling me back down. [Read: Mia is clearly starting to identify her avoidance as avoidance. Now the clinician can try to cultivate a different type of strategy for dealing with private experiences.]

Clinician: If running away from yourself isn't going to work, I wonder what would happen if you just stopped, turned around, and looked your visitors in the eye?

Mia: What do you mean?

Clinician: Just let the visitors be in the house. The stuff you don't want to have—can you just acknowledge that it's here without having to do anything at all to change it?

Mia: I don't know what you want me to do.

Clinician: Would you be willing to let go of running and just look at what's here?

Mia: I can try, but I'm just not sure I can deal with the anxiety. And I don't see how it's going to do anything except make me even more depressed and anxious. [Read: Mia is fused with the literal content of her private experience, which makes it hard for her to see why contacting her pain would be more effective than avoiding it. The clinician will amplify the meaning of letting go.]

Clinician: You aren't the same as your visitors. They speak to you, and you can choose to listen to them if you like. If you listen, the natural result is that you'll feel anxious, ashamed, sad, and depressed. An alternative is to just let go of any attachment to what the visitors have to say. You can just be aware that they're speaking to you without letting them dictate how you live your life. Your experience already tells you that you can't control whether you have contact with them. So maybe the alternative is to change how you relate to them when they show up.

Mia: I'm willing to try anything. This is pretty weird stuff, but what I'm doing isn't going anywhere either. [Read: This comment suggests that Mia is starting to incorporate the idea that her old avoidance strategies aren't working. She's indicating at least some openness to trying something new. The clinician will implement a brief skills training exercise in letting go.]

Clinician: If you're willing, we could do a little exercise for the next couple of minutes to give you some direct experience with what letting go feels like

in motion. We could even use some of those gnarly thoughts and feelings we've been talking about to see how it feels to actually let them go.
(*Proceeds to practice visualizing thoughts and emotions as clouds in the sky.*)

In this brief exchange, the clinician has succeeded in getting Mia to acknowledge the futility of her emotional avoidance and suppression strategies and to consider letting go as an alternative. The clinician first offers a rationale for acceptance as an alternative and then helps Mia make experiential contact with detachment skills.

Soften

Self-harming clients typically have to engage repeatedly in their unworkable behaviors, not only due to the emotion suppression problem, but also because their negative self-narrative generates a continuous stream of negative affect. Many of these clients have a significant history of trauma, were raised in emotionally abusive or neglectful family systems, or both. Therefore, they often didn't receive the emotional nourishment necessary for generating a positive self-image. Consequently, they walk the path of life believing that they're doomed to experience even more neglect and disappointment. Ultimately, the self-harming behavior itself becomes incorporated into their story as yet another example of how pathetic they are. Such stories are at the heart of clients' ongoing suffering and must be exposed for what they are by the clinician. This is exactly what the clinician will work on with Mia after concluding the clouds in the sky visualization.

Clinician: How did you do at putting stuff on those clouds and watching them move across the sky? Were you able to just watch your thoughts, feelings, and memories?

Mia: At first it was hard to picture them, and then I was able to do it for a little bit. Then I noticed that I was getting really anxious and feeling like something terrible was about to happen. [Read: Mia seems to be making some progress with thought-watching skills, but she fused with something in the moment. The clinician will explore this.]

Clinician: So you were making some progress, and then something showed up that you couldn't separate yourself from. That's usually what happens when people get lost in something. What showed up that pulled your attention away from cloud watching? What did you get lost in?

Mia: I guess you could say the story of my life. I feel as though no one could ever like me, much less love me. I've never felt loved. I had to perform to get any kind of approval. I did that by getting good grades, wearing nice outfits, sucking up to people, and stuff like that. When is it my turn to live? There are so many things that I'd like to have happen in life, but it's not possible. I'm broken inside and used up. I feel like I'm sixty years old and have lived a whole life already. *(Starts to cry silently.)* Look at me, crying and feeling sorry for myself. I thought this would help, but it only makes me feel worse. What's the point? [Read: Despite how much pain Mia is experiencing in response to fusing with her story, she's actually staying present with the story and the pain. She isn't shutting down or engaging in other escape behaviors. The clinician will take full advantage of Mia being in the present moment.]

Clinician: So, it sounds like that cloud blacked out the sun and the entire sky. When that story shows up, does it feel like everything goes into darkness—like you can't see two feet in front of you and you're completely lost?

Mia: That's a good way to describe it, blinded—not by the light, but by the darkness.

Clinician: You know, no matter how big and dark that cloud is, behind it is the blue sky. If you mistake the cloud for the sky, you somehow have to figure out how to make the cloud disappear, and you can get completely lost in your head if you try to do that. If you see the cloud as a cloud, though, you don't have to do anything but watch it move across the sky. The nature of clouds is to move. However slowly, they always move.

Mia: So you're saying my life story is a cloud in the sky?

Clinician: I'm saying you can make your life story into whatever you want to make it into. You can make it into a cloud that blacks out everything and defies the laws of nature, or you can make it a cloud that behaves just like all the other clouds do. You get to pick.

Mia: And I've been picking to make it the ginormous cloud that blacks out everything. [Read: This is high-level perspective taking, indicating that Mia might be ready to receive a subtle reframing that can redefine the functions of her self-story.]

Clinician: Well, think about where we started. You told me that your life had no meaning or purpose. But you aren't emotionally dead about this issue; you're actively hurting inside, and you're using all kinds of strategies to mask that hurt. That's one way to deal with huge, dark clouds when they appear. Another way is to lean into your emotional pain because it will tell you what's important to you in life. That's the clear blue sky sitting behind the big, dark cloud.

In this brief exchange, the clinician has succeeded in getting Mia to rethink the function of her well-rehearsed self-critical life story. The clinician didn't try to convince Mia that her story was distorted or inconsistent; rather, the clinician treated it as a psychological process that doesn't come with built-in meaning. Mia learned that she could make the same story be part of her suffering or part of her drive toward living a valued life.

Expand

As noted at the beginning of this chapter, self-harming clients enter therapy as lost souls primarily because they're so preoccupied with their ongoing negative self-narrative and the time- and energy-consuming need to control the emotional pain it produces. This prevents them from developing any sense of life direction, so they fall back into their myopic, avoidance-oriented lifestyle. Therefore, the ultimate goal is to engage them in specific present-moment activities that help them make contact with their values. When this happens, they can base their life activities not on the need to avoid emotional pain, but rather on seeking life outcomes that matter to them.

Clinician: Let's imagine that, for just a few minutes, you dropped the struggle with clouds and focused on the clear blue sky that contains them. Imagine that you could use your pain to tell you what really matters to you, instead of trying to avoid it. What kind of life could you imagine yourself living in a world where anything is possible?

Mia: Anything at all?

Clinician: Anything is possible.

Mia: I'd like to go back to school just to learn. It wouldn't matter if I didn't know what to major in. One thing I know is that I like being around kids. I'd like to have children of my own someday, and I could see myself working with children and parents. I'd like to have a real relationship with a guy instead of all these one-night stands where I'm just acting like I care to get sex. I'd also like to have more contact with my parents. [Read: This is a pretty rich response, showing that Mia is in contact with several important values. The clinician will try to package this as the antithesis of Mia's negative self-narrative to prevent it from being co-opted into the narrative.]

Clinician: And as you hear yourself telling me this, how does it feel—particularly your sense of having a mission in life compared with the dark predictions of your life story?

Mia: Well, I can honestly say that I haven't had any sense of hope in life for a long time, until today. I feel like the clouds have parted, and I can see a path here. I can see a way out. [Read: This response suggests that Mia has already drawn a mental comparison between a values-based view of the future and one that's based in her negative self-story. The clinician will try to fully amplify this distinction.]

Clinician: That's pretty damn cool to hear you say that! It's like, where do you want to put your precious life energy? Struggling with your life story, or going after things that matter to you in life? It sounds like you've grown weary of pouring sand down the rat hole of your life story and you want to move on to a more affirming life mission.

Mia: Yeah, that's the path out of my personal hell. I just about killed myself a couple of times fighting the life story. I know this stuff will probably come up again and again, but I'll tell you, I'm done with it. [Read: This is a very powerful statement, indicating that Mia understands that the story will reappear, and that she has the choice to relate to it in a different way.]

Clinician: Yeah, this isn't about getting rid of stories, because we all have them. I have mine too, believe me. It's more a matter of not letting the story control your behavior—continuing to go after things that matter, even if your story tells you that you won't win and shouldn't even try. Speaking of trying, where would you like to start with this journey?

Mia: I was just thinking about that a little earlier. I'd probably like to start with going back to school part-time. I'll need to enroll again and then see if I qualify for financial assistance. I'll probably take just one class the first quarter, so I can get a feel for how to be a student and hold a job at the same time. [Read: Mia is coming up with specific behavioral goals that seem well within her capabilities. The clinician will augment her goals to increase her motivation.]

Clinician: So, if you actually followed through and enrolled in school again, then determined if you qualify for financial assistance and started by taking one class, would that tell you that you were moving in the direction of that new life you imagined?

Mia: Yes, absolutely.

In this brief exchange, the clinician has succeeded in helping Mia defuse from her ongoing negative self-narrative by redirecting her attention to a set of values-based life goals. This involved asking Mia to dream, without restrictions, about a life worth living, and then to make direct contact with her underlying values. No promises were made that Mia's negative self-narrative wouldn't show itself in the future. At the same time, she can freely choose to have that story be present as she pursues what matters to her.

Summary

In this chapter, we've examined how to use present-moment-awareness interventions with clients who engage in self-harming and suicidal behaviors. In general, these clients habitually use high-risk behaviors to help control negative emotional arousal, yet over time they experience uncontrollable emotion rebounds that lead to chronic emotional crisis. With these clients, present-moment-awareness interventions need to evoke their painful, avoided emotions directly, in session, without allowing them to use their customary escape behaviors. These clients live in a world colored by a well-worn and intensely negative self-story, which must be called out during the intervention. The antidote is to help them connect with life values that are bigger than their need to control specific types of emotional pain. By helping them connect with their values, they can stand in the presence of their emotional pain and choose to engage in life-affirming actions at the same time.

CHAPTER 14

Using the Present Moment to Support Lifestyle Change

To keep the body in good health is a duty, otherwise we
shall not be able to keep our mind strong and clear.

—Buddha

The unsuspecting reader might be somewhat taken aback to see a chapter on promoting healthy behavior changes using present-moment-awareness interventions. Your immediate reaction might be, *This isn't really a clinical issue, and it isn't what we deal with in therapy. It's the job of physicians and health educators to help people with that stuff.* We would counter that vastly greater numbers of people are dying as a direct result of lifestyle factors than all mental disorders and addictions added together. We would also argue that lifestyle imbalance is a clinical problem that should be addressed with every client you see in therapy. Indeed, the level of difficulty involved in making healthy behavior changes, like quitting smoking or losing weight, is far greater than the level of difficulty for initiating new behaviors to overcome depression, anxiety, PTSD, or addictive and self-harming behaviors.

Why would present-moment-awareness interventions be an instrumental part of promoting positive lifestyle change? The short answer is that our contemporary lifestyle reflects the ideal of feel-goodism that dominates the cultural mainstream. Lifestyles obviously are influenced by a lot of different forces (economic, cultural, ethnic, religious, social, familial, and so on), and the function of those forces is to help people live in an organized way on a daily basis. Yet many of the mental experiences that show up on a moment-to-moment basis in daily life pull us away from the holy grail of "feeling good." Somehow, people have to come to grips with the daily grind of living with self-doubt, comparisons with others, fitting in, dealing with relationship stresses, anxieties, regrets, sadness, and a host of other common life challenges. To that end, an individual's lifestyle can function as a vehicle for promoting self-acceptance, awareness of the moment, and engagement in valued life activities, or, alternatively, it can function as a vehicle for emotional and behavioral avoidance. The reason there are so many people with out-of-balance lifestyles and the resulting elevated health risk is that our culture promotes lifestyles that are based in emotional and behavioral avoidance. The same basic cultural factors that have driven people into depression or anxiety in unprecedented numbers are also driving people to become morbidly obese, to smoke or chew tobacco, to be sedentary, or to fail to manage the behavioral aspects of their chronic health problems.

The last time we checked, the mind and body were still connected, so it makes complete sense to predict that individuals with lifestyle imbalances will also be susceptible to problems with their emotional health. Clinical experience suggests that a large percentage of obese clients also (and not surprisingly) suffer from depression. Both conditions are related to stress, and in addition, obese and overweight people are often the victims of stigma in our thin-is-beautiful world. Additionally, problematic eating patterns may play a role in both depression and weight gain. When people are depressed, their motivation to exercise, to engage in social or relaxing activities, or to take the time to prepare a nutritious meal may all be impaired.

In this chapter, we'll examine how to use the present moment to wake people up from this culturally induced slumber, take control of their daily behavior patterns, and preserve their health so they can pursue important life purposes. First, we'll discuss some general clinical guidelines for how to bring clients into contact with their avoidance-based daily behaviors and help them develop a values-based lifestyle devoted to promoting personal health and well-being. Then we'll use an extended case example to illustrate how to use each phase of a present-moment-awareness intervention to teach clients a new way of relating to their own mental chatter as they make daily lifestyle choices. This approach can be used with any health risk behavior; however, for the purposes of this chapter, we'll focus on one that's widespread—obesity.

Guiding Clinical Principles

The first and most important principle is to be aware of your own prejudices about people who are overweight. This is by far the biggest threat to being an effective clinician with such clients. In our thin-is-in culture, we're trained to view overweight people as unattractive and to fuse with blaming and shaming evaluations, such as "She must eat like a pig to weigh that much" or "He never met a grocery bag he didn't like." While most of us might deny holding these prejudicial and stigmatizing attitudes, they are, in fact, ubiquitous in our culture. As a member of this culture, you are very likely to hold some of these beliefs.

Furthermore, the person sitting across from you probably holds these prejudicial and stigmatizing beliefs too. Through a kind of mental osmosis, clients with weight issues gradually internalize socially transmitted self-rejecting attitudes. We now know that self-stigma is perhaps the biggest barrier obese clients face in their quest to control their weight (see Lillis, Levin, & Hayes, 2011, for an illuminating treatment of this topic). Most obese clients are already primed through their social training to join you in the process of beating them up mentally for being fat.

When you fuse with stigma, you unwittingly become an agent of social control. When you do, your words and actions will be guided by culturally instilled attitudes and beliefs about obesity, rather than by what clients need to help them succeed in their quest for a healthy lifestyle. Therefore, you must be willing to acknowledge that you hold stigmatizing and prejudicial attitudes while at the same time being open to the human being you're working with and genuinely curious about what kind of change might be possible for that person in the moment.

A second guiding principle is to be aware of the function of such clients' lifestyle behaviors, not just the form of those behaviors. Overeating and underexercising occur in a social and emotional context, so it's crucial to systematically assess the contextual cues that effectively control clients' problematic eating behaviors. When evaluated as "bad" behaviors, they aren't particularly interesting, nor is there a lot of clinical leverage to be gained by focusing on them. However, when you delve into the function of those behaviors, you can get to the heart of the clinical issue. For example, you might determine that some episodes of overeating are closely connected with the incidence of conflicts among other family members during which the obese client feels torn loyalties. Eating thus serves the very valuable function of helping the obese person calm down enough to navigate a difficult interpersonal situation.

Your functional analysis could even extend to the act of the client coming in to see you, ostensibly to get some help. Is the client here in an effort to reassure a worried physician or to get the physician to stop lecturing the client about weight issues? Is the client seeing you to assuage a pushy partner? Is the client here to convince yet one more clinician of the hopelessness of ever getting in control of the weight problem? All too often, obese clients have an ambivalent relationship with the health care providers they work with, and this could easily extend to you, the clinician. This is a terrible contextual formula for producing any kind of sustainable change. Plus, not surprisingly, most obese clients have tried multiple weight control strategies on multiple occasions, usually with minimal results. Losing weight to get others off their back—or worse yet, to get themselves off their back—isn't going to work in the long haul.

A third core principle is that repeated problematic lifestyle choices generally originate in emotional avoidance and behavioral inertia. Behaviors that are grounded in emotional avoidance generally help alleviate aversive physical or emotional states. For example, psychological experiences of anxiety, sadness, anger, or loneliness often commingle with poor lifestyle choices. These negative affects generally result from bottom-up attention being dominant in the task-positive or default mode networks. When clients are under the sway of bottom-up attention, they are much less likely to be aware of the choices they're making. In this instance, food offers a convenient and immediately available strategy for calming the nervous system, and because food is readily available for most people in the United States, overuse of this strategy is common. Then, as they gain weight, most people experience a surge of negative self-evaluations related not only to their body image, but also to their repeated failures at self-control.

This self-defeating narrative is reinforced by the social environment. When coming into contact with an obese person, most people have a conditioned reaction of disgust and disdain that's hard to conceal. People generally believe that fat people get that way because they lack self-control and are basically to blame for being fat. This predictably creates even more emotional turmoil in the obese person and creates even stronger triggers for deploying the short-term coping strategies that tend to populate imbalanced lifestyles. Depression, resulting from excessive dominance of the brain's default network, may set in and obstruct personal problem solving or goal setting. The resulting lack of contact with emotional experience resulting from rumination and mind wandering may freeze obese clients in patterns of self-isolation and inexorably diminishing health.

Behavioral inertia can be thought of as the habit strength, or psychological momentum, associated with engaging in the same lifestyle behavior over and over again. As behavioral inertia increases, the level of voluntary control over a behavior decreases. There is ample evidence to suggest that most of us gradually turn over control of common daily habits to the environment. Everyday lifestyle behaviors are triggered by environmental cues, not necessarily personal choice. Eventually, individuals are no longer attending to the choices they're making because their behavior has become automatic. Many overweight people spend decades vacillating between anxiously attending to dieting and checked-out periods of emotional eating. When you find such clients in a mindless, checked-out state, it's crucial to stimulate active participation in the moment—where all of their stigmas and negative self-evaluations will be waiting.

The final guiding principle is to use mindfulness-based interventions to wake these clients up, and then help them expand their ability to choose every behavior so that mindfulness becomes a core element of a new daily lifestyle routine. Clients often benefit a great deal from even a two-minute experience of successfully directing and sustaining their attention on thinking, sensing, feeling, or remembering. Ongoing practice in these skills will provide the foundation for acting mindfully even when the SNS is highly activated and the drive to engage in an unhealthful behavior is strong. Most substantial shifts in lifestyle behavior occur when clients repeatedly and successfully apply present-moment skills during challenging choice points in their daily routine.

• Case Example: Destiny

Destiny is a forty-eight-year-old married African-American woman who was referred by her doctor for help with weight loss. Her weight has ranged between 150 and 170 pounds over the past fifteen years. She'd like to lose twenty pounds and has tried numerous diets with varying success over the past thirty years. After a recent diagnosis of diabetes, she's decided to lose weight in order to improve her health.

Destiny has been married for twenty-four years. She and her husband, James, have been arguing more often over the past three or four years. James retired several years ago from a career in the military. He has missed the military community and finds it difficult to be at home with Destiny on a full-time basis. Destiny and James have two children: a daughter in her junior year of college and a son who's a senior in high school. Her daughter gained twenty pounds in her first year of college, and this is a concern for Destiny. Her son isn't interested in either college or a military career. He wants to move in with a group of older friends when he graduates and make a living as a drummer in a band. This also worries Destiny.

Destiny has had intermittent problems with her mood for much of her adult life. She started taking Prozac at the recommendation of her primary care provider fifteen years ago. She took it for several years but stopped due to weight gain. She's currently taking Lexapro but reports periods of depression, even with the medication. Her hobbies include cooking and sewing. She's from the South and loves to cook Southern food. She doesn't exercise on a regular basis.

Notice

Clients with chronic lifestyle imbalances tend to be out of touch with the entire array of physical and mental cues needed to make healthy choices. For example, many clients with weight issues fail to recognize hunger and satiety sensations in a way that would lead to balanced eating. Instead, they may respond to a small subset of cues that provoke poor eating choices, such as overfocusing on the warm rolls and butter dish on the table. They may strategically place a pair of sneakers by the front door in the evening so they'll go for a walk the next morning, and then overlook them when they go out to pick up the newspaper. Clinicians need to help these clients widen their field of attention to include a larger array of inputs so that each input is given its due in the process of making a choice. It's also crucial to teach these clients to flexibly shift their attention between salient cues as a way of countering the perceptual narrowing that leads to a certain subset of cues exerting undue influence on their health choices. Both of these aims are reflected in the following dialogue.

Clinician: So, Destiny, how do you go about making choices to engage in healthier or less healthy behaviors as you go through a day? Let's just say it's a workday for you and you wake up. What's the first thing you notice that might be a trigger for you?

Destiny: Honestly, I think it's when I first wake up. Sometimes I let myself lie in bed and wake up slowly, just warming up to the day, thinking about my children and my husband and what I want to do. Other days, I push myself from the beginning: *Get up, get going, you aren't going to have enough time…* That kind of sets the tone, if you know what I mean. [Read: This response indicates that Destiny has the ability to self-reflect on different ways of organizing herself mentally. The clinician will try to amplify this.]

Clinician: I do know what you mean. It's kind of like the difference between noticing that you have opportunities all day to live in an intentional way versus feeling like you're on a hamster wheel—kind of like that?

Destiny: Yes, I guess I need to do something to encourage the slower start.

Clinician: Let's imagine you're having one of those slow-start days. Just try to imagine that you're there lying in bed, taking your time with things. What do you notice going on in your body—things like sensations in different parts of your body, emotions, messages from your mind about food, or anything else related to how you want to live your day?

Destiny: When I wake up slowly, it is more like I don't feel urgent about moving. I guess you could say it's being calm inside, not anxious about what I need to do. I might notice I'm hungry because I haven't eaten in a while. I also enjoy the feeling of lying in bed in the soft sheets, and that the temperature is just right. I notice that when I gently stretch my legs and arms, it feels good. If I were rushing, I'd be focusing on have-tos and eating in order to get the day off to a fast start. [Read: Destiny is showing a good deal of somatic and mental self-awareness that the clinician will try to expand upon.]

Clinician: Interesting. So if you let yourself slow down, you come into contact with a whole bunch of physical and emotional sensations that kind of put being hungry in a different light. It's like, *Yeah, I'm hungry, and I also really like cuddling with these soft, warm sheets, just being awake and being here and gently warming my body up.* I'm guessing this has a huge impact on your sense of urgency about eating something right away. What do you think would help you start your day more mindfully more often?

Destiny: You're right. I usually stuff myself quickly if I'm feeling urgent. I could set my alarm five minutes earlier and maybe use soft, slow music as the alarm, rather than the klaxon alarm I have programmed on my phone. [Read: Destiny is tracking the basic idea of trying to slow down and be more deliberate as a way to reframe her hunger cues.]

Clinician: That sounds like a really powerful change in how you start your day!

In this brief exchange, the clinician has helped Destiny understand that her state of mind (being calm and purposeful versus being urgent and pressured) directly influences how she processes present-moment cues that might influence her eating behavior. This will allow Destiny to start better isolating the cues that are most likely to do damage.

Name

Once clients understand that the emotions, images, and urges associated with and often triggered by hunger sensations are actually situated in a larger array of physical and mental experiences, clinicians are in an excellent position to help them learn to discriminate between workable and unworkable cues. Often, the next challenge is to quickly assess which cues most trouble a given client and then help that client apply verbal labels to these events. Here's how the clinician tackled this phase of the present-moment-awareness intervention with Destiny.

Clinician: When we try to make changes in our daily habits, a lot of stuff can show up. Powerful emotions, negative images of the past or future, or strong-willed thoughts can show up and lead you to make choices you don't want to make, if you let them. Have you noticed this in the past when you've tried to lose weight?

Destiny: Yes, I have. I actually feel kind of fragile, really vulnerable. I don't like that feeling and I try to cover it up, I think. My life requires me to be strong, you know. I have a lot of responsibilities with my children, and my husband isn't a touchy-feely kind of guy. [Read: Destiny looked down while answering this question, suggesting that something uncomfortable showed up. The clinician will explore this further.]

Clinician: When you said you felt fragile, you looked down. What's the feeling that goes along with being fragile and vulnerable?

Destiny: I guess I'd say it's a mix of fear and sadness—sad that I'm alone, fear that I won't be able to take care of myself, and fear that things around me will start to fall apart. I think those feelings probably go way back in my life to when I was little and my parents divorced. Back then, I really did have to take care of myself, and I had two little sisters I had to take care of too. That's probably when I started using food to comfort me. Does that make sense—using food for comfort and strength? [Read: Destiny is showing good verbal discrimination abilities here, along with a good deal of insight into how her childhood programming has affected her relationship to food. The clinician will try to reinforce this.]

Clinician: It sounds like you're saying there are two ways you use food to help you. One is that eating comforts you and allows you to feel strong and in control of your fear and sadness. And the other is using food to give you the physical energy to take care of all your duties and responsibilities.

Destiny: Well, I don't think I focus on eating to have a strong body, but I'm pretty sure I eat to feel in control when I start to lose weight and feel fragile.

Clinician: We need to come up with a name for that part of you, something that will help you relate to it differently when it shows up—because right now it commands you to eat in ways that you don't like.

Destiny: Well, I guess I could name it Baby Girl. That would be a shift from my usual evaluation of it as some kind of fault or defect. Baby Girl is just scared. She feels very vulnerable and is looking for someone to comfort her. [Read: This is a strong start in using verbal naming skills to help Destiny take a more detached stance with urges to overeat. The clinician will try to enlarge upon the baby girl analogy.]

Clinician: And even as she becomes an adult, Baby Girl still has that sense of being fragile. She still wants to be loved and accepted for who she is and not be teased about what her body looks like.

Destiny: (*Starts to cry.*) Yeah, Baby Girl still has her needs.

In this brief exchange, the clinician has succeeded in getting Destiny to identify and attach verbal labels to a group of highly salient cues that trigger her unhealthy eating behaviors. The clinician achieved this outcome by giving Destiny plenty of space to approach these cues, discriminate between them verbally, and then supply an emotionally salient name to the entire complex.

Let Go

Most clients who are overweight avoid activities that might trigger busy mind's negative chatter about weight-related issues such as body image, self-blame, and social rejection. They may avoid grocery stores and shop only at odd times of the day or night when the store is less crowded. They may also avoid health clubs and parks in an effort to avoid social cues, such as looks of disgust or feeling embarrassed by their body in comparison to others, that may trigger unhealthy eating. To help clients relate to such cues differently, it's important to reframe the problem as one of attachment to self-evaluations and arbitrary social standards, as the clinician does with Destiny in the following dialogue.

Destiny: You know, I love food and I love to cook, and my children and I have had lots of fun in the kitchen for as long as I can remember. But I cringe at the grocery store sometimes. I feel like people are looking at what I'm buying and judging it. It makes me kind of mad. [Read: Destiny is showing up with her core process, presenting a good opportunity for the clinician to delve in.]

Clinician: Yes, there's a lot of chatter in our culture about weight. It doesn't do anyone much good, but we can't seem to make it go away. And actually, the more we try not to think about something, like *Being overweight is bad and a sign of weakness*, the more it sticks in the mind. Have you ever noticed this?

Destiny: Well, I have noticed that if I start thinking about pecan pie, all warm and served with ice cream, and then I try to get it out of my mind, I can't… It just keeps creeping back in. [Read: This statement offers a good opportunity to introduce the paradox of emotional control and thought suppression.]

Clinician: Maybe that's how some of this works. You have these images of food and how good it tastes, how you can't eat it, and how you'll get fatter and then people will see you as even more pathetic, and you just get lost in your own wheels. And that makes you even more inclined to eat because Baby Girl needs to be comforted and feel less vulnerable. These thoughts you're carrying around are anything but comforting if you take them at their word. They're downright scary. And we know what Baby Girl needs to be comforted, don't we?

Destiny: That's it in a nutshell. That's what happens all the time. But how do you stop thinking like that? [Read: This comment probably reveals that Destiny's typical strategy is to try to suppress and control cues for food consumption, so the clinician will suggest an alternative.]

Clinician: Maybe the goal isn't to get rid of Baby Girl and her needs, but to relate to them a little differently. I find that when I have thoughts and feelings I don't want, if I just try to allow them to be there, I don't have to spend energy trying to get them to stop. They can just come and go as they please. Are you willing to experiment with me on this? *(Destiny nods yes.)* What I'd like for you to do is think about a recent situation where this came up in your life. What did you feel? How did you handle it?

Destiny: Well, I made chicken-fried steak and mashed potatoes the night before last, and my husband made a salad. When we were eating, my husband got on me about putting butter on my potatoes, saying, "Why do you do that? You already put a lot of butter in them in the kitchen when you mashed them." I felt he was judging me—that he didn't like me because of my body. I felt really hurt, and I kept trying not to feel it or think those things. It really ruined dinner, and I didn't eat everything on my plate. But then I got up in the middle of the night and fixed myself a big plate and ate it alone. I know I need to let these things go, but they hurt. How do you let go of things that hurt? [Read: Destiny is clearly engaged and is seeking new information, suggesting that she's ready to try a new strategy.]

Clinician: Sometimes I use my breath to let go. I just notice my breathing, and then I start to breathe air into the thoughts that trouble me, the emotions that hurt, or painful memories—even physical sensations, like hunger or urgency. I try to imagine each one and then put a circle of air around it, almost like a soft, warm padding surrounding each one. I'm aware of each one being there inside of me. Would you like to try practicing this strategy with me for just a few minutes?

In this brief exchange, the clinician helped Destiny realize that accepting the presence of self-critical evaluations and social rules is a viable alternative to simply avoiding making contact with them. Further, the clinician has succeeded in making a link between unhealthy eating behaviors and failed attempts at emotional control and suppression. The clinician then offered a specific strategy for letting go that Destiny can use in situations in which she's emotionally troubled and prone to overeating.

Soften

As we mentioned, many triggers for overeating, such as shame, self-consciousness, and self-blame, are basically social stigmas and prejudices turned inward. Clinicians must help these clients understand that no one intentionally tries to create an unhealthy lifestyle, and that being overweight isn't a sign of weakness, lack of willpower, or self-absorption. It's the result of emotional and behavioral avoidance—something everyone in our culture is trained to do and falls prey to at one point or another. For obese clients, normalizing the knee-jerk response of self-criticism is an intervention that can help them soften in relation to their self-stigma, as demonstrated in the following dialogue between the clinician and Destiny.

Clinician: As we were coming to the office, you mentioned that you went to the gym and had your first appointment with a personal trainer. And I guess you discovered you could stuff your mind in your gym bag and put it in the locker, right? (The clinician and Destiny both laugh.) So what showed up during your time at the gym?

Destiny: Yeah, I wish I could check my mind somewhere. I was pretty critical of myself, especially how I looked in workout clothes. And my mind was also trying to read other people's minds—what they were saying about me. But you know what I did that worked? I focused on the trainer. Her name is Ebony. She's really excited about her work, and she seemed to genuinely enjoy getting to know me and trying to figure out what we could do—what level I could start at.

Clinician: Good for you, Destiny. What else did you notice during your time at the gym?

Destiny: I noticed that I'm completely out of shape and that I'm not very flexible. Well, my legs are flexible, but the rest of me isn't. I was upset and angry with myself for losing the strength and flexibility I used to have. And the next day, when I was sore, I felt more upset, sad, and discouraged.

Clinician: Does that theme of being angry and upset with yourself and being your own worst critic show up in other areas of your life?

Destiny: To tell the truth, it shows up pretty much everywhere. My husband and even my kids say I'm way too hard on myself. [Read: This is a very useful response as long as Destiny doesn't get lost in a story about it, so the clinician will change the angle of the conversation to prevent storytelling from taking over.]

Clinician: And it probably doesn't help a whole lot to see people reacting to your physical appearance, making snide comments about your weight, or being patronizing in different ways.

Destiny: That's one reason I really don't like going out of the house that much, except to run errands. It was a huge step for me just to go to the health club, and I felt pretty bad when it was all done. [Read: This is a good, honest self-disclosure that provides an opportunity for the clinician to work on self-compassion.]

Clinician: So, the next thing we have to tackle is how to turn the negative energy of being hard on yourself and being your own worst critic into something useful in your quest to improve your health, because, lord knows, people are going to judge you by how you look. There's nothing you can do to stop that. But you can do something about being your own worst critic. I know you have compassion for your husband and children from what you say about them, so it's just a matter of taking what you already know how to do and directing it toward yourself. Here's an idea: For five minutes at the beginning of your next trip to the gym, how about you just sit down, put a sock in your inner critic's mouth, and praise yourself for putting in the time and effort to try something that makes you feel vulnerable and fragile? In that exact moment, imagine treating yourself like you'd treat your children if they were trying something new and difficult for them. How would you help your children in such a situation?

Destiny: I'd tell them how proud I was of them, that they can do it if they keep trying, and that I will be there to pick them up if they fall. I'd tell them, "No matter how it turns out, I love you."

Clinician: So, might you be able to show a little bit of that love for yourself during those five minutes of self-acceptance at the gym?

Destiny: I can try to. Believe me, it's bound to feel better than beating myself up.

In this brief exchange, the clinician has helped Destiny adopt a more flexible, self-accepting stance toward her long-term struggles with self-criticism and imbalanced lifestyle behaviors. The clinician achieved this by putting Destiny's self-stigmatizing beliefs into a bigger social context that would allow Destiny to treat herself with self-acceptance even while being the object of stigmatizing evaluations by others.

Expand

When helping clients make significant, long-lasting changes to imbalanced lifestyles, it's wise to help them develop a larger life vision within which the new lifestyle is seen as furthering their life goals. Promoting physical health isn't an end in itself; it's a means to an end. As the old saying goes, "Health is the one thing you take for granted, until you don't have it anymore." If clients aren't able to preserve their health, a lot of life options are taken off the table. However, an equally important question is what they'll do in life if they have a body that's functioning well. Just because a person loses eighty pounds doesn't mean a vital life awaits. The best way to promote lifestyle change is to link it to the ability to more fully participate in daily activities that produce a sense of vitality, meaning, and purpose, as demonstrated in the following dialogue with Destiny.

> *Clinician:* I love the fact that you're going through with this personal trainer thing. It gives you one way to structure your daily routine. My first general rule is that what people weigh doesn't make or break them. It's all about what you do with your body once you get it into shape. You could weigh 200 pounds and be fit as a fiddle, full of energy, and ready to rock and roll. Or you could weigh 130 pounds and not have a clue about what you want in life. My second general rule is that people can't have too many relaxing or interesting activities in their life. So, if you were to expand your vision here, what else would you like to see come into your life? What would give you a sense of purpose and joy? What other activities interest you and pique your curiosity?

> *Destiny:* Well, I've always loved to dance, and when I was young, I was really good at it.

> *Clinician:* Tell me more about what dance does for you.

> *Destiny:* I feel alive, like I can move. I feel free. I love soul music, and I have good rhythm. I just feel one with the music, I guess. [Read: Destiny is imbuing this activity with a lot of positive valence, so the clinician will try to get her to commit to trying it.]

> *Clinician:* Wow, that sounds great! Is it possible for you to do some kind of dancing on a regular basis?

> *Destiny:* I'm thinking I'll look for a video that I can use at home, or maybe I'll just buy me some new tunes and dance for ten minutes when I get home from work... That would be a nice transition from work. My husband used to love watching me dance when we were young and fit. It might blow his mind a little bit to see this fat lady shakin' it! [Read: This response reveals that Destiny is already practicing self-compassion simply by being willing to put herself on the line and exercise in front of her husband, who has been critical of her weight in the past. The clinician will strongly reinforce this and try to build on Destiny's positive momentum.]

> *Clinician:* Wow! I like it! I have another simple suggestion. Remember we talked earlier about taking it slow when you wake up and how it kind of puts things into perspective? What would you think about taking two or three of those "slow-down" periods during the day? Maybe before lunch

and before dinner—say just five minutes. Maybe you could use the alarm on your phone to cue you to slow down, listen to some music, and scan your body for cues about what your body needs at that moment—food, rest, social activity, physical activity, stretching, or whatever. What do you think?

Destiny: That sounds interesting. So you're saying don't just rush from work to lunch and try to get back as quick as I can? Sometimes the same thing happens when I come home and cook after work. It's a duty, and I try to get it out of the way. Maybe taking it nice and slow would help change the way I eat at lunch and dinner.

In this brief exchange, the clinician has succeeded in getting Destiny to adopt a values-based perspective on contemplated lifestyle changes. Rather than making changes out of fear of health consequences, Destiny will be making them to bring her life trajectory into greater alignment with her personal values. Throughout, the clinician links contemplated lifestyle changes back to Destiny's larger life goals to imbue them with positive motivation. This makes it far more likely that Destiny will follow through with these changes and integrate them into her new lifestyle.

Summary

In this chapter, we've explored how to use present-moment-awareness interventions to help clients make long-lasting lifestyle change. Helping clients understand emotional and behavioral avoidance patterns that limit their success in changing health-related behaviors is of fundamental importance. By helping clients come to their senses, you allow them to be aware of the daily choices they're making. To this end, they must learn to notice and name painful emotions that may serve as cues for making unhealthy choices. Once these cues are in their awareness, they can learn how to detach from their literal meaning so the cues no longer regulate their behavior.

Many lifestyle problems are also packaged with socially acquired stigmatizing beliefs and attitudes. These attitudes are often internalized by clients who are struggling to control their lifestyle behaviors. In this case, they must learn how to practice self-compassion, even as they're being judged by others. Finally, preserving one's health is not an end in itself; it must be done in the service of living life more fully, rather than simply in an attempt to avoid negative health consequences. To succeed in lifestyle changes, clients must be able to see how new behaviors fit into their larger, values-based life goals.

References

Baer, R., Smith, G., Lykins, E., Button, D., Krietemeyer, J., Sauer, S., et al. (2008). Construct validity of the Five Facet Mindfulness Questionnaire in meditating and nonmeditating samples. *Assessment, 15*, 329–342.

Barbey, A. K., Colom, R., & Grafman, J. (2014). Distributed neural system for emotional intelligence revealed by lesion mapping. *Social Cognitive and Affective Neuroscience, 9*, 265–272.

Barrocas, A., Hankin, B., Young, J., & Abela, J. (2012). Rates of nonsuicidal self-injury in youth: Age, sex, and behavioral methods in a community sample. *Pediatrics, 130*, 39–45.

Braboszcz, C., Hahusseau, S., & Delorme, A. (2010). Meditation and neuroscience: From basic research to clinical practice. In R. A. Carlstedt (Ed.), *Integrative clinical psychology, psychiatry, and behavioral medicine: Perspectives, practices, and research* (pp. 1910–1929). New York: Springer.

Brass, M., & Haggard, P. (2010). The hidden side of intentional action: The role of the anterior insular cortex. *Brain Structure and Function, 5*, 603–610.

Brefczynski-Lewis, J. A., Lutz, A., Schaefer, H. S., Levinson, D. B., & Davidson, R. J. (2007). Neural correlates of attentional expertise in long-term meditation practitioners. *Proceedings of the National Academy of Sciences, 104*, 11483–11488.

Brewer, J., Wohunsky, P., Gray, J., Tang, Y., Weber, J., & Kober, H. (2011). Meditation experience is associated with differences in default mode network activity and connectivity. *Proceedings of the National Academy of Sciences, 108*, 20254–20259. doi: 10.1073/pnas.1112029108.

Buckner, R., Andrews-Hanna, J., & Schacter, D. (2008). The brain's default network: Anatomy, function, and relevance to disease. *Annals of the New York Academy of Science, 1124*, 1–38.

Carriere, J. S., Cheyne, J. A., & Smilek, D. (2008). Everyday attention lapses and memory failures: The affective consequences of mindlessness. *Consciousness and Cognition, 17*, 835–847.

Chiles, J., & Strosahl, K. (2004). *Clinical manual for assessment and treatment of suicidal clients.* Washington, DC: American Psychiatric Publishing.

Compton, W., Thomas, Y., Stinson, F., & Grant, B. (2007). Prevalence, correlates, disability, and comorbidity of *DSM-IV* drug abuse and dependence in the United States: Results from the National Epidemiologic Survey on Alcohol and Related Conditions. *Archives of General Psychiatry, 64,* 566–576. doi:10.1001/archpsyc.64.5.566.

Davidson, R., & Begley, S. (2012). *The emotional life of your brain: How its unique patterns affect the way you think, feel, and live—and how you can change them.* London: Penguin Books.

Gortner, E. T., Gollan, J. K., Dobson, K. S., & Jacobson, N. S. (1998). Cognitive-behavioral treatment for depression: Relapse prevention. *Journal of Consulting and Clinical Psychology, 66,* 377–384.

Hayes, S., Barnes-Holmes, D., & Roche, B. (Eds.) (2001). *Relational frame theory: A post-Skinnerian account of human language and cognition.* New York: Kluwer Academic/Plenum Publishing.

Hayes, S., Strosahl, K., & Wilson, K. (1999). *Acceptance and commitment therapy: An experiential approach to behavior change.* New York: Guilford Press.

Hayes, S., Strosahl, K., & Wilson, K. (2012). *Acceptance and commitment therapy: The process and practice of mindful change,* 2nd edition. New York: Guilford Press.

Hölzel, B., Carmody, J., Vangel, M., Congleton, C., Yerramsetti, S., Gard, T., et al. (2011). Mindfulness practice leads to increases in regional brain gray matter density. *Psychiatry Research: Neuroimaging, 19,* 36–43.

Kabat-Zinn, J. (1994). *Wherever you go, there you are.* New York: Hyperion.

Kalisch, R., Wiech, K., Critchley, H. D., Seymour, B., O'Doherty, J. P., Oakley, D. A., et al. (2005). Anxiety reduction through detachment: Subjective, physiological, and neural effects. *Journal of Cognitive Neuroscience, 17,* 874–883.

Kensinger, E., & Corkin, S. (2004). Two routes to emotional memory: Distinct neural processes for valence and arousal strategies. *Proceedings of the National Academy of Sciences, 101,* 3310–3315.

LaBar, K., & Cabeza, R. (2006). Cognitive neuroscience of emotional memory. *Nature: Neuroscience Reviews, 7,* 54–56.

Lang, P., & Bradley, M. (2010). Emotion and the motivational brain. *Biological Psychology, 84,* 437–450.

Lillis, J., Levin, M., & Hayes, S. (2011). Exploring the relationship between body mass index and health-related quality of life: A pilot study of the impact of weight self-stigma and experiential avoidance. *Journal of Health Psychology, 16,* 722–727.

Lutz, A., Brefczynski-Lewis, J., Johnstone, T., & Davidson, R. (2008). Regulation of the neural circuitry of emotion by compassion meditation: Effects of meditative expertise. *PLOS ONE, 3,* 3: e1897. doi:10.1371/journal.pone.0001897.

Lutz, L., Greischar, N. B., Rawlings, M. R., & Davidson, R. J. (2004). Long-term meditators self-induce high-amplitude synchrony during mental practice. *Proceedings of the National Academy of Sciences, 101,* 16369–16373.

McHugh, L., & Stewart, I. (2012). *The self and perspective taking: Contributions from modern behavioral science.* Oakland, CA: New Harbinger.

Morath, J., Gola, H., Sommershof, A., Hamuni, G., Kolassa, S., Catani, C., et al. (2014). The effect of trauma-focused therapy on the altered T cell distribution in individuals with PTSD: Evidence from a randomized controlled trial. *Journal of Psychiatric Research, 54,* 1–10.

Neff, K. D. (2003). Self-compassion: An alternative conceptualization of a healthy attitude toward oneself. *Self and Identity, 2,* 85–102.

Posner, M. I., & Rothbart, M. K. (2007). Research on attention networks as a model for the integration of psychological science. *Annual Review of Psychology, 58,* 1–23.

Quirk, G., & Beer, J. (2006). Prefrontal involvement in the regulation of emotion: Convergence of rat and human studies. *Current Opinion in Neurobiology, 16,* 723–727.

Raes, F., Pommier, E., Neff, K. D., & Van Gucht, D. (2011). Construction and factorial validation of a short form of the Self-Compassion Scale. *Clinical Psychology and Psychotherapy, 18,* 250–255.

Raichle, M. (2010). The brain's dark energy. *Scientific American, 302,* 3, 44–49.

Rawal, A., Park, R., & Williams, M. (2010). Rumination, experiential avoidance, and dysfunctional thinking in eating disorders. *Behaviour Research and Therapy, 48,* 851–859.

Robinson, P. J., Gould, D. A., & Strosahl, K. D. (2010). *Real behavior change in primary care: Strategies and tools for improving outcomes and increasing job satisfaction.* Oakland, CA: New Harbinger.

Schuyler, B., Kral, T., Jacquart, J., Burghy, C., Weng, H., Perlman, D., et al. (2014). Temporal dynamics of emotional responding: Amygdala recovery predicts emotional traits. *Social Cognitive and Affective Neuroscience, 9,* 176–181.

Segal, Z., Teasdale, J., & Williams, M. (2013). *Mindfulness-based cognitive therapy for depression,* 2nd edition. New York: Guilford Press.

Shea, M., Elkin, I., Imber, S., Sotsky, S., Watkins, J., Collins, J., et al. (1992). Course of depressive symptoms over follow-up. *Archives of General Psychiatry, 49,* 782–787.

Sheppes, G., Brady, W., & Samson, A. (2014). In (visual) search for a new distraction: The efficiency of a novel attentional deployment versus semantic meaning regulation strategies. *Frontiers of Psychology, 5*, 346.

Shiota, M., & Levenson, R. W. (2012). Turn down the volume or change the channel? Emotional effects of detached versus positive reappraisal. *Journal of Personality and Social Psychology, 103*, 416–429.

Smallwood, J., Beach, E., Schooler, J. W., & Handy, T. C. (2008). Going AWOL in the brain: Mind wandering reduces cortical analysis of external events. *Journal of Cognitive Neuroscience, 20*, 458–469.

Smallwood, J., Fitzgerald, A., Miles, L. K., & Phillips, L. H. (2009). Shifting moods, wandering minds: Negative moods lead the mind to wander. *Emotion, 9*, 271–276.

Smieja, M., Mrozowicz, M., & Kobylinska, D. (2011). Emotional intelligence and emotion regulation strategies. *Studia Psychologiczne, 49*, 55–64.

Spreng, R. N., Sepulcre, J., Turner, G. R., Stevens, W. D., & Schacter, D. L. (2013). Intrinsic architecture underlying the relations among the default, dorsal attention, and frontoparietal control networks of the human brain. *Journal of Cognitive Neuroscience, 25*, 74–86.

Strosahl, K., Robinson, P., & Gustavsson, T. (2012). *Brief interventions for radical change: Principles and practice of focused acceptance and commitment therapy.* Oakland, CA: New Harbinger.

Strosahl, K., & Robinson, P. (2008). *The mindfulness and acceptance workbook for depression: Using acceptance and commitment therapy to move through depression and create a life worth living.* Oakland, CA: New Harbinger.

Strosahl, K., Linehan, M., & Chiles, J. (1984). Will the real social desirability please stand up? Hopelessness, depression, social desirability, and the prediction of suicidal behavior. *Journal of Consulting and Clinical Psychology, 52*, 449–457.

Van Vugt, M., Hitchcock, P., Shahar, B., & Britton, W. (2012). The effects of mindfulness based cognitive therapy on affective memory recall dynamics in depression: A mechanistic model of rumination. *Frontiers of Human Neuroscience, 19*, 257. doi: 10.3389/fnhum.2012.00257.

Zettle, R. (2007). *ACT for depression: A clinician's guide to using acceptance and commitment therapy in treating depression.* Oakland, CA: New Harbinger.

Kirk D. Strosahl, PhD, is cofounder of acceptance and commitment therapy (ACT), a cognitive behavioral approach that has gained widespread adoption in the mental health and substance-abuse communities. He is coauthor of *Brief Interventions for Radical Change* and other core ACT books. Strosahl works as a practicing psychologist at Central Washington Family Medicine, a community health center providing health care to medically underserved patients. He also teaches family medicine physicians how to use the principles of mindfulness and acceptance in general practice. Strosahl lives in Zillah, WA.

Patricia J. Robinson, PhD, is director of training and program evaluation at Mountainview Consulting Group, Inc., a firm that assists health care systems with integrating behavioral health services into primary care settings. She is coauthor of *Real Behavior Change in Primary Care* and *The Mindfulness and Acceptance Workbook for Depression*. After exploring primary care psychology as a researcher, she devoted her attention to dissemination in rural America, urban public health departments, and military medical treatment facilities. Robinson lives in Portland, OR.

Thomas Gustavsson, MSc, is a licensed psychologist and cofounder of Psykologpartners, a company providing residential psychology and psychiatry services for self-harming clients in Scandinavia.

Index

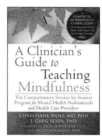
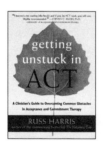